NEW ARENAS
FOR COMMUNITY SOCIAL WORK PRACTICE
WITH URBAN YOUTH

WITHDRAWN

WITHDRAWN

NEW ARENAS
FOR COMMUNITY SOCIAL WORK PRACTICE WITH URBAN YOUTH

—

Use of the Arts, Humanities, and Sports

Melvin Delgado

COLUMBIA UNIVERSITY PRESS   NEW YORK

Columbia University Press
Publishers Since 1893
New York   Chichester, West Sussex

Library of Congress Cataloguing-in-Publication Data

Delgado, Melvin.
New arenas for community social work practice with urban youth : use of the
arts, humanities, and sports / Melvin Delgado.
p.   cm.
Includes bibliographical references and index.
ISBN 0-231-11462-1 (cl : alk paper) — ISBN 0-231-11463-X (pa : alk paper)
1. Social work with youth—United States 2. Urban youth—Services for—
United States   3. Urban Youth—Education— United States.   I. Title.

HV1431 D44 2000
32.7'083'0973—dc21   99-086564

Casebound editions of Columbia University Press books
are printed on permanent and durable acid-free paper.
Printed in the United States of America
c 10 9 8 7 6 5 4 3 2 1
p 10 9 8 7 6 5 4 3 2 1

This book is dedicated to Denise (my spouse),
and Laura and Barbara (my daughters).
Without their support and inspiration this book
would not have been posssible.

CONTENTS

—

ACKNOWLEDGMENTS

—

It is impossible to write a book without the support, guidance, and effort on the part of a countless number of individuals. *New Arenas* is no exception. I wish to acknowledge the support provided by Boston University School of Social Work—Wilma Peebles Wilkins (dean), who provided support throughout all phases of this book, Suzanne Hogan (department administrative assisstant), and Danielle Arcidiacono (research assistant).

Numerous individuals and organizations outside the university provided valluable time, expertise, and materials. Mark Bolen (Parks and Recreation Department, Kansas City, Mo.); Tricia Bowen-Young (Moving in the Spirit, Atlanta), Kirsten Brandt (The Junior Players, Dallas), Jill Gurr (Write Now! Hollywood), Dan Manken (Make*A*Circus, San Francisco), Christina Koenig and Susan Fleminger (Henry Street Settlement House, New York), Carrie Friedmam (Galery 37, Chicago), Robin Smith (Video Action Fund, Washington, D.C.), Carolyn McKenzie (Soccer in the Streets, Jonesboro, Ga.), David Hernandez (Inner-City Games, Los Angeles), and Herlinda Zamora (Mexic-Arte Museum, Austin, Texas).

I also want to thank the anonymous reviewers of the book prospectus and its final draft. Their insights and suggestions were most appreciaated. Finally I would like to thank John Michel of Columbia University Press for his support throughtout all phases of the prospectus development and review.

NEW ARENAS
FOR COMMUNITY SOCIAL WORK PRACTICE
WITH URBAN YOUTH

—

Use of the Arts, Humanities, and Sports

PART I

—

BACKGROUND AND CONTEXT

Part I consists of four chapters that provide the reader with a variety of perspectives on the challenges and abilities of youth to influence their lives. These chapters make use of case illustrations to help the reader develop a better appreciation of what practice within new arenas looks like. This section also sets the stage for later chapters by defining many of the key concepts that inform the central goals of the book itself. Chapter 1 sets the overall context by introducing the reader to the author's background and interest in this topic. Chapter 2 provides a sociodemographic picture of the challenges youth face, particularly those residing in urban areas. Chapter 3 takes a different perspective from that of chapter 2 by approaching youth from a strengths perspective. In addition, it examines key principles that youth-focused organizations and services must utilize to engage and work with youth. The four chapters in this section provide the reader with the requisite foundation and context setting for better appreciating the struggles and strengths urban youth face in negotiating life's major transition junctures. Chapter 4 introduces the reader to the arts, humanities, and sports as arenas for social work practice and community development.

CHAPTER 1

—

URBAN YOUTH IN THE TWENTY-FIRST CENTURY:
PROBLEMS AND PROSPECTS

Much has been written about impending changes in social work practice and education as we approach and enter the next millennium (Abramovitz 1998; Haynes 1998; Witkin 1998). Globalization trends along with dramatic changes in technology, demographics, migration patterns, and economies, have profound implications for any society and any form of practice involving the helping professions. The approach of the twenty-first century milestone, however, provides professions with an opportunity to pause and examine past approaches, successes, and challenges (Abramovitz 1998; Haynes 1998; Swenson 1998; Witkin 1998). Further, it provides a natural juncture for examining where social work hopes to go in the future, and what kind of changes will be required to take it there. Further, the turn of the century coincides very closely with the century mark for professional social work practice, further lending significance to the next millennium.

A concurrent retrospective and prospective examination will undoubtedly result in much soul-searching and speculation about what strategic moves must be planned in order to increase the relevance of the profession in the future. In addition, it will result in a close examination of currently used practice paradigms and result in a call for new and more "contemporary" and "relevant" paradigms that will result in new approaches to social work education and practice. These new paradigms, however, will also cause a great deal of debate, with resulting tension within the profession concerning what is "best" for the profession, consumers, and society. If these new paradigms impinge on the practice of other helping professions, a debate involving these other professions can be predicted. The fact that social work practice is very broad, although still primarily clinical in nature, makes any form of examination arduous. This entire process is unavoidable and will ultimately result in a profession that is much more in tune with the environmental changes that are occurring within society and globally.

Effective social work practice is only possible and relevant when the practitioner designing the intervention is firmly grounded in the reality of the life of those he/she wishes to change. Urban-based community social work practice, a particular area of interest for me, too, must be firmly grounded in the operative reality of residents. Urban areas of the country are in the forefront, and some would rightfully argue bearing the brunt of the major changes that are transpiring in this nation (Cisneros 1996b). Consequently, there is a tremendous need to examine how urban communities are faring as a result of these trends. To accomplish this and other goals, social workers must be up to date on how issues and problems are manifested and perceived by the individuals experiencing them; practitioners must also not lose sight that these individuals, their families, and the community they live in, also have strengths. Thus, it becomes imperative for social work to be firmly grounded in how the profession has historically viewed urban communities and youth (the focus of this book), in order to better understand how it currently responds in this arena and with this population; and, in order to better understand what the future may bring if the profession resists significant changes, or if there are no major new perspectives and paradigms to guide practice in the future.

The reader, too, deserves an opportunity to be firmly grounded in the reasons why the book was written. This chapter, as a result, will provide a rationale and goals for the book, and outline why the topic of new arenas for social work practice with urban youth is so important for the profession. In many ways these "new arenas" are not so "new," "with historical roots dating back to the birth of the profession in this country. However, the newness of these arenas has more to do with the almost total abandonment of these forms of practice in social work practice today, even though urban-based youth still continue to be a significant sector of the populations we work with just as they were over 100 years ago.

New Arenas relationship to two other urban-based community practice books written by me should be identified in order for the reader to better understand how this book relates to community practice with nontraditional settings (Delgado 1999) and community capacity enhancement (Delgado 2000). Community social work practice covers an enormous amount of territory, with countless number of possibilities for practice, particularly with undervalued groups in urban areas (Hardcastle, Wenocur, and Powers

1998). Finally, I will describe the research approach and methods used to generate the case studies used to illustrate practice involving the arts, humanities, and sports. The case studies serve to bring the reader right into the middle of a current form of practice that has few social workers involved, with a glimpse of all its rewards and its challenges for the profession.

WHY NEW PRACTICE ARENAS FOCUSED ON URBAN YOUTH

There is little question concerning the importance and role of leaders and professions providing a vision for how society can utilize its strengths and assets as a means of redressing past or current injustices. There is arguably no group that is in greater need than youth, as it will be noted in chapter 2, particularly those residing in low-income urban areas of the country. Williamson (1997:123) very eloquently stated the importance of leadership exercising leadership qualities in addressing the needs of urban youth:

> The plight of the poor in America today, and the desperate conditions of life in our inner cities, form a tinderbox just waiting for a match. Our political leaders, many of whom are aware themselves that the tinderbox exists, seem to think they won't be reelected if they mention it. They spend more time and money investigating one another than on addressing the critical social and economic injustices that rage among us and threaten our children.

The nation's youth, in turn, have rarely been thought of as an asset, but instead have been thought off as a dangerous liability and a drain on national resources. This prevailing perspective has had a profound influence on shaping prevailing wisdom on how services and education have been conceptualized, particularly when targeting urban youths of color (Breggin and Breggin 1998).

The political will to address the needs of youth residing in urban areas across the United States is necessary before bold, creative, and much needed initiatives can be developed. The Carnegie Council on Adolescent Development (CCAD 1994:6) overview of the challenges facing adolescents places their fate squarely in the hands of society:

> During the past few decades, dramatic changes have profoundly affected the daily lives of young adolescents. Instead of safety in their neighbor-

hoods, adolescents often face physical danger; instead of economic security, they face uncertainty; instead of intellectual stimulation, they face boredom; in place of respect, they are neglected; lacking clear and consistent adult expectations for them, they feel alienated from mainstream American society.

Katz (1998:142) echoes much of the same sentiments as those expressed by the Carnegie Council on Adolescent Development and takes it one step further by placing the blame squarely in the hands of adults within society:

> The adult world is often inattentive to youth except to oversee them or to exhort consumption, conformity, and "good" behaviour. There are, of course, class, national, gender, ethnic, and racial dimensions to these problems. For some young people the best that they can hope for themselves is rather narrow, and this is more punishing now than ever before because of how much more they have learned to want thanks to the reach of globalised cultural production. These issues, which are environmental in the broadest sense, have deep, and largely unexplored, effects upon young people's constructions of identity, in how they see their "place" in the world, and ultimately, in how they produce the world to come.

Society's almost total disregard of the talents and wishes of its youth, as a result, may represent one of the greatest barriers that must be surmounted before youth can take their rightful place at the "negotiating table" concerning their future (Sarri 1996).

If and when the nation wishes to seriously address the needs of its youth, it doesn't necessarily mean that youth will be waiting with open arms and be willing to take us seriously. Many youth have developed cynicism concerning adults and the need that is often expressed for us to "rescue" youth from themselves (Males 1999). Thus, for any initiative to be successful, it must have youth at center stage as both players and recipients; adults must learn to plan with, rather than for, youth! Such a shift in perspectives may be very arduous to make, but essential nevertheless.

The engagement of urban youth in productive educational and developmental enhancing activities will undoubtedly be one of the main challenges facing this country as we enter the twenty-first century. The context, or what Skelton and Valentine (1998) refer to as the "geography of youth cultures," plays an influential role in determining how youth, particularly those belonging to marginalized groups, view themselves, each other, and how adults view them. Katz (1998:135–136) argues that restricted or lack of public space for youth to gather and feel accepted and safe has serious implications for their development:

> Young people have fewer opportunities for autonomous outdoor play or "hanging out." This lack has implications for many aspects of their healthy development related to such diverse processes as gross motor development, the building of culture, and the construction of their identity . . . the restricted access to the public environment, and with it many opportunities for forging and negotiating peer culture and acquiring the various social skills associated with there negotiations.

Thus, youth need their "own" space in which to develop their "own" identities and enhance their "own" skills, and they need to have a decisive voice in determining where these spaces are located and what transpires within them.

Numerous books and reports (government, university, and foundation) attest to the needs of youths, particularly those who are low-income, of color, and residing in large urban areas (Breggin and Breggin 1998; CCAD 1992; Children's Defense Fund 1994; Dryfoos 1990; Fraser 1997; Huston 1992; Jill, Winquist, and Loomis 1995; Kellogg Foundation 199?; Marshall and Wheeler 1996; McWhirter et al. 1993; Lerner 1995; National Research Council 1993; Poinsett 1996; Seefeldt 1993; Sharff 1998; Simon and Burns 1997; Upchurch 1996; Urban Institute 1993). These sources present an alarming picture of youth that is often described as "precarious," "endangered," and "critical," and issue challenges for the public and private sector to seriously consider the consequences of ignoring this population group if the country hopes to be competitive in the global market place well into the next century (Dryfoos 1995:vii):

> You don't have to be a rocket scientist to figure out that all is not well on the home front. Appalling statistics . . . portend terrible suffering . . . . But the general public does not just get up in the morning highly motivated to address social issues. Most are focused on their own welfare, worrying about their own kids, maintaining their own relationships, and keeping their taxes down. They have little insight into how those misery statistics affect the quality of their lives and the lives of generations to come.

Much has been written about the role of families and schools in addressing youth. However, it is becoming painfully clear that these two systems, important as they may be, are not sufficient to meet the challenges youth experience on almost a daily bases. The stressors all families experience, regardless of income, are further exacerbated for families who are undervalued in this society because of their income, ethnic/racial backgrounds, sexual orientation, etc. These challenges, in turn, have increased to the point that for some youths, particularly those who are low-income, of color, and residing in certain areas of cities, can encompass life or death at a very young age. As a result, additional partners must join in a concerted effort to assist families and schools. This undertaking will necessitate collaborative initiatives involving new partners and different configurations than have historically been the case. These efforts, in turn, will have youth playing significant roles in shaping the relationships, goals, and structure of activities.

SOCIAL WORK RESPONSE

The social work profession, like other helping professions, has struggled to better address the needs of this population group. The concept of empowerment, although widely accepted by social workers, has not found its way into practice with youth to the extent that is both expected and warranted (Morrison, Alcorn, and Nelums 1997). The profession can no longer view and address the needs of low-income urban youths of color from a narrow perspective, and use intervention strategies that are not based on the operative reality confronting youth within this context. The profession, in addition, can no longer view this population group from a deficit perspective; namely, an age-group in tremendous need without any assets (skills, knowledge, energy, and hope). Thus, the profession is challenged to develop, or rediscover (as the case may be), innovative, capacity enhancing community-based approaches for engaging youth in activities that systematically build upon their talents and energy (Jason 1997:103): "Much of the attention of community theorists has been directed to the skills and abilities that children and adolescents need, as well as, to a somewhat lesser degree, the opportunities they have to display such competencies and be rewarded for engaging in positive behavior." Consequently, if capacity enhancement interventions are reality grounded, conceptualized, and implemented, youth will become community assets rather than "drains" on families and communities. Further, they will play instrumental roles throughout all facets of the intervention.

The youth development work addressed in these pages has great appeal to social work when placed within an ecological context (Sarri 1996). This perspective, as noted by Greene and McGuire (1998), is multitheoretical, and is sufficiently flexible to take a holistic view of individuals, families, groups, and communities. Thus, these multiple viewpoints allow practitioners to both examine individual as well as societal factors systematically. An ecological framework, as a result, not only has applicability to different age groups, in this case youth (Watkins and Iverson 1998), different ethnic/racial backgrounds (Greene and Barnes 1998), but also different social work methods—micro- as well as macro-practice. Its relevance to community-based social work practice is, therefore, not bound by method.

NATIONAL CONCERN

A number of books and national reports have also addressed various aspects for reaching youth (Burt, Resnick, and Novick 1998; Carnegie Corporation 1994, 1996; CCAD 1989, 1992, 1995; Frank 1996; Health and McLaughlin 1993; Magid and McKelvey 1989; Marshall 1996; Pittman and Wright 1991; President's Commission 1996; Millstein, Peterson, and Nightingale 1993; Simon and Burns 1997; Upchurch 1996). These publications have been very informative in identifying key programming principles, listing important considerations, and projecting into the twenty-first century. However, they have made observations and recommendations that have not been widely examined from a skills perspective that can be incorporated by the social work profession. This step, although fundamental in nature, is best accomplished by a social worker.

THE POTENTIAL OF NEW ARENAS
AND YOUTH DEVELOPMENT

The avenues that the arts, humanities, and sports open up for social work practice increases the profession's competence to undertake interventions within undervalued urban communities (Sarri 1996). Jane Alexander (1995:ii), former chair of the National Endowment for the Arts, eloquently stated the potential role of the arts in reaching out to and engaging youth:

To save our children, to open their lives to new possibilities, we as parents and family members, teachers and volunteers, civic and religious leaders must marshal all our resources, public and private. The arts are one such resource, rich and inexhaustible. Disciplined and creative work —in music, dance, and theater; in visual arts and folk arts, in film and video, in literature and design—and help instill values, create pride in our cultural heritage, and engender a sense of self-worth. Children who pick up a paintbrush or a pen, a clarinet or a fistful of clay, are less likely to pick up a needle or a gun. They've got better things to do.

It does not mean that the profession must abandon conventional clinical and macro-practice approaches. However, it does mean that a social worker's skills encompass much more than those traditional forms of practice. This need takes on increased relevance for practitioners who have an interest in serving youth within a community context and positive development perspective.

The additions to a practice "toolbox" will necessitate a change in how we teach social work content in schools. For example, instead of traditional forms of clinical practice (individual, family, and group), another branch must be offered that is "nonclinical specific" and focus on use of activities that enhance youth abilities. It does not mean that important clinical services are not delivered in this new form of practice; however, it is done through integration into activities that on the suffice may not appear too "social work" in nature. Such a change requires new methods of intervention.

This "new" form of practice may not be so "innovative" in some schools of social work and undergraduate programs. However, instruction in those instances is generally done through field placements and rarely reinforced through classroom instruction. Work with the arts, humanities, and sports requires classroom instruction with appropriate scholarly material being used, just like it is done with any other form of intervention. This form of practice reinforcement is critical in order to better prepare students and future practitioners.

NEW PARTNERSHIPS AND YOUTH DEVELOPMENT

This book seeks to serve as a bridge between social work and other professions, particularly those associated with the arts, humanities, and sports.

This partnership is essential for better serving urban-based youth in the United States. The benefits of the forms of expression addressed must be viewed from a multifaceted perspective—personal and community. Personal transformation takes many different forms when using the arts and music, for example (Brown 1997:xii):

> This book is about changing yourself by working with the arts . . . looking at pictures, reading poems and stories, listening to music and watching drama can help you feel better; and how to paint pictures, write and create music that will boost your morale and help you problem-solve creatively . . . There are other art forms . . . : Dance gives you enormous powers of expression, and connects directly with the body. Clearly, the power of the arts and music have a way of helping individuals transform themselves. From a community perspective, these forms of expression serve to energize participants, their families, and the community in general. They not only enrich the quality of life among residents, but also serve as testaments to the external community of indigenous talents.

The field of youth development has much to offer the profession and can serve as a bridge for the profession. Probably the best definition that I have come across defining "positive youth development" was provided by a practitioner (Lawrence 1998:9):

> Positive Youth Development is an approach to working with youth that operates from the premise that all youths engage in a developmental process by which they seek to meet their needs and build their competencies. The model suggests that the way to assist youth in achieving positive outcomes from this process is the design of environments and services that emphasize strengths, asset building and youth/adult relationships.

This definition of positive youth development is based upon a set of values, principles, and beliefs that are not alien to the profession of social work. Further, the definition provides a path for social work to engage in this form of practice, and opens up possibilities for social workers to collaborate with other types of providers we typically would not enter into partnerships with.

The profession of social work must actively look toward other arenas in the hopes of developing interventions that are capable of reaching, and effectively serving, "at-risk," "high-risk," or "hard-to-reach" youth. The field of "positive youth development," versus the more limiting construct of "youth development," is not closely associated to any profession, least of all social work (Hahn 1998:54):

> Through every nook and cranny of the youth service field, activities unfold, day-in, year-round. Youth development professionals prowl through tough streets and suburban malls, they ply their craft managing storefront facilities and administering big downtown youth-serving agencies. Surely there is a field of youth development. But is this field a profession—or just an occupation? When youth workers are polled, some identify with youth work as the central organizing principle of their professional lives. Others say that they are social workers, program planners, or even accountants. Still others define themselves in terms of setting: "I am a lifer in the YWCA system."

The lack of close affiliation to any one profession serves both to facilitate and hinder the advancement of this perspective and the methods of intervention that result from it (Morrison, Alcorn, and Nelums 1997:323):

> Free from the paradigms and methodological boundaries of existing professions, the movement remains focused on social advocacy for youth. Yet, it does not contribute to the transformation of any one discipline or gain from knowledge forged out of professional experience.

Further, the lack of affiliation with a profession results in the lack of lobbying for additional resources that is often associated with professional membership organizations.

The concept of youth development is complementary with the use of the concept "developmental perspective," which focuses specifically on community. Midgley and Livermore (1997) note that despite an impressive growth in the professional literature on this perspective, the approach has only now resulted in more tangible conceptualizations that lend themselves to operationalization and evaluation. Social work, as a result, is in a propitious position to adopt a developmental perspective with an asset foundation at the micro and macro level of practice as part of its central mission to serve urban-based populations.

Important advancements have been made in the field of substance abuse prevention, for example some (even involving social workers) that combine the arts, humanities, sports, and are community-based. The lessons learned from these and other experiences will inform this book, and hopefully provide the reader with multiple avenues from which to implement this "new found wisdom" in their daily practice. Much of my practice experience is in the field of substance abuse prevention. This form of practice lends itself very well to using new arenas with urban youth.

RATIONALE

My interest in using the arts, humanities, and sports to outreach and serve urban youths of color started in the early 1990s when I was principal investigator on a federal substance abuse prevention grant. This grant served Latino, primarily Puerto Rican, youngsters in a mid-sized city (Holyoke, Mass.) located approximately 100 miles west of Boston. The project conceptualized substance abuse prevention by utilizing youth and community strengths and assets, and systematically developing youth self-esteem by emphasizing cultural heritage and pride. Cultural pride, in turn, was addressed through the learning of Puerto Rican history and culture (Taino, African, and Spanish influences) through a variety of means—readings, music, dances, arts, poetry, etc.

I was able to witness firsthand the power of development-focused activities for reaching, engaging, and transforming youth; the arts, music, and humanities, when relevant to the life of urban youth, serve to influence youth behavior and attitudes beyond what would be typically expected. These activities also served to reaffirm ethnic identities, and did so in a way that involved families and the community at large. Further, these activities play a transformation role within the community they are based in and reaffirm the importance of ethnic identity.

The project's goals and methods brought me into contact with numerous other prevention, early intervention, and youth development projects across the United States employing similar methods, including sports, chess teams, etc. These contacts reaffirmed the potential of such activities for other urban youth. The Holyoke project, like its counterparts across the United States, was very successful in achieving its goals (Delgado 1997; in pressb). However, the experience struck me in a variety of ways: (1) Why weren't there more social workers involved in these programs and activities? (2) Why weren't there more schools of social work and undergraduate programs teaching students how to use the arts, humanities, and sports, as methods for reaching urban-based youth? (3) Why wasn't the professional social work literature addressing this topic?; and (4) To what extent can social work collaborate with other professions in addressing urban youth in a more holistic manner—namely, social, economic, psychological, recreational, and artistic dimensions?

In essence, there was a tremendous need for the profession to seriously examine "alternative" and nonstigmatizing ways of serving urban youth, particularly those youth who were at greatest risk for failure in schools and after school hours—periods of high risk-taking. *New Arenas* focuses much of its attention on preadolescent and adolescent youth. However, I am ever mindful of Fassler's (1998) argument that the youth development field has virtually ignored younger children in the development of models and strategies for engagement. I have focused on preadolescent and adolescent youth because of the perceived threat that they present to the general public. Increased national efforts to treat youth criminal offenders as adults represents a very serious threat to this age group. Also, most efforts in the field of youth services tend to emphasize this age group, making selection of field examples of programs easier to accomplish for this book.

GOALS

There is a need for a book in social work that examines ways of engaging and serving urban youth through nonstigmatizing and culturally competent ways. Further, there is a need for a book that draws upon practice wisdom from a multidisciplinary perspective and in so doing, serve as a bridge between different helping professions. This book seeks to bring together activities that on the surface may appear not to share very much in common. After all, what do sports and music share besides being appealing to youth? However, upon closer scrutiny, they share many key principles. The implementation of these activities are not beyond the scope of any community in the United States. Further, as it it will noted in several later chapters, activities such as sports can serve to help communities organize intra-, inter-, and transnationally. Bringing together youth from throughout the country can be a very powerful experience for youth participants.

Greater collaboration between organizations sponsoring youth-focused activities such as the arts, humanities, and sports, should result in a more holistic and nondeficit approach toward serving urban youth. Such a unifying perspective minimizes conflictual perceptions between organizations and maximizes youth-focused resources. Further, it stresses the importance of youth activities being community-based. These collaborations must also break from the conventional sources of collaboration. New forms of partnerships will be necessary in order for communities to reach and assist youth.

Youth in general, and youths of color in particular, have historically been viewed negativing in this society. Youniss and Yates (1997:5) attribute this to adults having negative doubts about society:

> It may be that this negative view of youth reflects adults' own doubts about society. Is it youth who manifest unbridled self-interest or is it adults who, in the commercial and political sectors during the 1980s, violated public trust in the quest for excessive wealth and power? Is it youth who lack moral direction or adults who, for example, fail to meet child-custody agreements or publicly promote racial divisiveness in the name of managing government programs more efficient? Numerous violations of public and personal trust are evident to any informed adolescent, and the gap between ideals and actual behavior could easily be a source of embarrassment to adults and confusion to youth.

A book focused on youth as the world enters the twenty-first century is both timely and critical if we are to enjoy a future worth living.

New Arenas, as a result, will accomplish three goals: (1) highlight the importance of the profession systematically using the arts, humanities, and sports for reaching and serving urban-based youths of color; (2) conceptualize and operationalize a model that builds upon youth strengths and community assets that can be incorporated into intervention initiatives by drawing upon practice experiences of various types of helping professions; and (3) identify the necessary knowledge and skills (competencies) for practice using the arts, humanities, and sports.

The youth-focused activities addressed can transpire in a variety of in-school and out-of-school settings. However, the book emphasizes a community and after-school perspective. It is highly recommended that for urban youth to receive the maximum benefit of participation in the arts, humanities, or sports, both settings—school and community—must work closely together in pursuit of common goals (CCAD 1994). The dual approach toward community and school will necessitate social workers collaborating with professions that they normally would not work with.

RELATIONSHIP TO OTHER BOOKS

New Arenas is complementary and a logical extension of two other books I have written. *Social Work Practice in Non-Traditional Urban Settings* (Oxford University Press) uses an asset paradigm to identify, engage, and collaborate with indigenous institutions such as grocery stores, beauty parlors, barbershops, laundromats, etc., in delivering culturally competent services. Utilization of an assets paradigm toward community practice brings with it numerous implications for social work education and methods of practice. *Community Social Work Practice in an Urban Context: The Potential of a Capacity Enhancement Perspective* (Oxford University Press) focuses on urban community capacity enhancement projects such as murals, gardens, playgrounds, and sculptures. That book complements the nontraditional settings book by focusing on an aspect of community generally overlooked or misunderstood by outsiders, providers being a prime example. Urban communities do not exclusively consist of individuals needing assistance or plagued with problems. Urban communities have assets just like their suburban and rural counterparts. Neither of these books specifically focuses on youth, although both have direct implications for work with youth. A book specifically focused on urban youth, as a result, highlights interventions that must take into consideration developmental needs within the context of community.

This book, like the two other community practice books, also uses an asset paradigm and is urban-based. Nevertheless, unlike the Oxford books, *New Arenas* examines how community-based organizations (formal and informal) targeting urban youth can use the arts, humanities, and sports, as activities to teach cultural pride, enhance skills (academic and social), and develop youth leadership. A focus on youth is justified based upon the sad state of affairs this age-group is confronting in this country, and the potential role they can play in helping to shape this country's future in the twenty-first century.

This country has absolutely no hesitation in targeting youth as a "market, and as an important source of capital for the consumption of media, clothes, etc." According to the Sporting Goods Manufacturers Association, for example, adolescents (13 to 17 years old), spend on average $311 per year on sports apparel, or 31 percent more than the average consumer ($193), making adolescents the biggest consumers of any age group in the country (Landre, Miller, and Porter 1997). It should not be lost on the reader when looking at these statistics on purchases of athletic and logo apparel, the role of gangs in dictating fashion (Landre, Miller, and Porter 1997:163):

> Selected businesses have profited considerably from the growth and popularity of modern street gangs. Millions of advertising dollars are aimed at large groups of young people who want to wear what is "in" for the season, and often what is "in" originates with street gangs. For example, the loose, baggy, low-hung pants and long T-shirts worn by gang members for several years became a fad when the media caught on. Suddenly, well-known retail stores were carrying these clothes, and many non-gang youths were happily buying the same apparel.

Nevertheless, the country is reluctant to target resources for youth focused on assisting them in further enhancing their capacities. In essence, youth can be viewed as "needing" and "wanting" but not capable of "doing." This bias must be corrected if youth are to have a productive and expansive role in the future of the United States. Nevertheless, I am under no illusion that such a shift in perspectives will be easy to achieve in a country dominated by adults.

Unlike other influential books on the topic of urban youth, most notably Health and McLaughlin (*Identity and Inner-City Youth: Beyond Ethnicity and Gender*); Lakes (*Youth Development and Critical Education: The Promise of Democratic Action*); Burt, Resnick, and Novick (*Building Supportive Communities for At-Risk Adolescents: It Takes More than Services*); Youniss and Yates (*Community Service and Social Responsibility in Youth*); Scales and Leffert (*Developmental Assets: A Synthesis of the Scientific Research on Adolescent Development*); and McLaughlin, Kirby, and Langman (*Urban Sanctuaries: Neighborhood Organizations in the Lives and Futures of Inner-City Youth*), *New Arenas* targets the skills (competencies) and knowledge areas that are necessary for social work practitioners to use the arts, humanities, and sports as "interventions." In addition, it is written for social workers (experienced practitioners as well as students), although it will undoubtedly appeal to other helping professions such as those in education, psychology, applied sociology and anthropology, and recreation.

It is hoped that new arenas for social work practice involving urban youth should have great appeal for practitioners and students seeking to find ways of engaging and mobilizing the talents of this population group. Like practice with any age group, youth present their unique sets of rewards and challenges, and thus require literature and practice approaches specifically focused on them—approaches that take into consideration their talents, needs, and wishes. This "specialized" form of practice is not only necessary but required in order for practitioners to feel relevant in carrying out their mission. To facilitate this goal, I draw upon material obtained from numerous youth programs across the United States. This effort to draw upon "real" field programs and examples will hopefully facilitate the identification of practice approaches and issues, making the book relevant to practitioners interested in this field of practice.

Although my primary targets are community social workers, there is relevance for other professions interested in urban youth, in stressing collaboration between social workers and other helping professionals. As a result, I draw upon material from other professions, making it easier for other providers to see the connections with social work and for social workers to see how other professionals conceptualize and address the same population group. *New Arenas*, however, is not intended to be a "textbook" in the conventional sense, addressing all of the basic elements of work with urban adolescents. Nevertheless, it should make a solid supplement to a generalist practice text at the graduate level. Although written specifically for a method (practice) course, it can also be used in a variety of other types of courses such as human behavior and the social environment , or in racism and oppression. Further, it can be used in conjuncture with a field placement when it is not used in the classroom.

COMMUNITY CONTEXT

The concept of "community" has been with us since the beginning of time. The process of defining what is meant by "community" can easily result in a book onto itself, if not multiple books (Minkler and Wallerstein 1997). A significant number of scholars have devoted major portions of their professional lives to studying and defining community (Abrahamson 1996; Badsah 1996; Chavis and Wandersman 1990; Fellin 1995; Flanagan 1993; Haymes 1995; Keating 1996; Unger and Wandersman 1995).

The definition of community by former Secretary of Housing and Urban Development Cisneros (1996:50–51) captures the dynamic nature of this concept and places it within a practical domain:

What does "community" mean? We know what community is not. It is not streets darkened by the shadows of vacant buildings, deserted by people who fear sudden and vicious attack and know no one who will help. It is not giant housing projects where children die in the crossfire of rival gangs and security guards crouch around staircases to avoid Uzi-wielding drug sentries . . . So, what is "community"? . . . . it must be a stable place from which we can create opportunities for people; opportunities to go from homelessness to rental housing to homeownership; opportunities to go from joblessness, without education and training, to acquiring skills and self-sufficiency. Building community means helping neighborhood residents organize and develop partnerships with local government, nonprofit agencies, and business organizations. . . . If, as the old African adage says, it takes a whole village to raise a child, then it also takes a whole region to make a good community.

Community, according to Cisneros, encompasses much more than buildings, geography, and people. It represents that the total experience of these and other factors coming together.

The concept of community has currency from within and without helping professions. It is virtually impossible to pick up a local newspaper or not to see a plethora of books in a local bookstore on the "decline" of community in the United States (Blakely and Snyder 1997; Brown 1995; Chavis 1997; Garr 1995; Jason 1997; Oldenburg 1991; McKnight 1995; Moe and Wilkie 1997; Schwartz 1997; Williamson 1997; Wuthnow 1991, 1995). For my purposes here, the definition will be simple and restrict itself to what are the essential elements of community. The term "community" holds many different definitions. Urban community can be simply defined as a geographical area located within a city (small, mid-sized, or central), all of its residents and institutions (formal or informal). This geographical area is dynamic and represents a unit of analysis; the exact definition of geographical, however, is greatly dependent upon local circumstances.

I prefer a definition of community that encompasses up to possibly four key dimensions: (1) geographical; (2) ethnic-cultural-socioeconomic class; (3) psychological; and (4) concentration of facilities. Community, as a result, can consist of anyone, all, or a combination of these factors. The greater the presence of these dimensions, the greater the "sense of community" that will result. In situations where all four dimensions apply, practitioners who were not born in the community will be instantaneously considered "outsiders." One art director stated her definition of community quite eloquently, and comprehensively, and captured what "community" means in this book (Barker 1995:38):

> Community, in this case, includes everyone that the project touches: the youth, their parents, the buying public, and the people who live in the surrounding neighborhoods where the students might be painting a mural or having a show. As difficult as it may be to understand, in some cases the community has to be persuaded to buy the idea that its youth can be valuable contributors to society.

COMMUNITY AND YOUTH

The concept of community is not totally alien when looking at youth. The community context is necessary in order for programs to foster youth empowerment and development. The literature on communities is very clear about the importance of demographics, economic opportunities, institutional (formal and informal) capacities, and physical environment affecting outcomes in a variety of areas that are important to youth development—economic self-sufficiency, citizenship, positive family and social relationships (Sipe, Ma, Gambone 1998). Social work's active involvement of community in creating initiatives is not a modern day phenomenon (Simon 1994:105): "In community work of the interwar and war years, social workers considered community residents to be the indispensable source of initiative, power, and imagination in any successful collaboration between professionals and citizens."

Community is the context that is needed in order to develop a better and more in-depth understanding of youth. How the broader community views youth, as assets or a group to fear, influences how youth, in turn, view the broader community. Katz (1998) argues that restricted or lack of public space within a community for youth to gather in, prevents youth from exercising opportunities for autonomous play. Watt and Stenson (1998:252–253), too, reinforce the importance of the concept of localized (community) space for urban youth:

> Despite the postmodernist claims about the declining significance of local neighborhoods as important for young people's identities and lifestyles . . . , empirical studies of youth have demonstrated the ways in which young people continue to identify with local places . . . By "place"

we mean a space which people in a given locality understand as having a particular history and as arousing emotional identifications, and which is associated with particular groups and activities.

Thus, Katz's and Watt and Stenson's definitions of place within a youth perspective draws upon the four aspects of community (geographic, eth-nic/cultural/class, psychological, and concentration of facilities) that will be used in these pagaes. This holistic perspective toward youth serves to ground them within a foundation that can both be used to better understand youth and the challenges they face as well as a target for youth to change to make it more responsive to them.

URBAN FOCUS

My focus on urban areas is not meant to detract from the challenges and needs youth face in other contexts, most notably suburban and rural ones. However, there is little dispute that youth living in urban areas of the United States are at increased risk for experiencing a whole host of social problems, when compared with their counterparts in other settings (Feagin 1998). Austin and Willard (1998:1) note how an urban context shapes the experience of youths, particularly those of color:

> Urban youth, particularly youth of color, inherit cities where employment, adequate education, and the basic necessities of life are increasingly difficult to obtain. These conditions inform contemporary "urban problems," many of which are specifically related to youth . . . Atrocity tales appearing in newspaper headlines, on magazine covers, and during television newscasts ask us, with alarming regularity, to see young people as animalistic, alien Others. The decline in state education funding is matched by the increase in funding for prisons. We are left to wonder whether the new "Evil Empire" will be located in our schools, streets, and homes, among our friends, siblings, neighbors, and children: "youth."

Cisneros (1996a:1), in turn, summed up the importance of a focus on cities as settings when stating:

The American city—historic gateway to social and economic mobil-ity—has become home to many of the most disadvantaged people in America. Labor force detachment, lack of education, welfare depen-dency, drug abuse, teenage pregnancy, high infant mortality, and eco-nomic independence are virtually unknown. We are in danger of becom-ing two nations: one with highly skilled, well-paid workers and profes-sionals and the other with a low-skilled, low- or even no-wage, permanent underclass. This spatial isolation of people by income and race in our metropolitan areas has become America's Achilles' heel and is spawning Third World conditions in our very midst.

As it will be noted in chapter 2, statistics related to youth, and more specifically to youths of color in economically distressed areas of a city, make my focus that much more relevant to social workers. The status of their existence requires that they be a focus of a concerted strategy to elim-inate the barriers they confront in seeking a safe and productive future in this society. One does not need to be an "urban expert" to witness how the lives of youth in sections of major urban areas such as Chicago, Dallas, Detroit, Los Angeles, Miami, and New York differ dramatically from the lives of youth in other settings. The magnitude of the problems they encounter, combined with the extent of residential segregation, marketably separates them from their counterparts in suburbia and rural America.

RESEARCH METHODS

Stake (1995:1) very eloquently sums up what practitioners and researchers hope to get out of reading a case study:

> For the most part, the cases of interest in education and social service are people and programs. Each one is similar to other persons and pro-grams in many ways and unique in many ways. We are interested in them for both their uniqueness and commonality. We seek to under-stand them. We would like to hear their stories. We may have reserva-tions about some things people . . . tell us, just as they will question some of the things we tell about them. But we enter the scene with a sin-cere interest in learning how they function in their ordinary pursuits and milieus and with a willingness to put aside many presumptions while we learn.

In essence, be they highly detailed and structured or brief glimpses, cases allow us to enter a scene without having to be there in order to enjoy it, as well as struggle and endure. Most importantly, they allow us the privilege of learning by watching others.

New Arenas draws on field-based examples of social workers and other professionals planning, administering, and practicing using the arts, humanities, and sports. The "voices" of social workers in this field of practice are very important here because they are in the best position to advise other professionals and educators. Unfortunately, there will be instances where the profession is not playing any significant role at all; in these situations, the voices of those who are will be used to illustrate the importance of their work. These case examples will be approached from a multifaceted perspective: (1) goals of intervention; (2) key theoretical concepts; (3) facilitating and hindering factors; (4) key skills that are essential for practice; and (5) words of advice to practitioners.

Various types of case materials will be integrated throughout as a means of allowing the reader an opportunity to better appreciate new arena-type activities. I present nine case studies in chapter 9. A number of community organizations, schools, and city governments have been creative in tapping artistic talent. Graffiti artists, for example, have usually been looked upon unfavorably by authorities. However, initiatives have been developed to identify and enlist these artists in socially constructive projects (Pring 1997; Trust for the Public Land 1994).

Case vignettes and case studies are the two primary types of field-based illustrations used. The former provides a brief glimpse into a setting or activity, and are generally intended to highlight a key point or raise a series of considerations; the latter, in turn, are of considerably greater depth in detail, and provide sufficient information to allow the reader to develop a greater understanding of organizational and community context, programmatic approaches, issues, and considerations. Further, the cases also serve the purpose of integrating many of the themes addressed throughout. This integration is of critical importance if community social work practice is to be enhanced (Yin 1994).

Chapter 8 is devoted specifically to case studies representing different geographical areas of the country, activities, and organizations. In addition, every effort was made to draw upon a diverse sample, taking into account ethnicity, race, and gender. However, because of financial limitations, New England, Boston, and the Greater Boston area will have more than their fair share of citations. I hope that this "limitation" does not detract from the generalizablity of the key points and themes raised throughout.

The use of case studies provides me with an opportunity to tap into the impact of national trends concerning funding of the arts, etc. Case studies were selected based upon the following criteria: (1) is the agency is actively engaged in "innovative" forms of practice? (2) does the agency's mission specifically target urban-based youth? (3) do activities not only involve the forms addressed here but also seek to provide youth with an opportunity to receive additional services? (4) are the organizations located in different geographical regions of the country? and (5) does the organization express a willingness to assist me by sharing materials and granting access to youth and staff for interviews?

Information was gathered utilizing the following approach: (1) key informant suggestions; (2) telephone contact with key organizational personnel; (3) review of organization documents, newspapers, and scholarly articles where applicable; (4) interviews by telephone, or in person, with selective personnel; and (5) actual field visits in circumstances where it was possible. This multifaceted approach was both economical and efficient.

The nation and, indirectly, the profession, are now facing, and will continue to face, major challenges in reaching disengaged urban youth in the twenty-first century. Youth, particularly adolescents, look outward from the home and family to develop a better understanding of their identity and their place in the world (CCAD 1989). Consequently, there is a tremendous need to develop new and comprehensive initiatives targeting youth at a point in their development when critical choices are made concerning paths they can take as they enter adulthood.

These initiatives must employ practitioners who are not reluctant to reconceptualize practice and use new paradigms that systematically build upon youth assets. However, the field of youth work, too, is undergoing major changes as we approach the twenty-first century (Krueger 1998:51):

Perhaps people shy away from speaking about youth work as a process of interaction because it is so complex . . . as the field moves toward best practice, managed care, and outcome and competency-based approaches to youth development, it seems wise to give more consideration to knowing youth works. That means to shift from focusing so much on results, competencies, outcomes, best practices, assets and proving something, to understanding youth work as it presents itself in daily interactions.

Initiatives, in turn, must also seek to create partnerships between professions, and between professions and communities, as means of marshaling the nation's talent to work in the same direction and toward the same goal—namely, maximizing youth potential. The globalization of the nation's economy requires that all of its residents are actively engaged and shaping the nation's future; failure to achieve this goal will have disastrous consequences for this country. We cannot afford to systematically "write-off" a high percentage of its population (urban youths of color), if we are to compete on a global level. Further, "writing-off" a significant segment of our population will result in considerable sums of money being allocated to remedial education efforts and the criminal justice system.

Joseph Marshall Jr., nationally recognized youth worker and cofounder of the Omega Boys Club of San Francisco, expressed my sentiments when stating (Marshall 1996: xxvi–xxvii):

Many people . . . as I have told many audiences many times, seem to believe that it's easier for young people today. Well, it's not. The lack of employment, the availability of weapons of all types, and the presence of crack cocaine have all combined to make things interminably worse for them, especially in the inner cities of our nation. But—and the sentence is very key, people—armed with the belief that young people want a way out but just don't know how to get out, we have been able to save individual lives, and better yet, to empower others to reach out and do the same. This is a terrible thing to say, but I am almost convinced that as a society we would rather let those young men die than do something to save them. But we can't say anymore that we don't know how to save them, or that we don't have a successful model we can emulate. The success of the Omega Club demonstrates that it is not necessarily they who have given up on us, but we who have given up on them. The ball is in our court.

New Arenas for Community Social Work Practice with Urban Youth is about providing youth with alternatives that have cultural meaning, enhance self-esteem, result in obtaining meaningful skills, and help them make the transition from productive youth to productive adults in their community and in society. The profession of social work must be on the front line in helping to provide these alternatives and, in so doing, "rediscover the field of youth development," reaffirm our urban mission, and focus our practice with undervalued communities.

CHAPTER 2

DEMOGRAPHICS AND NEEDS
OF YOUTH IN U.S. CITIES

In this chapter I draw on numerous foundation and government studies to increase an understanding of the challenges facing urban-based youths of color in our society. To develop an in-depth appreciation of youth, and particularly those who are urban and of color, it is necessary to examine demographic information. This information, in turn, can be used to develop a profile of urban youth across the nation that will reveal who these youth are, an important yet disturbing picture of their needs, and the challenges facing helping professions in reaching, engaging, and serving them.

I present a picture of youths' needs and their issues, as a means of setting the context for community-based interventions (Collins 1998). Consequently, the reader is warned that this chapter presents a very dismal picture of the issues confronting many urban youths across the United States (Henderson and Champlin 1998). The statistics presented, as noted by the President's Committee on the Arts and Humanities, could not have been imagined two generations ago (1996:11):

> Children live in a different world today from that of their grandparents. In some ways, it is a better world. More children today are better fed, better educated and free from dangerous childhood diseases. However, this progress is not shared equally by all children. Today's children face new hazards that were not even imagined by previous generations.

Last, specific attention will be paid to adolescents, although other age-groups will also be covered, but not in the same depth.

The professional literature is rich with studies and examples highlighting the relationship between the incidence and extent of stressors and social consequences for adolescents (de Anda et al. 1997). Stressors, however, must be examined within the context in which they occur. Thus, the stressors urban youths of color may encounter in their daily lives will have relatively minor resemblance to those of suburban and rural white, non-Latino, youth. This is not to say that suburban and rural youths are not facing incredible challenges. However, the magnitude of the problems, and the resources available to reach and assist them, present a very different picture than that for urban youth (Breggin and Breggin 1998).

First, suburban youths do not have the same degree of problems, particularly those that often cluster together for urban youth. Further, the resources at their disposal far exceed those available to youths of color in cities. It is important to note as McLaughlin and Heath (1993:214): "They, like their more advantages peers, make choices based on what seems best for them at the time. Alternatives for inner-city youths are few, vision is limited, and the self-confidence necessary to 'make it' is often lacking." Last, the stigma and consequences youths of color face if they fail in surmounting these two sets of barriers can prove to be life-altering and life-threatening. Consequently, urban youths face multiple jeopardies that are further compounded by racism and classism in this society.

A DEMOGRAPHIC PROFILE OF THE NATION'S YOUTH

The number of youths aged 17 years or younger increased by 6 percent (4 million) between 1990 and 1994 from 64 million to 68 million, with approximately 25 percent of the country consisting of youths under 18 (De Vita 1996). It is estimated that the size of the school-age population (ages 5 to 17) will increase by 10 percent by the year 2006. By the year 2020 youths (ages 10–19), which numbered 34 million in 1992, will grow to 43 million (Kellogg Foundation 1998a). The adolescent population is expected to increase by as much as 20 percent in the next decade, with low-income youths of color experiencing an even greater increase. Consequently, youths will continue to represent a greater and greater percentage of the country's overall population well into the twenty-first century (De Vita 1996).

Youths of color (Asian, Black/African-American, Latino, and Native American) present a dramatically different demographic profile from that of the country as a whole and this is in large part the result of where they live, specific geographic areas within urban settings, the impact of racism and classism that results in limited opportunities for advancement, and the development of a pervasive attitude that the "cards are stacked against them" (McLoyd 1994:59–60):

> In view of these demographic changes, rendering minority children virtually invisible in the annals of knowledge about the conditions that facilitate and disrupt development is indefensible ethically. That some of the most pressing problems now facing America affect, disproportionately, children and youth from ethnic minority backgrounds makes it all the more so. It is also inimical to the long-term self-interests of the nation because minority youth's fraction of the total youth population is increasing precisely at a time when the proportion of youth in the total population is dwindling . . . . The economic well-being of the nation will depend even more than at present on its ability to enhance the intellectual and social skills of all its youth, as these will be crucial for maximum productivity in the workplace.

Thus, the future is replaced by the present; old age is defined as being in one's 20s, 30s, or 40s; and, for many youths of color, the only viable career option is that associated with prisons!

Youths of color accounted for 33 percent of the total population under the age of 18 in the United States by 1995—a much higher percentage than the 25 percent found in the white, non-Latino sector (De Vita 1996). Distinctive demographic trends are also evident within communities of color that have direct implications for the overall composition of the nation in the beginning of the next century. In 1995, black/African-American youths accounted for 45 percent versus 41 percent for Latinos of all youths of color. Asian-American youths were the third largest group, representing 11 percent of all youths of color (De Vita 1996). However, by the year 2000, a demographic shift is expected to occur with Latino youths surpassing black/African-American youths numerically. Projections for the year 2030 show youths of color under the age of 18 representing the vast majority of all youths in the United States (De Vita 1996).

It is important to pause and note that not all Latino groups are equally as young, with Mexican-Americans (39 percent) having the highest percentage of individuals under the age of 18, closely followed by Puerto Ricans (38 percent), with Cubans (19 percent) at the opposite end of the continuum with a very small percentage of the population within this age category (Del Pinal and Singer 1997).

One influential trend in the United States, with a profound impact on their economic and social well-being, is the number of children under the age of 18 since 1990 who live in female-headed households. According to the most recent statistics (1996), 27 percent lived with one parent, an increase from 12 percent in 1970. The number of households headed by an unmarried or divorced black/African American were equal. However, in 1996 unwed households among black/African Americans outnumbered divorced mother-headed households by 3 to 1. Since 1990, 25 percent of all white, non-Latinos, 30 percent of Latinos, and more than 50 percent of black/African Americans under the age of 18 lived with one parent, usually the mother (Wright 1997).

Since the vast majority of youths of color reside in urban areas across all regions of the United States, cities take on added significance as influential arenas for addressing the social-educational-psychological-political needs of these communities. In examining New York City, for example, it has been estimated that over 20,000 young people between 14 and 21 were homeless, up to 125,000 students are absent from school every day, with nearly 40 percent failing to earn a high school diploma; the unemployment rate for youths between 16 and 19 was 35 percent (black/African Americans and Latinos had close to 50 percent), and one in three youths grow up in a single-parent family (Quinn 1990).

NEEDS OF YOUTHS IN CITIES

When the term "youth" is combined with the term "urban," it invariably elicits a wide range of responses among the public, government, and helping professions. Unfortunately, few of these responses are positive (CWLA 1998; Magen 1998; Males 1999; McKnight 1995; Simon and Burns 1997). However, the needs and aspirations of marginalized urban youth in the nation's cities do not differ dramatically from their white, privileged, suburban counterparts (Fine and Mechling 1993).

The mere mention of social work practice with urban youth, and more specifically, adolescents, strikes fear in the hearts of most practitioners. There is no denying that youth, regardless of their circumstances, present challenges to social work practitioners. However, these challenges are no more or less demanding than work with any other age group. Thus, it would be unfair to label youth as particularly challenging. The challenges increase when the racial and ethnic background of the youths are of color and those of the practitioner are white, non-Latino. This gap represents a significant barrier in the establishment of respect and trust between the parties; further, it severely limits communication, perceptions, and the establishment of a working relationship.

Practitioners have age groups and social problems that they are committed to working with as well as groupings that they do not enjoy working with, regardless of their level of success. Thus, practitioners must find their "niche" in the field of practice as a means of maximizing their potential for change. In the youth arena, this may mean working with any of the following social problems—gangs, substance abuse, school dropouts, pregnancy, etc. It would not be unusual to be working with multiple "problems," necessitating developing a comprehensive approach involving other providers. Consequently, I contend that youths are no more or less challenging to work with than any other population subgroup. The ability to engage and work with youth is ever-dependent upon the "gifts" of the practitioner and his/her patience, tolerance, and commitment to this age group.

Numerous books have been written sounding the alarm about the future of urban youth and the need to redouble and refocus the nation's efforts at "saving this generation" from an external initiated self-destruction(Canada 1998; Marshall and Wheeler 1996; Simon and Burns 1997; Upchurch 1996). These books have generally served to identify the unique set of pressures facing urban youth as we enter the twenty-first century (Burt, Resnick, and Novick 1998; Heath and McLaughlin 1993; Kotlowitz 1991; McLaughlin, Irby, and Langman 1993; Skelton and Valentine 1998).

Statistics on youth-related problems, as will be noted later, have generally indicated an increase in most problem areas, particularly among urban youths of color (Leventhal and Keeshaw 1993:276): "The conditions in America's inner-cities pose a variety of complex challenges to intervention. Consequently, a closer look at promoting alternatives within this unique environment clearly illustrates the necessity of a multi-level approach." It is artificial to separate the lives of youths from the life of the community. In essence, the state of this age-group is inextricably related to the place they live in.

Although Leventhal and Keeshaw's (1993) comments are directed to providing healthy alternatives to substance abuse, their sentiments are also applicable to all other social problems experienced by low-income youths of color residing in urban areas of the country. The solutions that are often proposed address the importance of socialization—emphasis on creative ways of channeling aggression, particularly for males, the need for access to constructive activities during critical hours and days of the week, and the importance of youths having "dreams" that are achievable—in essence, don't count on making it in professional sports!

Historically, statistics focused on youth have generally been scarce. It used to be easier to find out the primary cause of death among cows than to find out how many youths were homeless (Lantier 1998). Recently, however, there has been a rapid increase in data related to youth, challenging organizations to be creative in substantiating service needs and helping them to plan services with a clearer profile of who they are trying to reach (Lantier 1998). Unfortunately (as will be addressed in chapter 3), statistics, when available, rarely look at youths from a positive perspective. Strength-focused statistics are not exclusively the opposites of negative statistics, such as percentage of high school dropouts, smokers, etc. These forms of statistics are important and useful. However, new forms of statistics are in order to capture aspects of youths that are necessary for enhancement capacity programming.

Substance Abuse: Alcohol, Tobacco, and Other Drugs

The subject of substance abuse is often synonymous with adolescents and drug experimentation. Substance abuse among adolescents has recently experienced a dramatic increase after several years of decline. Eighth graders, for example, who reported using illicit drugs in prior 30 days during 1997 witnessed an increase to 13 percent from 6 percent in 1991 (Lantier 1998). More specifically, alcohol and tobacco have shown the greatest increase in use (Feber 1996; Wren 1996). Tobacco's reliance on nicotine, an addictive drug, has facilitated the process of addiction (Immen 1996). It is estimated that 25 percent of all adolescents smoke on any given date (Hutchinson and Poole 1998). In 1992 it was estimated that 17 percent of all twelfth graders smoked cigarettes daily. In 1995, the percentage had increased to 25 percent (Lantier 1998). Heavy drinking among twelfth graders, for example, showed an increase from 21 percent in 1992 to 25 percent in 1997 (Lantier 1998).

Among African-American and Latino youths there has been a substantial increase in smoking rates since 1991. Among African-American youths, this signifies a reverse trend with rates of smoking increasing by 80 percent during this period (Stolberg 1998b). It is estimated that if current trends continue, approximately 1.6 million African-American youths will become regular smokers and 500,000 will die as a result (Stolberg 1998c). Recent research suggests that this increase in smoking is also closely tied to the use

of marijuana; the decision to smoke is tied to the belief that cigarettes pro-
long the euphoria associated with marijuana use (Gross 1998). Consequently, cigarette smoking takes on added significance for African-American youths.

Tobacco companies have recently come under public attack for their
practices of targeting adolescents as an important market (Jimenez 1997;
Meier 1998). Recent court-obtained documents involving one major
tobacco company (R. J. Reynolds) show the importance of adolescents to
the future of the cigarette industry (Meir 1998:A12): "Internal records . . .
provide new evidence of the extent to which the company for decades
courted young smokers . . . Viewed together, the R. J. Reynolds documents
indicate that the top tobacco industry executives long believed that people
under 18 were its most crucial customers because by that age, minors who
smoked had chosen the brand that they would stick with and smoke even
more as adults." A *New York Times* editorial (January 16, 1998, p. A26),
summarized the findings from numerous documents concerning R. J.
Reynold's campaign:

> A 1976 10-year planning forecast . . . called for a new brand for children
> as young as 14, and a 1980 memo to the company chairman called for
> reversing the company's decline among youngsters 14 to 17. Repeated sur-
> vey's assessed the smoking habits of these young teen-agers. Other memos
> described the age group between 14 and 24 as "tomorrow's cigarette busi-
> ness" as vital to the company's long-term prosperity and survival.

Tobacco companies, facing increased limitations concerning advertising, have started to use promotional gear (clothing or accessories embla-
zoned with cigarette logos) as a means of promoting their brands among
youths (Jimenez 1997). It is not unusual to find youths wearing caps, back-
packs, T-shirts, and other items with cigarette brands prominently displayed on the clothing. One study based in New Hampshire and Vermont
found that youths who owned promotional items were more likely to
smoke than those who did not—among senior high school students it was
50 percent versus 23 percent of those who smoke but do not own items
(Jimenez 1997).

It is no mistake that the alcohol and tobacco industries have targeted
advertising in places and events frequented by youth. Select sports magazines, arcades, music concerts, racing events, have been very popular
sources for alcohol and tobacco advertising dollars (Maxwell and Jacobson

1989; Meier 1998). These industries have also played influential roles in sponsoring ethnic-targeted cultural celebrations, scholarships, and have even underwritten the costs of conferences specifically tailored to prevent the use of alcohol, tobacco, and other drugs (Hacker, Collins, and Jacobson 1987). Thus, the insidious nature of these two industries has played a role in increasing the use of alcohol and tobacco among youths. In so doing, they have also systematically quieted the role of human service organizations and ethnic/racial targeted magazines in speaking out against these industries through their monetary support.

Violence and Crime

The subject of violence and crime is highly emotionally charged, with newspapers and local news programs more than willing to devote space and time to stories related to youth victims, or perpetrators, of crime (Alexander 1998a; Belluck 1998). The mid-1990s was a period during which several prominent criminologists predicted that the late 1990s and early twenty-first century would have youths committing crimes at an unprecedented rate (Steinberg 1999). A new breed of "superpredators" would be largely responsible for a record number of youth-on-youth murders. Although this prediction has not come true and there is serious question about whether or not the next ten years will witness this crime sphere, violence is still a major issue among urban youth.

A 1998 national survey found that crime/violence was the considered the greatest problem (cited by 30.2%) facing the United States today (Horatio Alger Association 1998). The highest risk for initiation of violence behavior occurs around the ages of 15 to 16, and the greatest participation in violence occurs at 16 to 17, with the risk of initiating violence after the age of 20 being considerably lower, and participation rates drop dramatically after the age of 17 (Elliott 1994).

Rarely does a day or week go by without the appearance of some news story related to youths and the "danger" they pose to society (Sheley and Wright 1995:1):

> Violence committed by and against juveniles has come more and more to define the public's image of the crime problem and the larger political debate over anticrime policy. No longer adequately depicted as mere "juvenile delinquents," today's young offenders are frequently described as violent, hard-core felons . . . Not so many years ago, police officers and school principals worried about young "hoods" who drank beer and car-

ried brass knuckles and switchblades. Today, they are preoccupied with hardened youth dealing crack and carrying semiautomatic firearms.

Probably no city in the country has received more national attention regarding youth-on-youth crime, particularly involving very young children, than Chicago. In 1998 the case of an 11-year-old girl who was allegedly murdered by two boys ages 8 and 7, the charges were eventually dismissed (Kresnak 1998). Nevertheless, for a brief period of time, the children were the youngest murder suspects in the city's history, and raised serious concerns in the community and criminal justice system. In the same year a 14-year-old and a 9-year-old were accused of fatally beating their 5-year-old foster brother. In 1994 two boys, ages 10 and 11, dropped a 5-year-old to his death from a fourteenth floor window after he refused to steal candy for them.

Chicago also received national attention in the case of a young girl who was killed in a cross-fire between two gangs. The alleged perpetrator, also very young, was found dead a few days later, a victim of his own gang. His killing was an attempt to take public pressure off the gang as the result of the girl's murder. The latest case involving the 8- and 7-year-old boys caused the state of Illinois to reexamine its penal code. According to state laws, these boys can never be locked up regarding the current charges because of their ages (Brown 1998). The case of a California teenager accused of killing a 7-year-old girl in a Las Vegas casino restroom has also received considerable national attention (*New York Times* 1998a). This case, like those of Chicago and other cities, has highlighted the degree of violence youths can perpetrate on other youths, and raised deep questions about how children can kill other children, and what can be done to prevent such occurrences.

According to an analysis by the Children's Defense Fund (1998) of how the United States stands in relation to 25 other industrialized nations regarding key aspects related to guns for children under the age of 15, they are: 12 times more likely to die from gunfire, 16 times more likely to be murdered by someone with a gun, 11 times more likely to commit suicide using a gun, and 9 times more likely to die in a firearm accident. Sheley and Wright (1995:1) sum up the influence of guns quite well when stating: "It is a sobering possibility that many teenagers in today's cities know more about the technology and operation of a semiautomatic handgun than they know about personal computers or even automobiles. More disturbing still is the likelihood that their knowledge of firearms will prove more useful, at least as they see it."

It was estimated that in 1994 that there were almost 200 million guns in homes across the country, almost one in every home; not surprisingly, there was one out of every fourteen children who died as a result of gunshot— one every 100 minutes (CDF 1998). Currie's (1998:37) summary of statistics related to homicide are quite sobering:

In the mid-1990's, a young American man age 15 to 24 was 37 times as likely to die by homicide as his counterpart in England, and more than 60 times as likely as a young man in Japan. Three-quarters of all homicide deaths among children under 15 in the entire industrial world took place in the United States.

It has been estimated that the average age of an assailant involved in a youth murder was 14.5 years, and the victim 13.5 years (Alexander 1998a).

The consequences of violence on the lives of youths can be quite profound and go far beyond physical harm (CCD 1997; Goodwillie 1993; Guterman and Cameron 1997; Heide 1998; Kay, Estepa, and Desetta 1998; Loeber and Farrington 1998: Osofsky et al. 1993; McCord 1997; Mitchell and Logan 1996; Prothrow-Stith 1991; Pynoos and Nader 1988; Sampson 1997). Deaths due to firearms for white, non-Latino males between 1985 and 1995 increased from 18 per 100,000 in 1985 to 28 per 100,000 in 1995. However, among African Americans, it increased from 47 per 100,000 in 1985 to 120 per 100,000 in 1995 (Lantier 1998). Older African-American youths, for example, are more likely to die today than ten years ago, and in time more likely to die from homicide than their white, non-Latino counterparts (Hutchinson and Poole 1998; The Policy Exchange 1998).

Although the homicide rate among adolescents decreased 16 percent in 1997, it was still higher than ten years ago (Butterfield 1998; New York Times 1998d). The decline is widely attributed to a decline in the use of crack cocaine. More specifically, homicides committed by youth accounted for all of the growth in homicides in the post-1985 period. Crack cocaine, as a result, played a key role in this increase along with relatively easy access to handguns (Butterfield 1998a). Zimring (1998) argues that some of the increase in assault-realted statistics are the result of changes in the way assaults are classified. He goes on to argue that the increase in homicides, however, is the result of gun availability, making youths better armed rather than more "vicious" than before.

The number of cases handled by courts with juvenile jurisdiction has increased over the past ten years. In 1995 the courts handled 1.7 million delinquency cases, representing a 7 percent increase from 1994. Between 1986 and 1995, the number of cases increased 45 percent (Sickmund et al. 1998). The Department of Justice estimates that due to an increase in the number of adolescents between 1992 and 2010, juvenile violent crime rates will double during this period (Snyder and Sickmund 1995). Between the mid-1980s and 1995, the number of young adults (18 to 24 years) in jail doubled from 178,000 in 1986 to 359,000 in 1995, the Justice Department estimating that the number arrested from this age-group doubling by the year 2010 (Sum et al. 1997). In 1993, the financial cost of caring for young firearms victims ages 10 to 19 was $407 million (Kellogg Foundation 1998).

Guns are involved in 75 percent of all adolescent murders, with approximately 10 percent of youths between the ages of 10 and 19 having fired a gun or been shot at; 60 percent of youths state they can obtain a handgun; 20 percent claim they can obtain a handgun within an hour, and more than a third can do so within a day (CCAD 1994a). Philadelphia experienced a dramatic increase in the number of youths murdered during a forty-month period ending in March 1997, with 62 percent of the victims being under the age of 22 (Janofsky 1998b). Among African-American youths between the ages of 15 and 19, the increase has been prodigious, witnessing a triple increase between 1985 and 1990 from 37 to 105 per 100,000 (Sheley and Wright 1995). A 1991 study by the Centers for Disease Control found that 4 percent of all students in school carry a gun (CCAD 1994a). A more recent study of middle school students in North Carolina reported by Dubrant, Krowchick, and Kreiter (1999), noted that 3 percent of all students carried a gun and 14 percent reported carrying a knife or club to school for self-protection.

It is estimated that there are more gun dealers than gas stations in the United States, with 20,000 new guns subject to sale in these establishments on any one day (Moyer 1995). Even in situations where communities have been highly successful in reducing the number of adolescent deaths resulting from gunshots, this statistic may still mask a deeper unrest (Currie 1998:37):

A Boston street worker and former gang member explains . . . . that although juvenile gun deaths have fallen sharply because of the city's antiviolence programs, young people are still shooting one another, but "in the butt and the legs," not to kill. Why do they do this? The kids, he says, call this kind of shooting "representing"—as in representing their community—"because they've got nothing else to represent."

Exposure to violence often starts at a very young age for urban youths in the United States. One study of first and second graders in Washington, D.C., found that 45 percent had witnessed a mugging, 31 had witnessed a shooting, and 39 percent had seen a dead body resulting from violence (CCAD 1994). Schubiner, Scott, and Tzelepis (1993) estimated that 42 percent of Detroit's inner-city African-American youths (ages 14 to 23), had witnessed a shooting or stabbing and 22 percent had seen someone killed. These findings do not differ from those in Baltimore, where 42 percent of Baltimore's inner-city youths (ages 12 to 24) had witnessed a shooting and 25 percent had seen a stabbing (Sheley and Wright 1995).

A governmental report noted that between 1987 and 1991, juveniles arrested for weapons violence experienced a dramatic increase of 62 percent. African-American youths under the age of 18 was the group most frequently involved in violence, having a weapons law violation three times that of white, non-Latino youths, and a murder rate six times greater than white, non-Latinos (CCAD 1994). Concern about youth-related crimes, however, is not restricted to the United States. Crime rates and all of their consequences among youths have not only caused alarm in this country, but have also caused alarm in Europe (Cowell 1998:4): "The days when the middle classes, at least, could guarantee their offspring better, more prosperous times are over. And just as unemployment—particularly among the young—seems to have become endemic, slick advertising and peer pressure have come to exert enormous pressure to acquire the unaffordable and perishable icons of the consumption era." The precarious status of youth is much more pronounced in this country, however, with the access to guns having a tremendous impact on the consequences of violence.

Ironically, at the same time that the nation's homicide rates have decreased dramatically in almost all major cities throughout the nation over the past five years, adolescent rates have increased significantly—154 percent between 1985 and 1991 (Butterfield 1994). The same period also witnessed a corresponding increase for homicide arrest rates for adolescents—127 percent. Juvenile arrests for murder and manslaughter increased 60 percent in the 1980s, and an additional 45 percent between 1990 and 1993 (Chaiken 1998). Nationally, youths perpetrated 137,000 more violent crimes in 1994 than in 1985, and were responsible for 26 percent of the growth in violent crime over that period of time; more specifically, they accounted for 50 percent of the increase in robberies, 48 percent of the increase in rapes, and 35 percent of the increase in murders (OJJDP 1996).

Overall, homicide rates for blacks/African Americans is far greater than those for white, non-Latinos, with the former accounting for 125 per 100,000 in 1991 compared to approximately 9 per 100,000 for the latter (Butterfield 1994). That is, blacks/African Americans, particularly youths, are at a far greater risk for death by murder than any other ethnic/racial group in the United States. Based upon a three-year period (1989–1991), African Americans had the highest homicide rate in the United States with nearly 39 victims per 100,000, followed by Latinos (15.5 rate) and Native Americans (11.7 rate); white, non-Latinos and Asian Americans had rates just under 6 per 100,000 (Mackellar and Yanagishita 1995).

In 1994 there were 150 per 100,000 African-American males ages 15 to 19 who died from firearms—600 times the overall rate of deaths from firearms for others in that age group. Between 1985 and 1990, the overall death rate for adolescents in this age group rose from 80.4 to 89.0 per 100,000. However, the same period witnessed a dramatic increase for African-American youths 15 to 19 years old, from 125.3 to 231.6 per 100,000 (The Policy Exchange 1998). In essence, homicide is considered to be the leading cause of death among inner-city youths in the United States (Simmons, Finlay, and Yang 1992).

The number of juveniles arrested for violent crimes (murder, rape, robbery, and aggravated assault) has increased nationally by 27 percent between 1990 (91,317) and 1995 (115,592), causing an alarm in many states that has resulted in passage of tough sentences for youths convicted of violent crimes (Willing 1997). It is estimated that in 1995 over 84,000 youths were in secure custody. Thirty-eight states currently house juveniles in adult prisons without any special programs addressing the differences in age with the adult population (Alexander 1999).

Approximately 50 percent of rape victims are girls in their adolescence or younger. In 1992, approximately 17,000 preadolescent girls were raped, representing 16 percent of all reported rape victims that year (Chaiken 1998). The number of violent crimes committed by girls has also witnessed a dramatic increase since 1987. Girls under the age of 18, based upon F.B.I. statistics, increased by 118 percent (6,418 incidents to 13,995); aggravated assaults (124 percent) and robberies (117 percent) also witnessed significant increases (Ford 1998). In 1992 the average cost for an incarcerated youth was $33,000 (Kellogg Foundation 1998). Recent studies have shown that in early adolescence (ages 10 to 14), serious violent crimes are committed almost as frequently by girls as by boys; in some cities girls commit more violent crimes than boys in this age group (Chiken 1998; Kelly et al. 1997)

The number of arrests, like that of homicide rates, falls disproportionally on black/African-American youths as in the case of Jacksonville, Florida. In 1995, black/African American youths in that city represented 85 percent of all those jailed on a given day, even though they only accounted for 11 percent of Jacksonville's total population. The relationship between violent behavior and substance abuse, particularly crack, is very strong and makes the distinction of treating two social problems (drugs and crime) false. The wave of violence resulting from crack-cocaine during the 1980s was felt most strongly in large urban centers across the United States, with small and midsize cities escaping the consequences of the crack epidemic (Inciardi, Pottieger, and Lockwood 1993; Mieczkowski 1990). However, recent studies show that violence, particularly murder related to crack, has found its way to midsize cities in the late 1990s (Janofsky 1998).

Cities, when compared to rural areas of the United States, have a four times greater rate of having youths exposed to violence (Mitchell and Logan1996). Approximately 72 percent of city youths know personally someone has has been shot, 24 percent have witnessed a murder, 25 percent have been shot or threatened (Zinsmeiter 1990). Fort Worth, Texas, for example, experienced a dramatic increase in the number of gangs and gang membership between 1987 and 1992. In 1987 there were 77 gangs and 1,316 members. In 1992, the numbers had increased to 211 and 3,448 respectively (Zavala 1996). Consequently, urban youths, particularly those of color who live in low-income communities, have a disproportionate rate of exposure to violence and all of its ramifications when compared to youths in other sectors of the country (Isaacs 1992; Kay, Estepa and Desetta 1998).

Gangs

The impact of gangs on the nation's cities is well documented through numerous reports and newspaper stories (Gorov 1997; Lasley and Radin 1998; Short 1997, 1992; Terry 1994; Virgil 1993). Newsweek (June 1, 1998) recently highlighted the impact of gangs on urban areas and explored the role the faith community can play in addressing this problem. Short (1997) summarizes a series of studies that demonstrate that urban-based gangs have increased in numbers in cities with populations over 100,000. A 1992 study for the National Institute of Justice found that 72 out of 79 of the largest U.S. cities and 38 out of the 43 smaller cities reported gangs to be a serious concern for local law enforcement authorities (Landre, Miller, and Porter 1997).

Gangs take on added significance in communities of color since they often represent an attractive alternative for youths (Hagedorn 1996; Moore and Hagedorn 1996; Wilson 1996). When they are actively involved in illicit drug activities, the added element of violence makes them that much more formidable for the community and law enforcement authorities (Mieczkowki 1990; Moore and Hagedorn 1996; Waldorf 1993). These gangs, as a result, represent serious dangers to residents and gang members themselves. Conflict between rival gangs for the lucrative drug trade often results in innocent community residents being hurt or killed, destabilizing the community in the process (Mieczkowki 1990; Moore and Hagedorn 1996).

Boston, a city that has received increased national publicity as a result of its successful effort at reducing youth-related violence, has witnessed an increased presence of gangs (Radin 1998). Gangs are by no means endemic to urban areas and, as a result, can be found in suburban and rural areas of the country. However, there is no denying that they play a particularly significant role in dictating quality-of-life issues for urban communities (Jankowski 1991; Klein 1995; Martinez 1992; Mieczkowki 1990; Moore 1991; Padilla 1993; Short 1997).

In essence, gangs take on added significance in communities of color since they can represent an attractive alternative for youths. When gangs are actively involved in illicit drug activities, the added element of violence makes them more formidable for the community and law enforcement authorities . These gangs, as a result, represent serious dangers to residents and members alike. Conflict between rival gangs for lucrative drug trade increases the crime rate within the community (Lai, Lai, and Achilles 1993).

Teenage Pregnancy

The is little debate that pregnancy at an early age places both the parents and their child at a distinct direct and indirect disadvantage concerning their place in society (Corcoran 1998; Kellogg 1998b; NCPTP 1997; The Policy Exchange 1998). Although that may not be the case for all adolescent girls (Apfel and Seitz 1996), the experience is still life-altering. It is important to note that adolescent pregnancy is not related to other types of social problems such as drugs. However, adolescent mothers have a lower likelihood of staying in school—64 percent having completed high school compared to 90 percent for nonmothers (USGAO 1998).

Although adolescent birth rates have declined in the United States during the 1990s by 21 percent between 1991 and 1993, this social problem does not decrease in importance (Lewin 1998). Every year one million adolescent girls become pregnant, with 500,000 keeping their babies; 73 percent of those who are unmarried and give birth go on public assistance within four years of having done so (Lerner 1995). Even though statistics on adolescent pregnancy reflect an overall decline in the United States (Holmes 1998b; Ozer et al. 1997), there is still a disturbing trend among Latino adolescent girls, who have experienced an increase in births from 106.7 births per 1,000 Latino adolescent girls in 1995, compared to 100.8 in 1989. In fact, Latino birth rates exceeded those of African-American adolescent girls, who experienced a drop from 84.8 percent in 1989 to 74.5 (Holmes 1998).

School Underachievement and Dropouts

The importance of formal education has continued to increase as society moves to an information era that relies upon computers. Pervasive underachievement, or consistently meeting minimum requirements when the potential exists for far greater attainment, is rarely looked at in youth-focused studies. However, it has far-reaching implications for education. It is not, however, restricted to any ethnic/racial or socioeconomic group. Nevertheless, it is especially "stark" for children of color or low-income families in cities (CCNY 1996; The Policy Exchange 1998).

Youths who do not finish their secondary schools and continue onto higher education are at a distinct disadvantage in the market place, which results in the stigma of being a "school dropout" and undermines their self-esteem (Rathbone 1997; Del Pinal and Singer 1997). The diminished role of the manufacturing industry, combined with an increased role of a service industry for individuals without high levels of formal education, seriously limits upward economic mobility for the high school dropout (Aronowitz and DiFazio 1994; CCNY 1996; De Leon 1996; Ogbu 1997; Sum, Fogg, and Fogg 1997; Willis 1998).

The consequences of dropping out are much more severe for urban-based youths of color who normally face limited options in the work world (Dupper and Poertner 1997; McLoyd and Jozefowicz 1996; Richards 1996; Seidman and French 1997; Willis 1998). Lack of "marketable" skills, combined with an increased opportunity for engaging in high-risk behavior, increases the likelihood of these youths falling into the correctional system. It is estimated that youths who do not finish high school have a significant higher likelihood of being incarcerated (2.5 times higher) than their counterparts who graduate (Sum et al. 1997).

School dropout estimates of public school systems with high concentrations of youths of color are very alarming with cities such as Chicago, Detroit, and New York having more than 50 percent of their students leaving school before graduation (Schorr 1989). Students of color have a disproportionate likelihood of dropping out of school when compared with white, non-Latino youth; Latinos having a rate 300 times greater with African-Americans and Native Americans following with a 200 times greater likelihood (Lerner 1995). Among Latinos, U.S.-born have a higher likelihood to graduate from high school compared to non-U.S.-born. Nevertheless, they still lag behind other groups at all educational levels (Del Pina and Singer 1997).

Other Pressing Needs

Poverty   Poverty is closely associated with a wide range of social problems (Betson and Michael 1998). However, it takes a particular toll on children (Brooks-Gunn and Duncan 1998). It is estimated that approximately 20 percent of all children in the United States live in poverty, with 45 percent living in central cities (Kellogg Foundation 1996). Children of color, however, bear most of the brunt of poverty. Approximately 40 percent of all poor children are nonwhite Latino. African-American children account for 34 percent, followed by Latinos with 22 percent, and Asian, Pacific Islander, Native American, and Alaskan Native accounting for 5 percent (Kellogg Foundation 1996).

The number of children living in poverty, a key factor that has negative consequences for the future of these youngsters, is approximately 14 million, or one out of every five children (20.5 percent) in the United States, reflecting a steady increase in percentage from that of 14.4 percent in 1973 (Brooks-Gunn and Duncan 1998; Children's Defense Fund 1998; The Policy Exchange 1998). However, the number of children of color living in poverty is dramatically higher for Latinos (40.3 percent) and African Americans (39.9 percent). Puerto Ricans, among Latinos, have the highest percentage of youths under the age of 18 in poverty with 53.9 percent, compared to 49 percent for Mexicans, 41.8 percent for Central/South Americans, and 22.5 percent for Cubans (Children's Defense Fund 1998; Corcoran and Chaudry 1998; IPR Datanote 1998). Urban areas have the highest percentage of children living in poverty with 30.8 percent, followed by rural (22.4 percent), and suburbs (13.5 percent) (Children's Defense Fund 1998; Harris and Curtis 1998).

The Homeless   Families with children are considered to be the fastest growing segment of the homeless population in the United States, accounting for approximately 40 percent of all those who are homeless (NCH 1997). Children, according to a 1996 survey of 29 U.S. cities, accounted for 27 percent of the homeless population (NCH 1997).

Arson   The subject of arson among youths is not one that is widely discussed, and for that matter, is not well understood. According to 1995 FBI statistics, youths accounted for more than half (52 percent) of all arson-related arrests during that year (Alexander 1997). In fact, between 1986 and 1995, youth arson-related arrests increased by 40 percent, as adult arrests declined (Alexander 1997). Youths who commit arson can cover the entire youth age-spectrum: during the 1986 to 1995 period, 33 percent of youths arrested for this crime were under the age of 15; in 1994, almost 7 percent were under the age of 10 (Alexander 1997).

Sexually Transmitted Diseases   It is not possible to discuss adolescent needs without considering how sexually transmitted diseases (STD) are impacted in this population group. Adolescents account for 25 percent of all sexually transmitted diseases diagnosed each year (ASHA 1995). Each year more than 3 million adolescents contract an STD in the United States (Freudenberg and Radosh 1998). In New York City, for example, chlamydia is considered to be the most pressing STD with teenagers, accounting for 40 percent of the 25,000 cases reported each year (Stolberg 1998a). In 1995 according to the Center for Disease Control and Prevention there were 5,734 pediatric AIDS cases of children under the age of 13 in the United States (Bok and Morales 1997). It is estimated that every day at least 25 adolescents become infected with HIV. Approximately, 20 percent of the approximately 600,000 individuals diagnosed with AIDS are presumed to have become infected during their adolescent years (Freudenberg and Radosh 1998).

Youths of color, particularly African-Americans and Latinos, are disproportionately represented in the number of AIDS-related cases among youths ages 13 to 24; African-Americans represented one-third of all cases reported among males, and 55 percent among females. Latino males, in turn, represented 20 percent and Latinas 21 percent, with Puerto Rican children being the largest Latino subgroup (Kellogg Foundation 1998b). There are an estimated 750,000 to 1,000,000 youths who run away from home every year in the United States, approximately 6.4 percent (48,000 to 64,000) having tested for HIV/AIDS (Lerner 1995).

Health Care   A Commonwealth Fund study (Schoen et al. 1998) of adolescent boys in fifth through twelfth grades found a lack of ready access to health care or support for this population group. Child immunization has fallen as low as 10 percent in certain urban areas of the country, with children of color being disproportionately represented. American children in general are immunized at rates one-half those of Canada, Israel, and Western Europe (Kellogg Foundation 1996). Lower rates of immunization not only translate into higher rates of illnesses for nonimmunized children, but also higher rates of school absences as a result of illness. The United States ranks 70th in the world, behind Burundi, Nicaragua, Trinidad, and Tobago, when specifically focusing on the proportion of children of color who are fully immunized against polio is compared with overall rates of other nations (Kellogg Foundation 1996). As many as 40 percent of youths have at least one major cardiovascular disease risk factor, such as high cholesterol, high blood pressure, or inactivity; 68 percent do not meet all standards for cardiovascular endurance, abdominal strength, upper body strength, and flexibility (Collingwood 1997).

Lack of health insurance, in turn, further limits accessibility to quality health care. In 1996 the number of children without any form of health insurance reached a record high (11.3 million); that same year also witnessed 70 percent of all Americans who joined the ranks of the uninsured were children under the age of 18 (Children's Defense Fund 1998). Uninsured youths tend to be of color with Latinos making up 22 percent of all uninsured children, followed by African-Americans with 19 percent, and other groups of color making up 5 percent (Kellogg Foundation 1998b). The Commonwealth Fund study (Schoen et al. 1998) of adolescent boys found that boys without health insurance were far more likely to go without health care when needed when compared to boys with health insurance (29 percent compared to 18 percent). Lack of immunization and health care are just two indicators of the health challenges facing youths of color and their families in our society.

Abuse and Neglect   In 1993 there were over one million substantiated cases of children in the United States who were either abused or neglected, for a rate of 23.1 per 100,000 under the age of 18 (Lindsey 1994; Policy Exchange 1998; U.S. Dept. of Health and Human Services 1995). In 1996 over 500,000 children were in some form of foster care, an increase of almost 25 percent from 1990 (Children's Defense Fund 1998). In 1997 it was estimated that 1.3 million adolescents run away from their homes or become homeless. Over 60 percent of the youths in shelters and transitional housing facilitates had a history of physical or sexual abuse, and 25 percent had experienced some form of violence from family members (CWLA 1998).

Suicide   Rates of suicide among youths have also been increasing at an alarming rate the past few years—over 400 percent since 1980 with a current rate of 14 per every 100,000 adolescents each year (Choi 1998). The rate of suicide among 10-to-14-year-olds has more than doubled from 1980 to 1994, and quadrupled for African-American males in this age group (CWLA 1998).

Employment   The rate of unemployment for young people is often overlooked in an economic era that is widely considered to be outstandingly prosperous (Duster 1995). Unemployment among youths of color far exceeds that among their white, non-Latino counterparts (Williamson 1997):

> While the Labor Department released figures in June 1997 placing unemployment at a new low of 4.8 percent—prompting President Clinton to say that "America's economy is stronger than it's been in a generation"—the jobless rate . . . for teenagers . . . was 15.6 percent, while 32.6 percent of black male teenagers in the labor force were without jobs.

DEMOGRAPHIC PROJECTIONS FOR THE TWENTY-FIRST CENTURY

In 1990, 25.7 percent of the population in the United States consisted of children under the age of 17. This percentage is not expected to change dramatically in the next fifty years, with a projection of 25.7 percent in the year 2000, 24.4 percent in 2010, and 24.4 percent in the year 2050. The total number of adolescents is expected to be over 23 million by the year 2000 and 30 million by the year 2008 (CCAD 1992; Cobb 1998). These adolescents as a group, however, will not look like the adolescents in 1976 (Cobb 1998:C6):

> The image we carry of boomer youth culture is a white one, and for good reason. In 1976, approximately 85 percent of the US teenage population was white; today the figure is about 67 percent; by 2008, it is estimated, it will have dropped to 62 percent; and by the middle of the next cen-

tury, white teenagers are expected to be a minority. The largest growth will be among Hispanic teenagers, who will outnumber black teenagers by the year 2008 and whose number is expected to triple within 50 years.

Another dimension of demography will be the graying of the United States, which will significantly increase the median age of the total population from 33.0 years (1990), 35.7 (2000), 37.2 (2010), and 38.1 (2050). This increase in median age will also witness a dramatic increase in the percentage of the population age 65 or older—13.7 percent (1990), 14.2 percent (2000), 15.1 percent (2010), and 24.8 percent (2050), respectively (Wright 1997).

The demographic projections addressed in this section will have profound implications for all of the systems that currently target youth. For example, school systems will experience tremendous growth in high school enrollments. It is projected that in the year 2007 there will be 2 million more youths in high school than there were in 1997, and over 451,000 more graduates (Dobbs 1998). Clearly, this example can be multiplied countless number of times in order to draw an appreciation of how demographics will shape youth-focused systems in the twenty-first century.

As this chapter has highlighted over and over again, the nation's youths, particularly those in cities and in communities of color, are facing a multitude of social and health problems at a critical stage in their development (Symons et al. 1997). However, there is a prevailing concern in this country about youths, particularly those who are poorly educated. These marginalized individuals are considered to be more of a threat to the country than any threat from abroad (CWLA 1998).

Ferrell et al. 1996:105) make an important observation concerning the importance of youth-oriented organizations and the impact of funding cuts on their role within urban communities:

> Historically, such community-based social resources as the Boys and Girls Clubs, the YMCA, and the YWCA played a "mediating" role in inner-city communities. They encouraged the inner-city disadvantaged, especially poor youth, to pursue mainstream avenues of social and economic mobility and discouraged them from engaging in antisocial or dysfunctional behavior. But during the 1980s, those mediating instructions lost much of their financial support and became less effective precisely at the time that the problems confronting the urban disadvantaged

were worsening, and as a consequence of massive inner-city disinvestment on the part of major employers, financial institutions, and the federal government.

Failure to successfully meet and negotiate these challenges will require a greater and greater portion of the nation's gross national product to be devoted to remedial and criminal justice programs. Funding can be just as easily channeled into productive-generating activities for the nation's youth, and at a much better return on the investment dollar, too. The financial costs of many of the problems covered here can be enormous, not to mention their social costs. Recent law suits against manufacturers of guns by parents of youths killed by guns may prove to be an avenue that will substantially reduce gun availability (Fried 1999). These suits argue that gun manufacturers have deliberately marketed and distributed handguns in a manner that results in an oversupply of the legal market, causing guns to find their way from states with lax gun laws to supply states with strict gun laws.

In another area, according to the Carnegie Council on Adolescent Development (1989:29):

> Each year's class of dropouts will, over their lifetime, cost the nation about $260 billion dollars in lost earnings and foregone taxes . . . The United States spent more than $19 billion in 1987 in payments for income maintenance, health care, and nutrition to support families begun by teenagers. Babies born to teen mothers are at heightened risk of low birthweight. Initial hospital care for low-birthweight infants averages $20,000. Total lifetime medical costs for low-birthweight infants averages $400,000 . . . Alcohol and drug abuse in the United States cost more than $136 billion in 1980 in reduced productivity, treatment, crime, and related costs.

School security costs are considerable in many of the nation's cities as schools struggle to address violence within their settings. Los Angeles spends $25 million per year, Detroit, $4 million, and New York, $75 million, for example (Jordon 1996). When the costs of graffiti removal are added to school budgets, the costs are formidable—Los Angeles schools spend $10 million per year, San Jose, $1.2 million, Philadelphia, $1.2 million. Phoenix, $750,000, Seattle, $2 million (Boyle 1998). When viewed from a broader perspective, graffiti removal costs governments and businesses $7 billion a year—New York City subways, for example, spend $10 million on removal (Boyle 1998a).

It becomes very artificial to separate many of the social problems covered in this chapter from each other; their interconnectedness reflects a state of existence that permeates entire lives and requires interventions that take this reality into account (Barton, Watkins, and Jarjoura 1997). McLaughlin (1993:55) makes a similar observation concerning the interrelatedness of youth issues and needs:

> The needs of inner-city youth do not come in neat bundles or tidy problem definitions. Just as the identities of youth are embedded in the character and resources of the communities, neighborhoods, and families, so are their needs enmeshed and interrelated. Inner-city organizations that connect youth with larger society, promote a positive sense of purpose and person hood, and provide the resources that youngsters need to reach adulthood are not single-issue, single-purpose organizations . . . These organizations, in short, serve as 'family' for youth, meeting their needs and promoting their growth much in the inclusive way a family would.

Consequently, it becomes imperative that the needs of the "whole child" be addressed within one roof, so to speak, at a time when funding is becoming ever more categorical, severely limiting how services are structured and delivered (Reardon 1996a).

Nevertheless, community-based programs and organizations have become very creative in finding ways to circumvent these restrictions in order to engage and help urban youngsters. As it will be seen in chapters 4 and 8, community-based organizations have succeeded against incredible odds to develop innovative approaches to service delivery, fund raising, and setting the organizational structure to support these efforts.

The sociodemographics presented here provide a very clear, yet disturbing, picture of projections for urban youths, particularly those of color, in the twenty-first century, if the predicament that they find themselves in the late twentieth century continues without change. Their demographic profile, in turn, raises important considerations for policy makers and other practitioners, foremost being, how does the nation focus its attention on a population group that is often misunderstood and not usually given a voice in the decisions impacting on its well-being. Further, how do practitioners develop new initiatives that approach urban youths from a strengths/assets perspective rather than the conventional deficit point of view—namely, youths are without innate resources and not capable of making responsible and informed decisions about what is in their best interest. The challenges facing urban youths require that adults, and thereby professionals, continue to support services and programs that work, eliminate does those that do not, and search for new approaches.

A failure to maximize current resources to prevent or intervene early on in an adolescent's life can effectively serve to doom millions of youths in the twenty-first century. Such a short-sighted approach will result in an even greater portion of the nation's gross national product being devoted to late-stage intervention, and seriously reducing the quality of the nation's work force.

CHAPTER 3

—

URBAN YOUTH FROM A STRENGTHS PERSPECTIVE

Youths, particularly those of color, low-income, and residing in the nation's major cities, usually have been viewed by the media (Cabral 1994; Riggins 1992; Rubin 1980; Schwartz 1982; Wilson and Gutierrez 1985), the general public, and the professional literature from a deficit perspective (Cox and Powers 1998; Fassler 1998; Heath and McLaughlin 1993; Kotlowitz 1991; Leadbeater and Way 1996; McLaughlin, Irby, and Langman 1994; Rathbone 1997; Watkins and Iverson 1998). This perspective can best be categorized as "pathological," "deficit," "risk," or "problem-driven." The average person's reactions would be negative to the statistics presented in the previous chapter, and result in a punitive approach toward solutions designed for urban youths. The media will rarely present youth in anything but a negative perspective as witnessed by the rash of youths shooting youths throughout the United States. Application of a deficit perspective toward youths, although possessors of talents, abilities, and dreams, results in strategies that ignore these strengths and instead focuses on their problems and needs. Statistical systems, in turn, are developed to gather information on these problems, which in turn influences policy and programs (The Policy Exchange 1998). This chapter provides an overview of the subject of strengths, youth, and program development principles.

A STRENGTHS PERSPECTIVE

Strengths Versus Deficits

Finn and Checkoway (1998), in reviewing a series of case studies focused on tapping youth as resources, note that youth have historically been viewed by the general public as a group to be feared, as a problem to be solved, or as needing treatment for some form of pathology. Youths have rarely been seen as competent community builders, with vision or a stake in the future of a community. A shift in paradigms to one of assets has implications throughout policy and programming arenas, and how we educate social workers and other helping professionals (Blum 1995). Further, a deficit paradigm is based on the belief that adults know what is best for youth (Fassler 1998; Lawrence 1998). Adults experience of youth earlier on in their lives makes them "experts" on the experiences associated with this stage in the life cycle. This disempowering and naive perspective serves not only to demoralize youths, but also seriously undermines families and communities, essential elements in their lives and critical components that must play a significant role in any form of intervention.

A strengths perspective, when applied to youths, also has potential benefits for other groups related to or associated with them (Schorr 1997). Youths, for example, can play an influential role in programs that outreach to elders. Elders, in turn, can witness firsthand the skills and talents youths possess. There may be many instances where elders' views of youth may be shaped by what they read or see on television news. In essence, a deficits perspective permeates youths and all of those who come into contact with them. Youths, in turn, react negatively to this biased perspective. A vicious circle ensues that seriously undermines the development of good relationships.

An emphasis on identifying and mobilizing youths' strengths does not take away from, or minimize, youths' needs. A failure to take into account youths' needs and constraints will ultimately result in poor delivery of services (Simon 1994:14): "Social work that has failed to take full stock of clients' present limitations as well as strengths has been a form of wishful thinking that offers false promises and eventually leaves a client with deepened despair." No group, regardless of age, consists solely of strengths. However, no solution to its needs should be attempted without taking into account and mobilizing its strengths.

A deficit perspective is by all means not restricted to urban youth. This perspective plays a prominent role in how society categorizes certain groups who, by their characteristics and views, makes them undervalued in a capitalist society. A deficit perspective will rarely take into account the impact of institutional racism, "cultural corrosion," and disconnection that results from structural forces that marginalize communities of color in this society (Erkut et al. 1996). However, a deficit perspective takes on added significance when applied to this group of youngsters.

The organizations undertaking these failed efforts, in turn, have rarely focused their analysis on the "real" reasons why they failed—unfortunately, it has been much easier to "blame the victim," rather than the strategy (Coleman and Hoffer 1987; Schorr 1997; Simeonsson 1994). The need to question the fundamental premises of the strategy rarely, if ever, gets attention. As a result, more deficit-oriented and doomed-to-fail strategies are forthcoming, further reinforcing negative stereotypes of youth.

Burt, Resnick, and Novick (1998:274) argue that there is a tremendous need for new paradigms in the field, and this is the result of a convergence of greater forces necessitating new perspectives on services and at-risk youth:

> It is not a coincidence that the movement of some innovative programs toward comprehensive service integration has occurred at the same time that scientific research and theories on adolescent development and problem behavior have reached a significant watershed. We suggest that three recent trends in the literature—the ecological movement in child development, the findings about long-term effects of early intervention programs for infants and children, and the recognition of the overlap among risk factors—point to the need for a new theoretical framework to address the challenges of creating positive outcomes for young people. A new framework must integrate existing notions of risk with a positive youth development approach to help service providers, parents, teachers, and others identify vulnerable youth so that supports can be strengthened and negative outcomes averted.

Fassler (1998) goes on to argue that a shift in paradigms cannot be restricted to a particular age-group without it also having implications for other age groups. In the brief history associated with a strengths perspective, it has generally been applied to preadolescents and older groups. However, younger groups have not been addressed in this shift in thinking. It is almost as if very young children cannot possibly have strengths. Strengths, when available, appear only at the preadolescent or later stages of development. This shortsighted view seriously limits the theoretical and empirical work that must take place in order for a strengths perspective to really take hold in the youth development field (Pinto 1998).

A shift in paradigms to one that is strength-focused holds much promise in the field of community-based youth services (Morrison, Alcorn, and Nelums 1997:327):

To build functional communities where consistency of values and goals is emphasized, youth and family development services need to foster both human capital—"skills and capabilities that make individuals productive"—and social capital—"relationships, norms, and sanctions that make groups productive."

The field of youth services cannot utilize adult perspectives in designing youth services; it must utilize the perspectives of the population they seek to attract, in order to make the available resources meaningful to participants. Attainment of this perspective, however, cannot be accomplished without systematically involving those they seek to help—youths themselves!

The field of social work has discovered the importance of a strengths perspective in the last decade, and raised important arguments for a shift in paradigms away from deficits to strengths (Cowger 1992; De Jong and Miller 1995; Delgado 1996; Fraser 1997; Freeman 1997, 1998; Kaplan et al. 1996; Logan 1996; Saleebey 1992; Simon 1994; Weick et al. 1989). This shift in perspectives is not restricted to any particular age, gender, ethnic/racial, or geographical area of analysis, physically challenged, or affectional preference group. Thus, a strengths perspective toward youth as a population group does not specifically single out this group.

Nevertheless, I am hard pressed to think of any sociodemographic group that is more likely to be marginal than urban youths—after all, they do not vote in a society where the vote is possibly the most empowering act individuals can exercise, and they reside in areas of the United States that most decision makers have all but ruled out for significant investment of social and economic capital (Brookins, Peterson, and Brooks 1997; Johnson 1997; Tolan and Gorman-Smith 1997; Walberg et al. 1997). The interface of all of these critical factors further marginalizes this population group. Watkins and Iverson (1998) stress that as a result of a changing social environment that systematically undervalues youths' assets, the profession of social work, and other helping professions, must redouble their efforts at engaging in a dialogue focused on identifying and utilizing youths' strengths whenever possible. Clearly, there is a tremendous need for more asset-focused studies of youth (Howard 1997; Lerner 1999; Scales and Leffert 1999). Further compounding the picture is the fact that assets are interdependent, making simplistic approaches to using them arduous to achieve (Kimball-Baker and Roehlkepartian 1998). Burt, Resnick, and Novick (1998) stress the interconnectedness between youth development, strengths, and competencies. The interconnectedness between these different constructs serves to provide social workers with a foundation from which to examine what role we can and should play. It is not a question of whether or not we should play a role; it is a question of how do we conceptualize our potential contribution to the field of youth work.

Elements of Resiliency/Assets

A strengths perspective consists of a variety of key elements that, when combined, result in a view of individuals, in this case youth, that is empowering and self-esteem enhancing. It is not possible to achieve the goals associated with empowerment without tapping strengths (Simon 1994). Further, development of self-esteem and self-efficacy is very much influenced by a youth's relationship with caring and trusting adults (Cox and Powers 1998; Werner and Smith 1982). Thus, an ability to establish and maintain adult relationships is another dimension related to strengths. Werner and Smith (1982) developed three clusters of resiliency factors (temperamental characteristics and engaging social skills, strong relationships with parents or their substitute, and a community support network) that serve to help youth. Blum (1995), summarizing the literature on youth resilience, notes that factors associated with resilience fall into four categories: (1) personality traits (inquisitive, possesses social skills, highly verbal); (2) family traits (fewer children, spacing of at least two years between children, at least one caring adult in the home, and a stable family environment); (3) skills and values (belief in own capability to overcome the odds); and (4) other factors such as at least one close friend and supportive social network. These four factors are highly interrelated and serve to reinforce each other's potential contribution to youth development.

A strengths perspective is not limited to youth development. Poertner and Ronnau (1992) have used a strengths perspective with children with emotional disabilities. Their approach utilizes a set of seven principles to guide interventions: (1) an individual and his/her disability are not one and the same; (2) youths with disabilities also possess great strengths; (3) youths with disabilities possess the potential for continued learning and growth; (4) youths are and must be the primary informants of their experiences; (5) youths with disabilities should be an integral part of society and not marginalized; (6) society must welcome and integrate youths with disabilities; and (7) families must be considered the primary care givers and must play an active and influential role in any intervention. This set of principles, with minor modifications, can apply to work with any type of youth—typical and untypical.

Kaplan et al. (1996) have taken a strengths approach toward substance abuse prevention. Their program is one of the few in the field of substance abuse prevention that is explicitly based upon a strengths perspective. Benson (1996) developed a five-part framework consisting of thirty factors for identifying and working with youth assets (strengths). This framework, in turn, consists of two major categories of assets—external (support, boundaries, structured time use) and internal (positive values and social competencies).

Youth resiliency, or strengths, has also been conceptualized along a variety of areas by nationally based youth-focused organizations. The National Assembly (1994) has conceptualized youth resiliency as consisting of five domains that can be enhanced through capacity enhancement strategies: (1) physical competence—good nutrition, attitudes, and skills related to physical development; (2) social competence—interpersonal skills such as empathy, caring, communication skills, etc., that facilitate the establishment and maintenance of relationships; (3) cognitive competence—good reasoning skills that facilitate problem-solving and can engender alternatives to situations that can be classified as risky; (4) vocational competence—life options that can be realized through proper education and training and result in a sense of a promising future; and (5) moral competence—the development of character and values that results in individuals making a positive contribution to their community and society.

The Search Institute (1996) based in Minnesota, in turn, has taken a broader, and at the same time more detailed, perspective of youth assets and categorized them into two major categories (external and internal), and forty subcategories that lend themselves to a practice: (1) external assets (support, boundaries, and structured time use); and (2) internal assets (educational commitment, positive values, and social competencies). These broad domains, which when broken down into subcategories, systematically tap individual, peer, family, and community aspects, illustrate the importance of collaborative efforts involving individuals, families, communities, and organizations, working together in pursuit of a common agenda of not only addressing presenting social problems but doing so through capacity enhancement (Scales and Leffert 1999).

Cultural Dimension to a Strengths Perspective

There is little disputing the importance of culture in determining how strengths get operationalized. A society that values interrelationships as opposed to possessions, for example, will have these values operationalized in a certain way. Individual strengths, in turn, will be measured according to these set of values. Interestingly, most of the published works on strengths have not, with some exceptions, addressed the role of culture in the conceptualization and use of the construct. The concept of culture has been used in a myriad of ways within the helping professions literature. In fact, there is very little dispute concerning the importance of culture in helping to inform practitioners in their assessment and development of interventions. Nevertheless, the difficulty of capturing how culture influences perceptions and help-seeking patterns has made the study of this phenomenon arduous, at best. This challenge takes on added significance since the construct of culture is dynamic.

Freeman (1994) brings a different dimension to a discussion on culture by commenting on how a Eurocentric perspective of competence primarily focuses on the individual rather than groups. Competence, in turn, is defined in the Eurocentric, male-centered context as meaning one who is qualified, capable, or has the potential to perform in an "appropriate manner." A focus on the individual serves to emphasize this value at the expense of one that focuses on groups. Erkut et al. (1996) argue, like Freeman, that constructs such as "resilience," "protective factors," "strengths," "coping," "prosocial behaviors," and "personal assets," generally reflect white, middle-class cultural models, and may not be practical or valued in communities of color. Providing a cultural dimension to a strengths paradigm serves to broaden an important perspective and increase its relevance to communities of color. However, in so doing, it is necessary to view cultural strengths very broadly in order to allow sufficient flexibility for including strengths that may be unique to certain groups. Failure to do so may result in definitions of strengths that are narrow, and therefore biased.

Gutierrez (1990), in turn, draws a strong association between empowerment and strengths and notes the importance of these two perspectives. Identification and building upon strengths facilitates a practitioner in the empowering process by assessing a client's current level of functioning and current sources. Lazzari, Ford, and Haughey (1996), although not directly using the concept of strengths, highlight this perspective in their analysis of Latina women who were identified as leaders in their communities. The list of activities these women actively engaged in was extensive and quite impressive—promoting environmental changes to improve circumstances for people, creating, providing, and maintaining social services in the community, promoting self-esteem (self-pride), and encouraging and sustaining individual and collective approaches to change. These Latinas represented indigenous leadership and, as a result, were able to identify and mobilize both internal and external resources in service to their communities. A more "traditional" perspective on strengths in all likelihood would have missed these indigenous talents.

Stauss (1995:111) applies the concept of strengths to Native-American families and highlights the particular role it plays within the culture: "Indians and non-Indians share some family strengths, but the similarities often are overshadowed by major differences. Indian family strengths are sacred, cultural, and political—all at once." Dykeman, Nelson, and Appleton (1996) also stress the importance of family within Native-American communities, and note that one of the greatest strengths common to Native-American Indian culture is the extended family. McCubbin, Thompson, and Futurell (1998) have also identified strengths among Native Americans and new immigrants.

Aguilar's (1996:155) comments, although concentrated on Mexican Americans, have applicability to other groups of color: "Language, culture, family, personal characteristics have not been identified as strengths in youths at risk . . . Parents and at-risk youths possess strengths that have not been called forth or even acknowledged."

Logan (1996) has applied a strengths paradigm to African Americans and identified a multitude of ways this community has striven to help itself in the face of great adversity. Logan (1996), for example, does an excellent job of tracing the concept of strengths among African-American families from a historical perspective, and arguing that they do not need to be "saved." Instead, they need to be strengthened, empowered, and utilized as resources in the development of intervention strategies. Martin and Martin (1978, 1995), McCubbin, Thompson, and Futurell (1998), McRoy (1990), and Freeman (1990), also have documented the strengths of African-American families and communities in providing help to family members and community. Freeman (1990), for example, has operationalized a strengths perspective through use of an African-American family's life cycle, and in so doing, has integrated various community support systems such as the church.

As the concept of strengths gets incorporated into the literature on communities of color, it has undergone a critical transformation by taking into account the impact of culture and context, with an emphasis on urban community. This impact, as a result, has necessitated acknowledging the basic premises a strengths paradigm is based upon, with necessary changes to make the paradigm more applicable to communities of color. A strengths perspective of urban-based communities of color, for example, has resulted in practitioners and researchers reexamining ways of viewing community facilities. Delgado's (1999) book on nontraditional urban settings addressed the multitude of informal systems of care found in communities. Beauty parlors, barber shops, botanical shops, grocery stores, laundromats, for example, fulfill a variety of helping roles that have historically been overlooked by professionals. These facilities, in essence, represent a parallel social service system that is responsive to the needs of urban-based marginalized groups. His interest in nontraditional settings can be traced back to his earlier work with indigenous folk healers, another cultural-based source of strength in Latino communities.

Youths of Color from a Strengths Perspective

A strengths perspective must take context into consideration. Although there may be aspects of a strengths perspective that are common across ethnic/racial groups and geographical settings, these may be operationalized in a very different matter depending upon context. Further, there may be aspects of a strengths perspective that are specific to certain contexts and groups (McCubbin, Thompson, and Fromer 1998; McCubbin et al. 1998). As a result, it is not advisable to come up with a long list of strengths and simply check them off when viewing youths of color.

As already noted, a wide range of cultural factors may be playing influential roles in the lives of these youths. These factors may involve religious worship, extended family, family definitions of self that facilitate non-blood-related individuals joining families, values such as godparents, belief in metaphysical forces, etc., making generalizations difficult if not impossible. The extent of acculturation in the lives of youths must be taken into account in any assessment of strengths in order to eschew generalizations and stereotypes.

The universality and particularistic dimensions of a strengths perspective must be taken into account in reaching out to urban youths of color in the United States. An ability to "survive" in a hostile environment cannot be underestimated by social workers as a strength. Urban living presents a series of challenges for youths and their skills at navigating through potential dangerous situations must find a place in any form of strengths assessment tool or process (Seidman 1991).

Community Context to a Strengths Perspective

Youth strengths do not exist within a vacuum (Fassler 1998). A community perspective serves to ground these strengths within a broader context, and serves as a mechanism for uniting the wide range of strengths that youths possess (Benson 1996a). Thus, it is of critical importance to practitioners to take context into account in determining the type and levels of strengths of assets (Kimball-Baker and Roehlkepartian 1998).

Jarret (1995), in a meta-analysis of 26 qualitative studies on resilience among African-American youth from low-income families, noted that the process of "community-bridging" by families played a critical role in providing support to youth (Scales and Leffert 1999). Community bridging represents a concerted effort to provide safe haven for youths in their communities. This concept is very similar to "urban sanctuaries" coined by McLaughlin and Irby (1994). Swenson (1995) argues that for a strengths perspective to have any meaning for individual or family work, the practitioner must be able to view strengths from a broader perspective. namely, community. Contextualization of strengths serves to increase the likelihood that all of the strengths are identified and possibly mobilized.

Community strengths, or assets, have historically escaped the attention of most scholars, although they have been receiving increasing attention the past few years (Acosta and Hamel 1995; Delgado 1995, 1999a; McKnight and Kretzmann 1990; Kretzmann and McKnight 1993). The field of social work, as a result, is in a propitious position to make important contributions to this area based upon our extensive history of working within and with urban communities. It is impossible to view individual strengths without also examining how the environment, in this community or neighborhood, enhances these assets (Greene and Barnes 1998) . An ecological perspective toward youth can serve as a key conceptualization of how these two dimensions interact and support each other. Communities play a vital role in setting the context for individuals, along with youths cultural heritage. Consequently, any effort at better understanding the strengths of youths of color must do so from a community and cultural perspective (Greene and McGuire 1998). The contextualization of youths' strengths, as a result, serves an important role of informing organizations as how to best identify and tap these assets in programming activities (Smokowski 1998).

Strategies for enhancing youth capacities, in turn, cannot be divorced from enhancing community assets (Brown 1995; Guest 1995; Hughes and Nichols 1995; Wahl 1995). Masten (1994) classifies resilience-based intervention strategies into four types: (1) reduction of vulnerability and risk; (2) promotion of positive outcomes through reduction of stressors; (3) increasing resources targeting facilitating adaptive outcomes; and (4) mobilizing protective processes. These strategies, however, should not be conceptualized as mutually exclusive (Smokowski 1998).

Community development (as will be noted in chapters 5, 6, and 7, when examining arts, humanities, and sports) is closely tied to youth development. Watkins and Iverson (1998:182) tie the concepts of youth development with community development by stressing their interconnectedness:

> Taking the concept of goodness-of-fit one step forward, one realizes that not only do healthy communities contribute to the well-being of their youths, but healthy, prosperous youths can also simultaneously make a difference within their community. Therein lies the mutuality between the concepts of youth development and community development.

A strengths perspective, in turn, can further unify these two concepts, by specifically stressing assets and competencies in these two arenas (Brown 1995; Hughes and Nichols 1995). Guest (1995) points out how current youth development strategies have not reached deep enough into communities and have failed to gain community support. A focus on institutional support, in this case formal, is not sufficient to bring about a lasting impact on youths and their families. It is necessary for youth-serving organizations to reach out to informal community organizations as a means of tapping all potential existing resources (Delgado 1999a).

The following description of El Barrio (Spanish Harlem) in New York City brings the dimension of community assets into focus when describing this community (Cotter 1998:3):

> The neighborhood around 106th Street and Lexington Ave. is usually called East Harlem. But to its Spanish-speaking, largely Puerto Rican-born residents, it is El Barrio, and it offers the best and worst of New York, The streets have a vibrant extended-family feel. Friends hail one another warmly; children shout from stoops.
>
> And the spirit of Puerto Rico can be felt, in the clusters of men playing congas in front of bodegas on a Saturday, in the shops called botanicas, packed with a museum's worth of objects: sculptures, paintings, ritual utensils, old and new, mixing Christian, African, and Caribbean motifs.
>
> At the same time the Barrio has stayed grindingly poor. Tenements are crumbling. Schooling and health care are chancy. Crime, drugs, and diseases like AIDS have taken a heavy toll, as suggested by boxlike sidewalk altars with flickering candles and commerative murals painted on walls. But these murals and the botanica's treasures reveal another ele-

ment that binds the neighborhood: the connective tissue of art. For decades artists have lived here, turning out work in the streets and in railroad-style apartments, taking their talents and energies into the local public schools and community centers.

Cotter's description of the neighborhood provided a perspective that is often missing from the development of context by professionals —namely, the role art, religious beliefs, family values, cultural pride and strengths, and connectedness, that are often overlooked or misunderstood by community outsiders. These elements, in turn, do not exist in isolation from each other from individuals, regardless of the age of the person. These "symbols," in turn, are part of the context in which youths grow up within—in this case, Puerto Rican youths. The expressions that are manifested through these elements must be part of the fabric of a strengths perspective for youth. The rich texture that community provides for examining assets must never be overly simplified, nor overlooked by providers.

Strategies for Utilizing Strengths in Programming

A strengths perspective toward youth lends itself to involvement in many different strategies. In fact, there is no aspect of programming that cannot incorporate youth strengths. As will be shown later on in this chapter, strengths inform principles, which, in turn, inform how youth development gets operationalized. The shift from a needs perspective for organizations does not mean total abandonment of positive actions and activities being conducted. Taking an asset perspective to programming has a profound impact on all aspects of service delivery (Search Institute 1998:3):

> "What needs to be stressed . . . is that asset building is not another program; it's a philosophy that can be incorporated into the great programs [tutoring, life skills, recreation, and family support]." The idea of asset building is a call for a new perspective and a larger view of youths and the whole community's responsibility for them.

An asset perspective, as a result, represents a fundamental way of conceptualizing individuals and communities, regarding their potential for growth and contributions to society.

An asset perspective toward youths requires youth-serving organizations to rethink their language, methods for assessment, and the role youths play in the decision-making process throughout all levels of programming. An asset perspective, in essence, permeates an entire organization. It is not advisable to use this perspective only in one aspect of the organization and totally ignore it in all others. Such an approach will no doubt severely limit an organization's capacity to make significant changes in its participants and the community they come from.

The following are some examples of how this shift in thinking and operating from a deficit approach to an asset-building approach can influence all aspects of programming (Search Institute 1998). Instead of a deficit approach's focusing on problems, an asset approach focuses on positives; instead of a focus on remedial programs, there is a focus on positive relationships; instead of a reliance on professionals, there is a reliance on empowering youths themselves; instead of a focus on an individual youth separately, there is also a focus on a youth's family, neighborhood, community, and other systems. Deficit-approach programs generally rely on short-term intervention; asset approaches commit to long-term support and generally focus on youths' lack of problems and look for the presence of positive attitudes, behaviors, and competencies. These are just a few of the ways the two approaches differ and how they impact on programming.

Youth can play an important role in the area of community assessment (Freeman 1998). Delgado (1979, 1981, 1996) has reported on the use of Latino youths as research interviewers in community-based studies. He strategically used Latino adolescents because of their knowledge of the community, their willingness to undertake community-based research, their abilities to elicit information and contextualized results, the benefits of community capacity enhancement that result from employing youths, and the importance of highlighting indigenous results to adults. Youths have the potential to make significant contributions if permitted to do so by adults.

Leadbeater and Way (1996), in examining the subject of sexuality, note that the vast majority of poor urban adolescent girls do not fit the stereotypes the public has formed about them—most do not drink or use other types of drugs, engage in premarital sex, perpetrate crimes, drop out of school, or use public assistance. Musick (1993:13) takes a similar argument to that of Leadbeater and Way when commenting on adolescent childrearing:

> In order to avoid teenage motherhood girls growing up in poverty need to possess not just average but above-average psychological resources and

strengths, self-concepts, and competencies. Considering the many forces drawing poor females toward early unprotected sex and early parenthood, the scarcity of viable alternatives steering them toward school and work, and the responses of family and peers, which validate pregnancies once they have occurred, it is remarkable that rates of adolescent childrearing are not even higher.

The last decade has witnessed a number of prominent local, national, and regional foundations (Anney E. Casey Foundation's New Futures; Ford Foundation's Neighborhood and Family Initiative; Chicago Community Trust's Children, Youth, and Families Initiative; Boston Foundation's Persistent Poverty Initiatives) launching initiatives at addressing urban community problems by emphasizing comprehensive interventions based on a wide range of principles, one of which is a focus on community assets (Barton, Watkins, and Jarjoura 1997). These funding initiatives have attracted much attention from organizations working with youth. Scholars have also started to focus their attention on evaluating these initiatives and making recommendations for programming.

The concept of youth development has found greater currency in the professional literature, and incorporates a strengths perspective by focusing on abilities rather than deficits (Barton, Watkins, and Jarjoura 1997). Youth development, as a result, offers tremendous promise as a strategy for prevention of youth problems through a focus on enhancement of competencies (Pittman and Cahill 1991). Further, a youth development perspective can serve as a unifying construct that allows practitioners from various professions to come together through a focus on strengths—which, incidentally, may vary according to the practitioner's point of view. This unifying perspective can play an influential role not only in increasing collaboration across disciplines but also in serving as a way of developing a political constituency to lobby for more national and local funding and attention for youth. This coalition can accomplish goals that single organizations, regardless of their influence, cannot do alone.

Nevertheless, the concept of youth development can easily serve as a basis for comprehensive strategies (Fruchter and Cahill 1995). Youth development, after all, is not possible without also achieving community development (Hughes and Nichols 1995). These two constructs have very similar foundations and share similar goals. As a result, comprehensive strategies focused on youths will ultimately also benefit their families and communities. Consequently, for youth development to achieve its true potential, it must be placed within a community development or capacity enhancement set of strategies.

The very strengths of a youth development approach can also be its primary weakness, namely, it can be all things to all people. Thus, its boundaries and flexibility can easily result in a field of practice in search of boundaries. In fact, social work has been accused of being so broad that it has lost its meaning and purpose; so open that virtually any form of activity or method can be considered as part of the profession; so encompassing that no age-group is left out. Youth development, although targeting a particular segment of the life-cycle, is sufficiently broad to encompass a large segment of any population group, making it easier for a human service organization to embrace a strengths perspective for all segments of the populations it serves.

Strengths-Based Statistical Data

As noted earlier, strengths-based policy and programming decisions require the creation of data-gathering systems that can inform these arenas (Pittman 1998; The Policy Exchange 1998). The importance of strengths indicators, sometimes referred to as human capital, cannot be easily dismissed. If data represent one of the most critical factors in helping to inform interventions, in this case problem-focused, then they play an equally important role in enhancement initiatives that systematically build upon individual and community strengths. The creation of data premised on strengths is necessary if communities and, for that matter, the nation, are to shift in approaches. Thus, easily obtainable asset-related data can play a critical role in helping to facilitate this shift.

Healthy development and constructive behavior cannot simply be opposite ends of unhealthy development and risk-taking behavior. These indicators are important and readily available to practitioners and policy makers. However, there is a desperate need to create asset indicators at the individual, family, and community level, that can be used to inform community capacity development. These indicators, however, should be sufficiently flexible to take into account local circumstances, the adding or dropping of indicators as circumstances change, as well as have meaning for both providers and residents—namely, residents can relate to how these indicators reflect well upon the status of their youth.

Data related to thriving youth attitudes and behaviors such as valuing diversity, working well in groups, maintaining good health habits (nutrition and exercise), volunteering at school and community, succeeding at resolving conflicts without getting into fights, attending religious services, using leisure time productively, etc., are either not easy or impossible to obtain (Search Institute 1997). These types of data are rarely collected by institutions. A similar situation occurs with communities —the number of community fairs held during a year, attendance at community events, numbers of volunteers who do so on a daily, weekly, or monthly basis, quality of upkeep of local parks and other spaces, number of gardens and murals, etc. In essence, asset-based data generally must be gathered from scratch by organizations wishing to develop a well-rounded picture of the communities they serve—a picture that goes beyond deficit-oriented information.

Words of Caution

It is necessary to pause and make a few cautionary remarks concerning the central focus of this book. Garbarino et al. 1992:224) make a striking observation concerning the limits of a resiliency (or strengths) paradigm quite well when noting: "Children are resilient, but their resilience is not unlimited." The emergence of paradigms based upon strengths and assets such as strengths-based practice, community capacity enhancement, and youth development, for example, create a great deal of excitement for practitioners and researchers, as viable and attractive alternatives to deficit-focused paradigms and interventions. However, it is important not lose sight of the role of key factors operating in today's environment.

Our embracing an asset paradigm does not mean that government has no role in providing much needed external resources addressing low-income urban communities. Identification of innate individual and community resources does not translate into letting communities pull themselves up by their bootstraps (Delgado 1999a). A number of leading exponents of using assets raise concerns about the need for government and other private and public entities developing collaborative partnerships with communities as a means of maximizing innate resources (Gottlieb 1988; Olsen 1983; Logan 1996a; Popple 1996; Rothman 1994; Saleeby 1996; Schwartz 1997; Whittaker and Garbarino 1983).

In embracing youth development, any role we as providers can play in assisting youths in making a healthy transition to adulthood must be placed within a broad framework. This nation's shift from an industrial-based to a service-and-information-based economy must be taken into account in determining what viable alternatives youths face going into the twenty-first century. School transition to work programs, for example, must not prepare youths for jobs that do not exist or will not exist in the near future.

STRENGTHS PRINCIPLES AND YOUTH DEVELOPMENT

Engagement of youths in the arts, humanities, and sports can very easily represent ends in and of themselves. Youths' involvement in these activities keeps them out of the streets and situations that may result in risk-taking behaviors, particularly during periods of the day when the likelihood of involvement in these kinds of acts are at their highest. Further, these activities place them within a setting that has adult supervision. Protection of urban youth is a basic goal of any youth-focused organization. Protection, however, must encompass both physical and psychological dimensions.

Nevertheless, these activities must, and can, result in greater benefits for urban youths by seeking to link and support them with formal and informal institutions and resources such as schools, employment, and opportunities to meet their needs in making the transition to adulthood. They serve to promote youth development, or competence. Breitbart (1998:320), nevertheless, identifies the importance of the process associated with activities such as the arts as a means of engaging and assisting youth:

> Often, with public art, it is the process rather than product of art production that generates the most significant benefits and lasting outcomes . . . When young people are encouraged to reexamine the strengths and weaknesses of their surroundings and then act creatively to transform them, the experience can alter young people's attitudes toward each other and their future; it can also provide a much needed outlet for the expression of feelings.

The process, as a result, is even more important than the outcome in youth development.

The American Youth Policy Forum (see Halpern et al. 1995:1) defines youth promotion as "efforts specifically designed to bring about clearly defined positive outcomes, or designed to foster the development of skills and competencies in young people." Promotion (unlike prevention, eliminate harmful outcomes), productivity (efficient achievement of desired outcomes), and preparation (cuts across the other three), stress use of strengths and seek to use competencies as measures for evaluating success of interventions. Promotion is also based on the premise that youths have innate abilities and only need the opportunity and support to foster these talents.

Engaging youths, particularly when addressing those in high-risk circumstances, is quite complex because of the varied situations found in urban areas. The dynamic nature of cities, with ever-changing demographics, is further compounded by a host of other factors, factors such as socioeconomic status, acculturation level, ethnicity and race, gender, and the availability (or lack) of resources. Consequently, youth programming must be sufficiently focused so as to provide clear direction, but sufficiently flexible so as to take local circumstances into consideration. There are no "standard operating procedures" that can be applied, nor are there any "short-cuts" that can be recommended that are low-labor intensive.

This section is organized using a set of principles for effective youth programming. The fourteen principles provided here serve to illustrate how they play an important role in informing and directing programming. These principles are based on findings from various national commissions, including the President's Commission on the Arts and Humanities (1996), American Youth Policy Forum (1997), those of the Carnegie Corporation (1994 a, b, c), Kellogg Foundation (1998 a, b), an extensive review of the literature, key informant interviews, and my own experience in this field. They address various organizational and community aspects of programming, such as the type of activity that maximizes goals, the organizational factors that facilitate achievement of goals, and the community factors that should influence selection of activities.

These principles can best be conceptualized within a youth and community capacity enhancement perspective, and address four distinct yet interrelated levels—neighborhood residents, associations, organizations, and individuals. The strengthening of these four domains serves to identify assets, builds upon them, and provides a focal point from which to seek external resources to assist in capacity enhancement (Aspen Institute 1997). The fostering of collaboration and relationship building between these four represents an essential aspect of capacity enhancement. Although the principles addressed specifically target urban youths, they can only be achieved when involving community-based key organizations (formal and informal) and adults.

The concept of "community-based" has numerous connotations within the human service field. It can simply represent an organization being physically located within a community, and thus providing geographical accessibility to its constituencies. However, there is general agreement that for "community-based" to have significance within a youth and community capacity enhancement perspective, it must also be culturally (respect and understand cultural heritage), psychologically (youth feel secure and safe to be themselves), and logistically (periods of operation are tailored to the availability and needs of participants) accessible.

Local circumstances dictate how the the principles covered in this chapter get operationalized. Organizations following these principles do not have to have youth-focused services as their sole mission. Use of these principles assists organizations primarily serving adults to also serve youths, but in a much more limited capacity. I do not wish to convey to readers that they must be based in a youth agency in order to effectively practice in new arenas. The reality is that most youth services are delivered by adult-centered organizations.

Each of these principles, in turn, incorporates four dimensions: (1) an overview of the literature (identification of important themes); (2) a description of various activities that can be utilized to operationalize the principle; (3) key challenges in operationalizing the principle (individual, institutional, and community); and (4) special considerations. These dimensions are interwoven throughout the write-up of the principle. Youth workers, thereby, are challenged to take these principles and apply them to their practice. Some principles will not have to be modified in order to find applicability in practice; others will have to be modified. Nevertheless, it is hoped that readers will benefit from the guidance these principles provide in helping to inform practice with youth.

1. Programs must seek to deepen creativity, provide critical tools for negotiating developmental stages, and provide multiple avenues for the processing of cognitive information.

Any activity that provides youths with an avenue for channeling creative energies cannot be easily dismissed by professionals working with or teaching youth (Sum et al. 1997; Smith 1997; U.S. Dept. of Education 1998). There is little debate in the field concerning the amount of energy youths possess (Scales and Leffert 1999). Thus, it is not a question of whether youths possess this energy; it is question of how best to tap and direct in a constructive way. T. J. Smith (1997:x) effectively summarizes the importance of organizations employing creative forms of learning for youth:

Youth program settings need to make learning an ongoing challenge for young people. The joint tasks are to make learning engaging and relevant, with curricula and teaching strategies that are creative, substantive, and attuned to the interests of the learners; and to provide effective pathways for young people to finish high school and move successfully into college or other forms of postsecondary training.

Youths, as a result, must have creative outlets for their voices and talents (Lakes 1996). Murals, for example (Delgado and Barton 1998), not only provide urban youths with creative outlets, they also serve to help teach cognitive skills in the process. Youths must be able to have a solid grasp of math, chemistry, geometry, in addition to being able to undertake library research, interviewing, and conflict-resolution. Work habits related to punctuality and an ability to follow safety procedures take on added importance because the painting of a mural should never be an individual event—it takes a team working closely, and cooperatively, to succeed in painting a mural that has meaning for the artists as well as the community. Painting murals takes on added dimension that help prepare youths to undertake projects in other spheres of their lives.

Providing youths with an opportunity to learn more about their cultural heritage not only helps them increase their self-esteem because they are able to recapture a lost history, but it also helps communities in the process. Communities, particularly those composed of various ethnic and racial groups, are presented with an opportunity to share their backgrounds and learn from the backgrounds of others. There generally are very few organized outlets for groups of different backgrounds to come together, share and learn from each other. Consequently, youths and youth organizations can play an important role in helping communities come together and counter the forces that are often operating to keep groups apart.

2. Effective programs emphasize innovative, dynamic, and comprehensive approaches toward serving youth.

Provision of innovative, dynamic, and comprehensive programming is necessary in order for organizations to maximize their potential impact on youth-related issues. Further, for programming to be effective, it must be based upon a thorough understanding of a youth's assets and needs (Goplerud 1994; Smith 1997; Sum et al. 1997; U.S. Dept. of Education 1998). Activities, although focused on the arts, music, humanities, or sports must reach out to embrace goals that are holistic in nature as a means of facilitating a comprehensive approach toward youth (Langley 1996; McLaughlin and Heath 1993; Scales and Leffert 1999).

Program leadership should take into account local circumstances and seek to connect youths with available resources from within and from without the community. Failure to do so can seriously undermine the potential of a project (McLaughlin 1993:66):

> Effective leaders use local knowledge and credibility to craft programs and resources that provide the connective tissue between estranged, cynical inner-city youth and the broader social institutions essential to their productive futures and positive conceptions of self. This connective tissue is spun from personal knowledge of youngsters and their setting and from knowledge of social, political, and economic resources in the larger community. These effective leaders act as brokers, catalysts, and coaches, making the contacts and linkages necessary to enlarge the opportunities available to youth and providing the introductions and confidence necessary to access.

The importance of comprehensive intervention approaches toward youths is further reinforced by the notion that there is a common etiology for most risk-taking behavior (Elliot 1993). These interventions must be based upon the lifestyles of youths, with attention paid to key socioeconomic and cultural factors (Morrison, Alcorn, and Nelums 1997). Further, comprehensive interventions must also address all levels of the life cycle for youths in an effort to retain and assist them throughout all of the critical stages of childhood. A comprehensive perspective, in addition, serves to help organizations manage scarce resources and often necessitates the development of partnerships with other resources, formal and informal, as a means of ensuring that all needs are addressed, and that each party knows what the other is doing. This communication exchange maximizes resources and reduces duplication and, at times, counterproductive efforts (Burt, Resnick, and Novick 1998).

Clearly, there are few social service/recreational organizations that are capable of meeting all of the needs of youths because of funding limitations, mission, or willingness. Thus, it becomes necessary for the lead organization to marshal the necessary services, and to do so in a manner that is culturally competent, based upon local circumstances, and is accessible to those youths they seek to serve and their significant family members. Nevertheless, as Burt, Resnick, and Novick (1998) note, many youth-serving organizations are severely limited in providing comprehensive services because of limitations associated with categorical funding.

Comprehensive approaches, however, must be based upon a particular type of funding, admittedly rare, that facilitates a holistic perspective toward youths, families, and communities. Categorical funding, as a result, seriously impedes this type of approach (CCAD 1994:11):

> Existing programs find their services diminished by targeted funding for prevention of pregnancy, violence, substance abuse, and school dropout. Often they are not designated as appropriate providers for such services. One approach to reducing financial barriers to effective developmentally appropriate programs is to enact legislation that allows for consolidation of categorical funding streams for community-based programs for youth.

Thus, it may be necessary for organizations to actively seek funding with minimal restrictions, most likely from foundations and corporations, and/or initiate grassroots fund-raising drives to facilitate a comprehensive perspective of youth (Dryfoos 1998). Organizations wishing to take a comprehensive approach toward youths should be prepared to reach out to informal resources to complement the funding and support they get from other agencies. Each community, regardless of income, has an extensive network of nontraditional settings (Delgado 1999a) that can be organized to work on youth issues.

3. Effective programs provide youths with opportunities to succeed and contribute to their community.

Youths have tremendous potential for making important and lasting contributions to their communities—if given the opportunity and support. Youths must have access to social opportunities to actualize their talents and goals. Achievement of success for youth must be viewed from two perspectives—individual satisfaction and community benefits (Boyle 1998b; Fassler 1998; Smith 1997; Sum et al. 1997; U.S. Dept. of Education 1998). Service to community can be operationalized in a multitude of ways, one of which is apprenticeship (Osterman 1995; Partee 1996; Pennington 1995; Rosenbaum et al. 1994; Scales and Leffert 1999; Smith and Jucovy 1996).

Apprenticeship can be defined as work-related experience obtained through a formalized internship, which can vary in duration and intensity, and is under the supervision of someone with authority and knowledge to impart to the apprentice. Partee (1996), in an examination of schooling to employment in England, brings an international perspective to service, and notes that among several major differences between England and the United States is a national curriculum for youth ages 5 to 16, and a statutory basis for youth programming nationwide.

Youniss and Yates (1997) note that the concept of community service, or service to community, is quite encompassing in breadth, and can consist of tutoring and other educational work, environmental protection, and forms of health care. Breitbart (1995:47), too, stresses the importance of urban youths playing an active and meaningful role within their communities:

> Recognizing the importance of the social ecology of childhood in the context of the incredible environmental deprivation facing many children today suggests an even more important role for creative approaches to urban environmental action. Projects that encourage children to actively understand and intervene in local neighborhood life have the potential to provide them with greater visibility and the promise of becoming more meaningful members of the urban community. Such projects can also help to chip away at rampant stereotypes of urban youth that so negatively affect urban policy now.

According to Sagawa (1998), youth service has caught the attention of the public, national, and local officials, because it can serve as an effective mechanism for achieving multiple yet complementary goals. These goals, in turn, benefit all sectors of society: (1) increasing academic performance by providing hands-on opportunities for learning; (2) helping youths make the transition from school to the world of work; (3) teaching life skills within a community context; (4) providing valuable resources to address pressing local needs and issues that would otherwise go unaddressed; (5) serving to bridge gaps between youths of different backgrounds and preparing for work within a very diverse world; (6) better preparing youths to play active and meaningful roles within their communities; and (7) helping youths make the connection between rights and responsibilities.

The emphasis on performance within a public arena provided by the arts, music, humanities, and sports provides youths with an audience through which they can convey their sense of accomplishment and pride.

When the audience is composed of other youths, however, the contribution is that much greater (Archibold 1998). Youths can derive a tremendous amount of benefits while serving their communities in the process (McLaughlin 1993:59):

> Many aspects of program design signaled the positive value of youth and positive expectations for their future. Youth activities geared toward tangible products or performances provided a sense of accomplishment and success. These activities gave youth concrete evidence that something called "visible victories" for youngsters who have had few such positive experiences in school, in their family, or in the community.

The outcomes resulting from utilization of the arts, music, humanities, and sports lend themselves to programming for youth (Archibold 1998; Goplerud 1994). These arenas provide communities with the opportunity to take pride in their young people, and allow the external community to see youths as an asset rather than a drain on resources. Further, youths involved in these arenas can perform in other communities, facilitating their interconnectedness with other youths who may, or may not be, of similar backgrounds.

4. Effective programs build upon what youths value and their assets.

If programs and services are to be attractive to youths, making recruitment and retention easier, then they must be based upon what youths value (Brown 1995; Fassler 1998; Scales and Leffert 1999; Smith 1997; Wahl 1995). Consequently, staff must endeavor to develop mechanisms for identifying and mobilizing youths' assets in the planning and implementation of services (Crowe 1998; Gambone 1993; Lawrence 1998; Morrison, Alcorn, and Nelums 1997; Pinto 1998). These activities, in turn, should be accessible to youths geographically, psychologically, operationally, and culturally. Adults running these programs must be willing to listen to young people and their opinions. The greater input youths have, the greater the ownership of the program. One project director's description of the youth in her city captures the importance of an asset perspective toward this age-group (Barker 1995:35): "These teenagers—like most teenagers—are incredibly energetic, very quick-minded, perceptive, and resourceful. But the fact is that in New Orleans, like in most major American cities, these very talented, capable individuals are almost all unemployed."

The fundamental premise that youths have abilities and that the communities they come from have assets represents an important departure for many youth-serving organizations (Linden and Fertman 1998). As already noted, most youth-focused organizations experience great difficulty in viewing youths from a strengths perspective. Consequently, these organizations do not have the mechanisms through which to tap youth strengths. In addition, these same organizations will rarely look at the communities youths come from as possessing strengths. This biased perspective places the organization in the position of being a youth's "savior" because it may be the only "anchor" in his/her life. This deficit perspective, although well-meaning, effectively seeks to separate youths from their own communities.

Enrollment or intake forms rarely seek to identify strengths. Instead, these forms are usually focused on gathering demographics and deficit or problem-driven information. In fact, these forms play a prominent role in socializing youths to the central goals of an organization. In addition, these organizations are rarely inclined to hire staff who subscribe to a strengths perspective. Unfortunately, there are few university-level training programs across the United States that stress preparation of students for youth-service careers stressing use of strengths. Thus, the onus of preparing staff with this perspective invariably falls on youth organizations. This process is not only labor-intensive but also very expensive because of the cost of taking staff out of the field and the cost of paying trainers. Successful organizations develop the capacities to identify youth and community assets and successfully build them into constructing programming (Fassler 1998; Goplerud 1994).

Youth-serving organizations, as a result, must devise ways of honoring participants who are doing well within and outside the program, as a means of validating their strengths. Some organizations chose to do this by awarding completion certificates, publicly announcing school achievements, and holding recognition dinners and awards ceremonies. Youths can also be selected as participants of the week or month for outstanding performance during that time period (Gambone and Arbreton 1997). Thus, public recognition of youths' assets and accomplishments can play important roles within and outside of the program, and allow family and community to take pride in their accomplishments.

Further, it is very important that organizations allow youths to experiment with participating in activities that they normally wouldn't consider, because of fear of failure, coming from backgrounds where risk-taking is outside of cultural norms, or a lack of an opportunity (Griffth-Wiesner and Hong 1998). The experiences, positive or negative, in venturing forth into new areas will help prepare youths to take calculated risks in other areas of their lives. Youths can benefit from failure if the proper support is provided, and their lessons can be generalized to other areas. I am very fond of saying that I can learn more about youngsters by how they handle failure rather than by how they handle success.

5. Effective programs have multiple clear, high, and realistic expectations for participants.

There is tremendous value in programs having high, clear, and realistic expectations of participants, be they young or old. This clarity serves to focus resources and better prepares participants for what they can expect from the organization and what is required of them to be meaningful participants. Youth programs that have coherence and structure allow and expect participants to have a higher probability of achieving success (Fassler 1998; Smith 1997; U.S. Dept. of Education 1998). Expectations of youth should be high but reasonable, maintaining a healthy balance between high standards, yet allowing for individual interests and considerations (Griffin-Wiesner and Hong 1998). The ability to achieve this balance should be the goal of any youth program, particularly one that targets urban youths of color.

There is no question that youth programs must create criteria for membership and for judging behavior, with the appropriate consequences for those participants who violate established rules—limit-setting combined with sensitive and supportive adult guidance is essential. Having clear, high, and realistic expectations of urban youths, combined with providing the necessary resources to help them achieve their goals, must be communicated through all aspects of service delivery (Goplerud 1994; Morrison, Alcorn, and Nelums 1997; Scales and Leffert 1999; Smith 1997). The concept of membership must be examined from two perspectives—conditions for entry and conditions for staying in a program. The former may involve meeting residence requirements, age, test of motivation, and parental permission. The latter generally involves behavior, such as no drinking, drug use, gang membership, wearing certain clothes, etc. (CCAD 1994).

Urban youths from communities of color have historically faced people in authority who have not had high expectations for their achievement. Their experiences in having authority figures perpetrate injustices has socialized them into distrusting these individuals. Consequently, it becomes crucial for youth-serving organizations to employ staff that break away from these traditional biases—preferably staff who, too, have faced similar challenges in the past and succeeded. Their words of advice mean so much more than the advice of someone who never had to face such challenges. An ability for youth to relate to staff and for staff to relate to youth represents the cornerstone of relationship-building. Youths must, however, play a significant role in setting expectations for their behavior and performance. Involving youths in dictating their expectations does not necessarily mean that what they seek is irrelevant in their lives (CCAD 1994).

Excessive reliance on normative standards developed by "experts" (none of whom are young themselves) often leads to a very skewed and unrealistic view. Youths must have a strong voice in setting standards and expectations. The world youths inhabit has changed dramatically from that the practitioner has experienced. These changes, in turn, have had a profound impact on how current-day youths view their future. The Information Age, for example, has made advancement in this society almost impossible for youths who have not completed their high school or, for that matter, their college education. Service jobs are no longer unionized to the same extent as they were for previous generations, severely limiting income, advancement, and job security. These changes alone could overwhelm any urban youngster. This combined with the accessibility to guns, drugs, etc., makes for a formidable world.

6. Effective programs provide youths with a sanctuary from which to generalize their learning and do so in a fun manner.

It is a sad commentary on the current state of affairs to say that urban youths are in desperate need of safe places within their communities. As discussed in chapter 2, urban youths are in need of places where they can both feel and actually are safe (CCAD 1994; Goplerud 1994; McLaughlin, Irby, and Langman 1994; Scales and Leffert 1999; Smith 1997; U.S. Dept. of Education 1998). These places are often referred to as "urban sanctuaries" and meet a variety of important needs within a community, needs that not only encompass provision of a physical safe setting, but also a place where youths can be accepted and valued.

McLaughlin, Irby, and Langman (1994) coined the term "urban sanctuary" based upon their research in urban areas and the roles that community-based organizations play in shielding youths, primarily those of color and low-income, from physical and psychological harm. These types of sanctuaries may differ according to communities with houses of worship fulfilling this need in some, while libraries and youth-centered organizations may play this role in others. In essence, communities with multiple sanctuaries are in a better position to reach out to youths and protect them while nourishing them physically, intellectually, and emotionally. These sanctuaries also provide youths with an opportunity to interact with adults who are in positions to help them make successful transitions to adulthood.

Although provision of a safe environment is important, there must also be activities that can be classified as "fun" and "meaningful" by youth participants (Wertz 1994b). Youth-focused activities can involve any, all, or a combination of the following: arts, bowling, billiards, community service, creative arts performances, dance, goal- or production-oriented activities, interactive games, karate, music, Ping-Pong, rap group counseling, role-playing, sports, swimming, study assistance, theater arts, tutoring, video-tapping, and weight-lifting, to list but a few of the more popular types (Wertz 1994b). These activities can be both educational and fun if properly planned and carried out. However, they cannot exist separately from other forms of support such as guidance, counseling, development of positive peer-relations, conflict resolution, and academic preparation. In short, activities within sanctuaries should not be limited to "killing time" and providing a safe environment; the time spent in these sanctuaries should be maximized for participants. Learning opportunities are too important to be wasted. As a result, a safe environment must also be a learning environment. This necessitates an integration of the two.

Physical safety can be maximized if organizations are willingly: (1) to issue and require ID cards to participants; (2) to have written rules concerning expected behavior within the program, particularly regarding fighting and gang clothing; (3) to provide transportation to and from the program; (4) to see that the facility is well lit; (5) to monitor physical access to the program; and (6) to ensure that adult supervisors are available and easily visible to the outside world (Gambone and Arbreton 1997). In essence, achieving the goal of providing a sanctuary for youth is one that must be deliberate in nature, and essential if an organization is to be successful in meeting its mission.

7. Effective programs are voluntary and provide youth with decision-making powers in shaping programming.

Successful programming systematically seeks to utilize youth strengths and build upon community assets. This, however, can only be accomplished through the development of avenues for seeking youth participation in the decision-making process (Boyle 1997c; Gambone and Arbreton 1997; Fassler 1998; Goplerud 1994; Pittman 1998b; Simpson 1997; Simon 1994; Smith 1997; U.S. Dept. of Education 1998; Witt and Crompton 1996b). Adults must be prepared to share the power if youth programming is to be relevant (Scales and Leffert 1999). Youths, as observed by Witt and Crompton (1996b), are tired of having adults make decisions that affect them without seeking to tap their interest and input. As a result, the process of empowerment enables youths to take ownership and responsibility for their leisure-time activities.

One program based in New Orleans (Young Aspirations/Young Artists), for example, specifically sets youth involvement as a goal throughout all levels of the organization (Barker 1995:40):

> YA/YA's ultimate goal is for the students to become part of the organization's board and staff. To this end YA/YA has created the YA/YA Committee, composed of both high school and college students and staff. Participation on the committee gives students the experience they will need to manage the organization in the future. Napoli [director] believes that YA/YA belongs to the students. "I don't expect to be the lead of YA/YA. It's theirs," she says.

Rhode Island, too, has developed a youth advisory board for its Department of Children, Youth, and Families (Crowe 1998).

Input, nevertheless, is not possible without responsibility. In short, in order for youths to "own" the activity, they must play a significant role in developing and implementing it. The concept of empowerment, although applicable to all age-groups across the life cycle, is rarely used with youths (Rees 1991). However, the concept of empowerment must be firmly grounded in lives of youths. Rees (1991) notes that youths' feelings of despair can be converted to hope. The process of empowerment necessitates that practitioners comprehend the values and aspirations of youths. This awareness, however, can best be achieved through direct contact with youths and their key stakeholders. Reliance on newspaper accounts, formal studies, and task force reports invariably stresses the "adult" point of view and often seeks youths' input without their involvement in decision making. Egalitarian approaches that stress development of citizenship must be systematically integrated into all aspects of the organizations reaching youth (Morrison, Alcorn, and Nelums 1997).

Biographies, too, are commonly used activities to foster youth empowerment, and encourage youths to tell their stories regarding personal and social issues (Rees 1991). Youths telling their life stories not only provides them with a "voice," but also serves to create a group sense of belonging by allowing them to identify common themes among themselves. Poetry, music, art, sports, for example, are excellent biographical activities because of their potential to address issues related to identity, achievement, and general well-being.

Biographical activities (1) require youths to commit themselves to telling their stories; (2) necessitates research, learning, and goal setting; (3) requires a public forum for youths to share their stories and engage in dialogue with audiences; (4) engages parents and other significant adults in the process of discovery and sharing; and, with the possible exception of sports, (5) has a "product" at the end of the process.

Video, for example, can also be an excellent mechanism for empowering use (EDC 1994). Thus, new arenas such as those addressed in this book, can provide social workers with opportunities to employ techniques and approaches that enhance youths' abilities. Empowerment, for example, is not restricted to work with "clients" in the conventional sense of the word. Technology, as a result, can be a powerful tool for engaging youths, facilitating their communication with their community and outside world, and teaching them a skill that can result in a career.

It should be pointed out that youths rarely are given an influential role within schools. Consequently, nonprofit organizations take on greater importance because they present one of the few types of organizations with the possibility of involving youths in decision-making roles. Decision-making roles can be enhanced by providing youths with opportunities to determine programming, having them represented on the board or on advisory committees, using opinion boxes, surveys, and holding periodic sessions during which youths can provide suggestions and share concerns (Crowe 1998; Finch 1998; Gambone and Arbreton 1997; Gordon 1998; Pinto 1998). If youths are an integral part of all levels of the organization and their input is both encouraged and respected, the program benefits, and so do participants.

8. Effective programs are built upon quality staff and programming and are willing to invest the necessary resources to provide support.

Quality staff are essential if quality programming is a goal (James *1993*; U.S. Dept. of Education *1998*). Organizations can have the latest equipment and instruments and not be successful without proper staffing. Quality staffing, in turn, is much more than technical mastery. Quality staffing does entail technical mastery and having the requisite interpersonal skills to make an impact on youth that goes beyond the activity being addressed (Scales and Leffert *1999*; Smith *1997*).

The following description of an ideal staff member highlights the key factors that are necessary to successfully engage urban youths (Bemby and Tufono 1996: 84–85):

> The Department looks for role models with whom the kids identify. The role models will often be former gang members or former athletes. Hiring people who have lived in an environment where there are gangs, who have experienced what it feels like to be in a gang and what it feels like to get out of a gang is important. The people hired had the opportunity to get out and, therefore, are interested in creating similar opportunities for others . . . Program leaders have to show a passion for the work and commitment to it . . . "It is about going beyond the paycheck. They can't pay us enough to do what we do." Often the program leaders have not attended college . . . Hence, the staffing model is often an apprenticeship program through which staff are trained for the job.

A number of authors have identified the importance of personal qualities over professional credentials in the staffing of programs targeting urban youth (Delgado 1999 Goplerud 1994; McKnight 1995). This is not to say that technical skills and knowledge are not important. Nevertheless, professional credentials do not ensure that youths will receive appropriate services, particularly when professional education is not grounded in the reality that urban youths face. As noted, urban youths face tremendous hurdles in successfully negotiating life. However, they are not without strengths. These strengths, unfortunately, rarely get recognized in the professional literature and in the classroom instruction of future social workers and other helping professionals.

Bernstein's (1964:113) review of the literature during the 1950s summarized the qualities of an effective practitioner with gangs, and there has been very little change in thinking about these qualities almost half a century later): "Dedication, abundant energy, a sense of fun, good and quick intelligence, courage, inventiveness, ability to relate to suspicious teenagers, a degree of comfort with authority, and a firm set of values rooted in his own experience, all seem essential. Beyond these, the ice gets thin." These qualities will serve any provider well regardless of the population he/she is working with. However, these qualities take on added significance when addressing urban youths, particularly those of color.

Staff, in turn, must be provided with the necessary training and support in order to carry out their primary responsibilities. Education and training, in turn, should stress experiential methods whenever possible to ensure that instruction addresses the daily needs and perspectives of youths (Morrison, Alcorn, and Nelums 1997). Failure to provide the necessary support will ultimately result in high staff turnover, poor quality programming, and disengagement of youth for activities.

It can be argued quite convincingly that bureaucratic requirements dictating professional credentials make it very challenging to recruit the type of staff that would be effective in working with urban youth (McLaughlin 1993). The ability to understand the context youth are living in and make the necessary connections and caring relationships is often much more important than a paper credential. Finding staff that have the necessary personal qualities and professional training is often the ideal although such a search may prove difficult, if not impossible. Consequently, if staffing is conceptualized as a "team," then it is possible to have team members with differing backgrounds, abilities, and interests.

As a result, youth development programming must be sufficiently flexible concerning the minimum qualifications that staff must possess in order to be employed by an organization. The greater the flexibility, combined with the necessary resources to put into training and staff support, the higher the likelihood that a staff can be recruited that can meet the needs of program participants. Regardless of the innate abilities of the staff member, he/she must be backed by the organization through provision of training, supervision, consultation, as a means of increasing effectiveness and preventing burnout. This support, unfortunately, may be viewed as a "frill" by some organizations. However, support of this nature will prove invaluable in preventing staff burnout and turnover, costly consequences of poor support.

9. Effective programs emphasize positive intergenerational (mentorships) relationships.

Mentoring is often mentioned as a key component of youth programming, be it formal or informal in nature. Mentoring programs can come in many different shapes and sizes. A recent review of the literature found five types that varied according to length of time and nature of the relationship between the mentor and mentee (Saito and Blyth 1995): (1) traditional—typical arrangement (goal of being a positive role model) of having one mentor with one mentee where they meet once a week over an extended period of time such as a year; (2) long-term focused activity—a mentor is paired with a youth with a focus on a particular goal such as academic achievement; (3) short-term focused activity—very similar in nature to long-term but transpires over a much shorter period of time such as a summer, and can involve an activity such as tutoring; (4) team mentoring—a family or team establishes a relationship with a mentee as is common with kinship programs and usually covers an extended period of time; and (5) group mentoring—one mentor develops a relationship with a group of youths and can cover a very extended period of time, such as that of a Boy or Girl Scout leader.

The concept of mentoring is often used to characterize the relationship between someone receiving the guidance and attention (mentee) and someone providing it (mentor). A mentor is usually an older person who, by the nature of his/her life experiences and other qualities is in a position to assist young individuals develop their characters and skills (Freeman 1993; Smith 1997). The term "mentor" has evolved over the years to mean trusted and trustworthy nonparent counselor, guide, tutor, or coach (CCA 1997). However, it can encompass many additional roles. The concept of mentor has been described as: (1) counselor; (2) role model; (3) supporter; (4) sponsor; (5) champion; (6) benefactor; (7) advocate; (8) protector; (9) teacher; (10) exemplar; (11) patron; (12) pal; (13) guide; and (14) host (Collins and Scott 1978; CCA 1997; Freeman 1993; Lakes 1996; Scales and Leffert 1999; Sullivan 1996; Whisenhunt 1996).

Mentors can easily combine all or some of the above descriptions in how they carry out their roles. The role modeling that transpires will occur explicitly and implicitly over the course of a relationship. The length of time required will vary according to circumstances, such as the needs of the youths and their experiences with adults. Further, it will be influenced by the nature of the relationship, whether it has been formal or informal. However, regardless of how practitioners operationalize the concept, mentor still refers to an individual who is in the position of influence and importance. This individual, in all likelihood, would be an adult although he/she doesn't have to be, and preferably someone of the same ethnic/racial and socioeconomic class/background as the mentee (Whisenhunt 1996). It is widely believed that the more the mentor and mentee are similar in background, the greater the chance that a positive relationship will occur because of increased communication and an ability for the mentor to understand the circumstances and challenges facing the mentee. Ideally, the mentor should have been born and raised in the community where he/she is mentoring. However, achieving this match may pose an unnecessary burden on programs.

The benefits that youths derive from having a mentor are numerous: development of social skills, guidance in making decisions, prosocial alternatives to involvement with gangs, goal setting, communication enhancement, to list but a few (Lerner 1995; Mincy 1994). The following observation made by a youth participant captures the importance of an adult in the lives of youths (Wertz 1994:29): "Every program highlighted by the youth representatives mentioned a significant adult. This adult liked and respected the young person. Though many young people had limited family support and lives in high-risk environments, the caring adult made a difference in their lives. Many of these programs had mentors, tutors, or a trained young adult to act as a 'friend' to the young people."

Benefits, however, are not necessarily one-sided. Mentors, too, are enhanced from engaging in activities that promote personal growth in young people. Mentors, like all other types of volunteers, engage in the mentoring process because of some instrumental or expressive need. Most notably, the need to "give back" to the community is very common. Thus, it is important that youths realize that a mentoring relationship is never one-sided, namely, that the adult is doing the youth a favor. The reciprocal nature of a mentoring relationship plays a prominent role in fostering this type of contract.

10. Effective programs actively seek to involve parents and other significant people.

Supportive and caring relationships with adults play a more important role than programs do in the process of enhancing youths' assets (Higgins 1988; Kimball-Baker and Roehlkepartian 1998; Scales and Leffert 1999; Sum et al. 1997). Consequently, programs directed at youths must seek to involve adults in the community (Kellogg Foundation 1998:15): "Programs never treat a single person, grantees tell us. Each person is part of a family, neighborhood, or culture that has being on the young person's development." The board perspective advocated by the Kellogg Foundation serves to place youth within a constellation of other individuals, young and old alike. This ecological perspective, in turn, necessitates that youth programming also seek to involve and assist adults. Nevertheless, the primary focus is still on youth.

Successful youth programs have families and significant adults actively involved (CCNY 1994; Smith 1997; U.S. Dept. of Education 1998). For some youths it means supporting families who are actively involved; for others, it means having families reengage through parent participation in school and after-school activities (Barton, Watkins, and Jarjoura 1997). It is widely accepted that communities where adults have extensive social networks, sets of obligations, and effective communication patterns (horizontal and vertical) are also communities where children's behavior can be controlled and supervised, resulting in a decrease in health-compromising behaviors and an increase in health-enhancement behaviors (Elliot 1993; Wilson 1993).

Effective youth programming must find a way of involving parents and other significant adults as a means of reinforcing its goals for youth. It becomes a very delicate balance because youths may not want to involve parents and other adults. They may, however, wish to involve someone else's parents and not their own. They may have fears that once parents get actively involved, organizations will start to focus on parents and not youths, thereby eliminating an important alternative for participants who have very few options. Parental involvement, however, is essential if a program is to have a wide impact within the community and develop the requisite political support that comes from having "adults" believing in the program and the services it offers. Further, many adults are not engaged in organization-led activities. Thus, efforts at reaching out to adults through youth organizations may be an effective way of reaching adults and providing them with important services and recreational alternatives.

Youth organizations, however, must be careful in reaching out to parents and other significant adults because other community-based organizations may view such efforts as violating "turf," causing interorganizational conflicts. Nevertheless, youth organizations cannot afford to ignore potential influential people in a participant's life; influencing those individuals will have a positive impact on youth. As a result, the impact of the program may involve multiple generations beyond youths themselves.

11. Effective programs require long-term institutional commitment and seek to be comprehensive in nature.

The development of an organization's commitment to a population group such as youth must be conceptualized as long-term and comprehensive

(Burt, Resnick, and Novick 1998; CWLA 1998; Sum et al. 1997). Commitment, however, must also be multifaceted, covering a variety of organizational dimensions in order to maximize resources and prevent certain age-groups from falling between the cracks (Humke 1996; Smith 1997; U.S. Dept. of Education 1998).

Long-term institutional commitment is required if youth-focused services are going to be successful over a long period (Lerner 1995:80):

> Interventions must be designed to be longitudinal in shape . . . [with] continuity of programming . . . . maintained across development. Programs, conceived of as lifespan convoys of social support . . . , should be implemented to protect and enhance the positive effects of preventive interventions. Clearly, such continuity of effort is expensive.

Thus, conceptualizing programming across the lifespan serves to engage and maintain youth in prosocial activities throughout the difficult period of adolescence (Dryfoos 1990; Hamburg 1992; Lerner and Ryff 1978; Scales and Leffert 1999; Smith 1997).

The importance of long-term commitment goes beyond factors stressing efficiency, start-up costs, staff retention, etc., it also involves the time and energy that must be exerted by organizations in developing reputations among youths and their communities. Any practitioner who has been involved in developing a new program or service realizes that the recruitment or referral process is very labor intensive, particularly when seeking candidates with a history of not participating. Consequently, the outreach process tends to rely more on person-to-person contact rather than letters, leaflets, posters, etc. Reputations cannot be developed through well-orchestrated media campaigns, and must be achieved through word-of-mouth contact within the community. This process, as a result, tends to be very time-demanding and necessitates the hiring of staff who feel comfortable "working the streets" of a neighborhood, and meeting potential participants in their homes, places of worship, or favorite hangouts. This will mean that staff people must be flexible concerning where they will "practice" and when they will do so—weekends, holidays, and evenings are not necessarily exempted.

Consequently, programs cannot be implemented/unimplemented off and on again depending on whether funding appears or disappears. Organizational reputation allows youths and their communities to develop relationships with institutions and their staffs, regardless of the type of funding available. It must be stressed that youths and other community residents are not privy to the vicissitudes of funding. Consequently, they are not easily forgiving of an organization terminating a service or activity because of a decrease or termination of funding. Organizations, as a result, cannot initiate or terminate activities or programs without seriously considering the consequences of such actions on a community's trust and/or the impact it will have on future initiatives.

12. Effective programs serve as vehicles for delivering "conventional" services to youth, and if necessary, in unconventional settings and times.

Efforts to reach urban youth must not be saddled by having needs be conceptualized and structured in conventional ways. Services, as a result can, and must, be provided in a variety of ways and settings that take into account local circumstances (Smith 1997; Sum et al. 1997). The Kellogg Foundation's Safe Passages through Adolescence initiative found the greatest degree of success through service systems stressing multiple points of entry (formal and informal). These systems coveted community-owned and -located businesses, schools, houses of worship, agencies, and providers. It is highly recommended that access channels be increased rather than narrowed as a means of reaching adolescents who normally cannot be reached through conventional service points (Scales and Leffert 1999).

An organization's willingness to resist conventionality is an important ingredient in determining the ultimate success of its efforts. Culturally competent models of outreach and programming often necessitate "unconventional" approaches in hiring and deployment of staff (Kellogg Foundation 1998). Interventions, in addition, must stress recreational and other activities instead of conventional "talk-based" methods as a means of engaging youth. Much counseling and advice-giving can be systematically incorporated into the use of activities (Morrison, Alcorn, and Nelums 1997). However, these methods cannot be expected to exist either solely, or in isolation from other forms of activity that are nonstigmatizing and fun. Further, every effort must be made to have youths "give back" to their community either by community services or performance. Youth-targeted organizations such as those that are sports-oriented are not stigmatizing to program participants. This makes delivery of "conventional" talk-therapies more accepting if integrated in some form into the "normal" course of daily activities.

The movement to include conventional forms of social services within social settings illustrates the applicability of these types of settings for service delivery to communities (Dryfoos 1998). Schools have been one of the primary beneficiaries of the trust to include a variety of social service-type programs within these settings. Some of the services have caused controversy, as in the case of clinics where birth control is practiced. However, schools, with some notable exceptions (situations where students are bused), are generally easily accessible to residents because of their location in the community; in addition, visiting them is not a stigmatizing experience. Parents can drop of their children and access needed services in one stop.

13. Effective programs systematically involve other organizations (formal and informal).

The task of reaching and serving youth cannot be relegated to just a few organizations or individuals who have historically had this goal as part of their mission, nor can it be successfully addressed by any one institution. The issues, needs, and challenges facing urban youth require a much more concerted effort to involve other organizations and volunteers (CCNY 1994, 1994c; CCAD 1994; CCA 1997; Freudenberg and Radosh 1998; Langman and McLaughlin 1993; Scales and Leffert 1999; Smith 1997; Sum et al. 1997; Tyler 1996; U.S. Dept. of Education 1998). The delivery of services to youth leaves much to be desired in comprehensively addressing the issues and needs of this population group (Melaville and Blank 1991): (1) most services are crisis-oriented rather than preventive; (2) the problems of youths and their families are invariably divided into rigid categories that fail to reflect their interrelated causes and solutions; (3) lack of open communication and cooperation between agencies allows youths and families to "fall between the cracks"; (4) specialized organizations cannot easily create comprehensive solutions to complex problems; and (5) services, when available, do not have adequate funding to successfully address the issues and needs of youth.

Interorganizational partnerships represent one viable way of combining limited resources and deploying them in a coordinated fashion to reach urban youths within the context in which they live. Nevertheless, a series of factors or circumstances must converge in order for organizations to see the value of working together, and to seek collaborative partnerships (Melaville and Blank 1991): (1) a social or political climate within a community that encourages different groups working together; (2) a process that fosters creation of common goals, structures, and procedures; (3) collaboration between parties that have the requisite vision, commitment, and competence; (4) collaborating partners who have governing policies that value collaborative endeavors; and (5) resources that are necessary to achieve success are available.

The Carnegie Corporation's Task Force on Youth Development and Community Programs (CCAD 1992:43) concluded the following upon obtaining youths' input into what activities they valued:

> When the Task Force asked young adolescents what they wanted most during their nonschool hours, they replied: safe parks and recreation centers; exciting science museums; libraries with all the latest books, videos, and records; chances to go camping and participate in sports; long talks with trusting and trustworthy adults who know about the world and who like young people; and opportunities to learn new skills.

This list of wishes should not come as any great surprise to anyone who has worked with young people.

Further, no one organization can possibly meet all of these wishes. However, several organizations working together can address these wishes in a way that is comprehensive and complimentary. The enormity of the task necessitates communities thinking and acting in collaborative and strategic ways as a means of maximizing their talents and resources, and doing so in a manner that is culturally competent (Sullivan 1996).

Finally, creation of new ways of involving adults in volunteer positions and other informal organizations not only increases the amount of human resources addressing youth issues and needs, it also serves to create greater connectedness within the community, build a political constituency, and maximize ways of creating a "sense of community" involving organizations. These benefits cannot be achieved overnight. However, they require creation of partnerships in order to succeed over the long-term.

14. Successful programs stress the importance of interethnic/racial relations among participants by preparing them to live in a multicultural world.

Quality interactions and exchanges provide a conducive atmosphere where youth participants can share and learn from each other and program staff (Hansot 1993; Smith 1997). Unfortunately, there may be many youths who do not have such an environment within their lives, at home, school, or other places. Thus, a conducive environment takes on added importance in the lives of these youths. The time and thought that go into creating such an atmosphere is also greatly influenced by the size of the groups, the nature of the activities used in helping staff members to personalize services, increase their knowledge of participants, and have cultural awareness and acceptance of differences between participants (Scales and Leffert 1999). Any concerted effort at addressing these factors will no doubt facilitate positive exchanges between youth.

The world that most urban-based youngsters live in is one that is ever-changing in ethnic and racial composition. Demographic trends in the United States reflect a society that is ever-changing in composition. Urban areas of the country, in turn, have experienced the greatest amount of change in composition. Growing up in the South Bronx during the 1950s and 1960s, I learned very quickly that my community consisted primarily of three types of groups: African Americans, Puerto Ricans, and "others." This country, however, has experienced a prodigious amount of diversity in terms of race and ethnicity the last two decades. Consequently, programming must both recognize and provide young people with the necessary awareness and skills to live in a multicultural community.

Youth programs need to be keenly aware of how the ethnic/racial backgrounds of participants can severely limit relationship-building (Smith 1997). Youths themselves, after all, are not beyond harboring racist sentiments and stereotypes. As a result, successful programming cannot leave to chance youths surmounting racial barriers on their own. Adults can fill an important leadership role in this area. Although racial/ethnic relations play an important role in service delivery that is very crucial, it rarely gets addressed in an open and straightforward manner. It is as if one thinks the topic will go away if ignored. Organization employment of staff of similar racial and ethnic backgrounds to the participants is a critical aspect. Such staff can serve as role models for youth, as well as role models for interethnic and racial relations (Gambone and Arbreton 1997).

Youniss and Yates (1997) note, in their review of the literature on youth and community service, a lack of attention to the dynamics of race, class, and gender. A lack of attention to these key factors severely limits the effectiveness of programs because of the conflicts arising from these differences. They also found a general disregard for the interplay of various key sociodemographic factors. The success of youths with different backgrounds working together has far-reaching implications for relations within the community; their success in youth arenas can spill over into other arenas such as school. Thus, any effort at minimizing conflict due to

racial background will go a long way toward improving community relations. Creation of forums such as discussion groups can be an important
component of youth-focused programming.

Over twenty-five years ago a national panel of experts (NCRY 1974) identified the potential that youth possesses to make lasting and important contributions to society but that has generally been untapped. The potential of
a strengths paradigm for reaching and assisting youths, particularly those
in environments and circumstances that can be considered unhealthy, is
very promising. The construct of resiliency, or strengths, assets, protective
factors, can be effectively used in programming a multitude of activities
that seek to systematically build upon youths' talents and potential. Building upon youths' interests and potential, however, will have far-reaching
implications for their families, communities, and the systems that serve
them, particularly schools.

Youths' assets, in turn, cannot be fully recognized unless placed with a
sociocultural context that views this population group within the community in which youths live. Youth development, however, cannot be addressed
without also broadening the concept to community. Thus, enhancement of
one arena will naturally impact on the other. A conscious effort to bring
about this relationship will serve both immediate and long-term interests.
Nevertheless, much more work and research must be undertaken in this area
to more fully identify the set of factors and circumstances that lend themselves to maximum use of indigenous talents and resources. The philosoph-
ical stance that everyone has talents that can and must be identified and nur-
tured fits well within a professional value stance that stresses empowerment,
participation, collaboration, and capacity enhancement in the conceptualization of social work practice. This stance, which many practitioners and
scholars would argue is ideologically based, needs a solid research base before
it can rightly be more fully embraced by the profession.

Future research focused on examining the value of a strengths perspective will undoubtedly require close collaboration between practitioners and
researchers in order to succeed in capturing the impact of this paradigm
(Delgado 1999; Freeman 1998). Failure to develop and foster this type of
working partnership will seriously limit the appeal of a strengths perspective, particularly when funding agencies require careful and systematic
evaluation of initiatives premised on this paradigm.

Generation of data premised on strengths is critical for strengths-based
evaluation to succeed in capturing a true picture of how activities and

events have changed youths, their families, and their communities. Thus, a strengths perspective has the potential to revolutionize social work practice in general, and youth-focused work in particular. However, evaluation studies of initiatives based on strengths must be carefully planned and implemented if practitioners and scholars advocating this approach are to truly have an impact on social work and other helping professions.

Numerous foundations and national commissions have examined what makes for successful youth-focused organizations. These learned bodies have tapped the "national wisdom" on the topic and have generated numerous recommendations pertaining to funding, planning, and organizational structure and process. These recommendations in combination with recommendations culled through reviews of the literature have resulted in the set of fourteen principles.

The principles were not intended to be exhaustive. Practitioners may no doubt have additional principles that have "worked" for them. The principles capture the conventional wisdom on the topic of the arts, humanities, and sports, as vehicles for reaching out to, engaging, and channeling youth's energies and capacities into constructive avenues. No organization wishing to serve urban youth can possibly use all fourteen of the principles outlined here. However, no organization can possibly succeed without using some, if not many. Consequently, these principles not only guide staff in operationalizing their role, they also serve to focus their organization to better direct staff.

In addition, this chapter has provided an overview of the importance of arts, humanities, and sports, and the potential they have for engaging urban youth. The organizations planning and implementing these activities cover a wide range of types, and are not limited to the conventional types of organizations that are commonly considered to be youth-focused. The organizations covered in this chapter not only involved the "traditional" youth-focused organizations but also informal, or what I call "nontraditional settings." Houses of worship, merchant institutions sponsoring teams, settlement houses, etc., all can play important roles in reaching community youth. These organizations have been successful in carrying out their mission because of the principles they subscribe to, and their willingness to be creative in search of the right approaches and services they provide for urban youth.

CHAPTER 4

—

THE POTENTIAL OF THE ARTS, HUMANITIES, AND SPORTS

The potential of using the arts, humanities, and sports for reaching urban youth cannot be examined without taking into account historical and current forces that have operated and continue to operate in urban areas of the United States. These forces have had a profound impact on how families structure their daily activities, as well as how they view their future. Further, the potential of these activities is not restricted to anyone age- or at-risk group (Rook 1998). A message from a young person regarding the importance of art brings to the foreground the potential of this expressive form for achieving beneficial outcomes that go far beyond artistic expression (Francis 1994:45):

> As we move into the twenty-first century and are confronted with problems such as racism, poverty, AIDS, and crime, most young people in our society do not know about movements that are going on right now to end these problems. When young people learn about art, they learn about DaVinci and Botticelli. These artists are important but do not suffice for representing life in the present. It should be known by every student that there are thousands of people out there trying to better society . . . through their art work.

Art and other forms of expression provide a "voice" for youths to express themselves and share their hopes, frustrations, and fears.

The use of the music media, particularly radio or the music industry, to enhance adolescent health promotion behaviors is not an entirely new strategy (Flora 1990). There is no denying that music increases in significance for youths as they approach and enter their adolescent years. Consequently, it only stands to reason that this form of activity can be used to both reach and assist youths in meeting the challenges associated with this developmental stage. Music-related activities, in addition to actual performance, can involve any or all of the following: composition, directing, filming and recording, supervising, set design, and technical editing. Opportunities to be involved in all aspects of music, however, increases a youth's appreciation of the multifaceted nature of music and the possibilities of finding their "niche" in this arena. In fact, the combination of video and music serves to bring aspects of the arts and music, thereby making collaborative activities between these two forms of expression that much more likely.

The use of the arts, humanities, and sports counterparts, can be a mechanism for promoting multiculturalism within society (Cahan and Kocur 1996:xix):

> Over the past decade the body of literature on multicultural education in the United States has been rapidly growing . . . Despite this scope, literature addressing the visual arts falls into a narrow range . . . . within critical approaches to multicultural education, even interdisciplinary approaches, little attention has been paid to the substitutive roles art can play.

A number of cities throughout the United States have turned to building art centers within their downtown areas as a means of attracting businesses and institutions, and as part of their revitalization efforts (Weber 1997). Newark recently opened its $180 million New Jersey Center for the Performing Arts as a means of both exposing residents to the arts and economically revitalizing the downtown area of the city in the process.

One summer project director articulated the value of an arts program for at-risk youth of color very well when stating (Williams and Knoey-Li 1996:276):

> The Oakland Summer Performing Arts Day Camp provides a pivotal opportunity for Oakland-area 6- to 18-year-old youth to learn how to express themselves through dance, music, drama, and the visual arts. The program was established on the premise that cultures and societies have always created art as a vehicle for expression of their values, hopes, and beliefs. Every aspect of a person's life is touched by art in one way or another.

In essence, it is not to say that the arts, music, humanities, and sports are not important in and of themselves, because they certainly are (Archibold

1998b). However, they are also important as a result of their potential to serve as vehicles for reaching other critical social development goals for youth.

The concept of "social reconstruction" has been applied to the arts. This concept refers to an educational process that utilizes the arts as a vehicle for youths to become productive members of their community and society by relying on an "egalitarian ideology." This ideology, in turn, raises youths' consciousness of issues of inequality and injustice, fosters an appreciation of cultural diversity, and teaches them skills, political and academic, that they can use to combat oppression (Cahan and Kocur 1996). Urban youth are painfully aware of their physical surroundings and the threat to their well-being posed by crime and encounters with authority. The poor state of their environment also serves as a reminder of how the external world views them (Breitbart 1998). Thus, it is not possible for initiatives to just target youth without also attempting to change the physical environment in the process. The concept of play, as manifested through sports activities, serves to provide youth with socially constructive outlets for aggressive behavior, learning relationship-building, team work, communication skills, and developing a variety of motor skills. This learning and development serve both present-time and long-term needs (Hamburg 1990).

The role of these new arenas for urban social work practice must be placed within the broader goals of facilitating youths' transition to adulthood, the current roles and potential of organizations, the historical role of social work, and the factors that enhance after-school settings effectiveness in reaching youth. The interrelationship between these factors not only sets the context for social work practice but also influences the nature of that practice. Nevertheless, it is important to pause and take into account to what degree is it important to foster competition as a central part of participation in these new arenas . Alder and Alder (1998:110) make an important observation concerning the role of competition, individual or team-focused, when such competition effectively places those who can participate in an "elite" category:

> Children could progress from school plays or local dance troupes to participation in adult theater or dance performances, from the school band to the junior symphony, from local competitions to regional and/or national meets, and from competitively oriented league to elite leagues. The decision to pursue an elite activity meant allocating it a greater amount of time, making it a priority ahead of other activities, and eliminating other projects.

There is an increasing and impressive body of research extolling the role of structured out-of-school activities, recreation- and nonreaction-centered, in helping urban youth. In Phoenix, a midnight basketball program and recreational facility have been found to be responsible for a dramatic decrease (55 percent) in juvenile-related crime when kept open until 2 A.M. (Trust for the Public Land 1994). The Fort Myers (Fla.) STARS (Success Through Academics and Recreational Support) program for young adolescents reported a 28 percent drop in juvenile arrests since its inception, including a dramatic rise in school grades (80 percent of the 1500 youths who are enrolled achieve a grade of C or better). A recreation and mentoring program called Project HYDRA (Hart Youth Development Resource Association) reported a decrease of 14 percent in juvenile complaints and 25 percent incarceration rates during the first year of operation (Trust for the Public Land 1994). Consequently, there is ample data to strongly suggest the value of youth participating in after-school programs and activities.

IMPLICATIONS FOR SOCIAL WORK

Transition to Adulthood

Assisting youths to make the transition to adulthood is a very important goal for any organization. However, there is a significant difference between assisting them in the transition and considering them "adults-in-waiting." The former recognizes the importance of the "here and now" while the latter is primarily interested only in the future. Failure to take into account the operative reality of youths seriously undermines any efforts at engaging them.

According to the Carnegie Corporation (Poinsett 1996), transition to an effective adulthood for adolescents necessitates achieving the following goals: (1) finding a place in a constructive group; (2) learning how to form close, durable human relationships; (3) achieving a sense of worth as a person; (4) achieving a reliable basis for making informed decisions concerning major life choices; (5) having available and knowing how to use a support system; (6) being useful to others; (7) having hopes for a future that provides real opportunities for growth and achievement; (8) developing problem-solving skills and a mind for lifelong learning; (9) understanding what responsible citizenship entails and respecting democratic values; and (10) building a healthy lifestyle that is conducive for growth and achievement of happiness.

It is estimated that approximately 7 million youths, or 25 percent of all adolescents, can be considered at high-risk for school failure or engaging in high-risk behaviors, and another 7 million more can be classified as being at moderate risk for the same kind of consequences (Poinsett 1996). New arenas can serve as effective vehicles for helping youth make the transition to adulthood. One dance instructor stated this goal very simply and eloquently (Wade 1998:8): "We are teaching the kids about commitment—teaching them how to be young adults—through the discipline of dance."

Role of Organizations

Achievement of these critical goals is beyond the reach of any institution and family. Success in meeting these goals is only possible when there is a coalition of multiple sources such as schools, health care organizations, media, community organizations, governmental entities, recreational organizations, to list but a few, who are willing and able to work in collaboration (Lerner 1995:62):

How can American society foster these attributes of positive youth development? Clearly, given the multifaceted individual, interpersonal, and institutional character of these attributes, neither one person nor a single institution (e.g., the family) can be charged with sole responsibility in promoting the positive development of youth. Thus all segments of the community . . . . must collaborate in the raising of our nation's youth. Indeed, given the historically revolutionary changes that have occurred in the American family over the course of this century . . . , children's and adolescents' families are less able than perhaps ever before to act alone in fostering positive youth development."

The enormity of the task requires a corresponding enormity of resources! It is estimated that there are anywhere from 17,000 to 20,000 national and local youth-serving organizations operating in the United States (Poinsett 1996). However, all of these organizations combined can only reach less than one-third of the eligible youngsters. Thus, the need for the nation to focus its attention on youth is no simple task, yet an extremely important one that cannot possibly be left solely to youth-serving organizations.

Many cities across the United States have established specialized schools focusing on the arts as a means of reaching inner-city youth (Manning 1999; Wade 1998). These institutions address both artistic and academic aspects of education. Students usually must pass an entrance examination.

Graduates often continue their education or enter jobs in the arts. Professional classes often include acting, singing and dancing, set design, among others. These schools very often have partnerships with professional dance, art, and music organizations.

McLaughlin, Irby, and Langman's (1994) classic study of community-based organizations, and the potential that they can play in the lives of inner-city youth, further reinforces the importance of these types of organizations. As already outlined in painful detail in chapter 2, urban-based youths face incredible challenges in leading "typical" lives in this society— namely, a hope for a future; minimal chances of premature death; a sense that the world is fair; a believe in self-worth; a belief that the institutions that are there to serve youth will do so in a way that will ensure their effective transition to adulthood. The book, *Urban Sanctuaries*, documents why community-based organizations are so important, and how they are effective; in essence, it is not by chance, nor is it a miracle. These institutions, as noted in chapter 3, have a very clear sense of youths and their lives, in addition to involving them in decision making, and are staffed with the "right" kind of people (Marshall 1996). Further, in helping young people, adults as well as the community benefit directly from those efforts. A number of organizations have been created to specifically address the needs of youths and urban community residents through the use of the arts and other methods (Calamese 1999).

In New York City's Spanish Harlem a new organization has emerged called the Julia de Borgos Latino Cultural Center (named after a famous Puerto Rican poet who died in the streets of East Harlem), which has taken over a former school building consisting of over 60,000 square feet. This building has been renovated to include classrooms, rehearsal studios, offices, galleries, and a 225-seat theater (Cotter 1998). This arts center is intended to play an important role in providing avenues for residents and artists, by serving as a focal point of the community.

On the West Coast, California is very fortunate to have at least two arts organizations with national and international reputations that are exemplary in how they have used the arts as a means for involving and organizing the community in the creation of art, enhancing community capacity, and beautifying areas that were often considered "blights" on the community. These organizations have transformed a vision of achieving social and economic justice through the use of the arts, most notably mural painting. An interesting aside, both of these organizations were established during the 1970s, a time in U.S. history of great social upheaval.

In San Francisco, Precita Eyes Mural Arts Center was established in the late 1970s by a group of eight artists whose sole purpose was to build community through use of art, and art through community (Lawrinsky 1997). This goal is accomplished through the painting of murals that both seek to involve residents in all aspects of the project, but also to educate them while doing so. In Los Angeles, the Social and Public Art Resource Center (SPARC), like its San Francisco counterpart, was established in the mid-1970s and sought to combine the arts and community in creating positive social change. SPARC focused on using the arts, primarily murals, as a means of achieving cultural affirmation for groups that have have historically been marginalized in this society (Baca 1990).

The Chicago Public Arts Group (CPAG), too, has a national reputation for using the arts, primarily murals, sculptures, and mosaics, as a means of building community, enhancing the environment, and teaching and employing residents in the process. CPAG was formed, like its Los Angeles and San Francisco counterparts, in the 1970s by a group of mural artists that sought to organize residents through increasing their awareness of the role and potential of public art (Lakes 1996).

The Omega Boys Club (coeducational) in San Francisco, cofounded by Joseph Marshall Jr., has been immensely successful in reaching youths who would normally be classified as "hard core" delinquents utilizing a variety of methods (Marshall 1996:xxvi):

> I'll get right to the point. In just six years, the Omega Boys Club of San Francisco has been able to place 108 young people in college, many of them former gang members and drug dealers. We have been able to elicit community support to pay for their education. Six years ago we began with fifteen members. Today we have over three hundred [and as I write this, the number has nearly doubled]. We have since added a weekly radio call-in program which enables us to reach an additional two hundred thousand. We do peer counseling on a weekly basis in the juvenile detention centers of San Francisco and Oakland.

These organizations and their counterparts in other cities throughout the United States involving other activities such as music, sports, etc., bring a different yet very appealing alternative for social work practice with urban-based youth. These kinds of organizations, as will noted in other chapters throughout this book, provide venues for social work practice that are nonstigmatizing and easily accessible to the community. These organizations epitomize community accessibility: (1) geographical; (2) cultural; (3) psychological; and (4) operational. These four types of accessibility, when combined, play a very powerful role in bringing communities together in search of avenues for achieving social and economic justice.

> Geographical accessibility is just that, the location of the organization is in or near the community being served. Youth do not have to travel long distances to participate. Further, these organizations are often located in neutral sites within the community, minimizing possible dangers from crossing gang territories.
>
> Cultural accessibility refers to activities and personnel who reflect the cultural background of the youths, minimizing miscommunication resulting from not sharing similar backgrounds and experiences. Further, cultural accessibility also refers to language and activities that reinforce positive images of ethnic and racial heritage.
>
> Psychological accessibility, in turn, refers to the degree of comfort and safety that youths experience when participating in organizational activity. The degree of comfort that is derived from being accepted without condition is very important when involving urban youths, particularly those who have experienced pervasive rejection by society because of their background.
>
> Finally, operational accessibility focuses on facilitating youth participation by minimizing extensive intakes, filling out of forms, and operating hours and days that lend themselves to youth participation. Organizations sponsoring midnight basketball conferences, for example, epitomize logistical accessibility through their hours of operation.

The Role and Potential of Social Work

It would be false to think of social work as not having an historical role in using the arts, music, humanities, and sports as vehicles for delivering services (James 1993; Sanders 1998). Initially, by 1893 the settlement house movement offered community residents a wide range of activities, most notably a dispensary, nursery, gymnasium, and playground; shortly afterwards, the activities expanded to include theater, art, and music (Specht and Courtney 1994). The number and types of youth-serving organizations proliferated dramatically during the early twentieth-century, unlike any period prior to this era (James 1993).

Like Morrison, Alcorn, and Nelums (1997), I advocate the use of practice based upon many of the original principles that guided the settlement house movement, with the incorporation of recent developments such as empowerment, cultural competence, and strengths/assets. Simon (1994:75) notes that an embrace of multifaceted roles by social workers in settlement houses was based on "the importance of offering preventive and crises responses to the spiritual and psychological aspects of their neighbors' poverty and social dislocation." A belief in empowerment and client strengths were important factors in shaping these roles. These factors, however, have not changed in over a century of practice.

Social workers must have a historical understanding of how the profession used these approaches as activities in practice. For example, settlement houses and group work had arts, humanities, and sports activities. New York City's Henry Street Settlement, one of the oldest and best-known settlement houses in the nation, still maintains an active arts and humanities program. Their dance program was recently featured in a *New York Times* article describing the importance of dance for encouraging creativity among youth, increasing interracial/ethnic relations, fostering parent involvement, and increasing dance accessibility to all socioeconomic classes (Dunning 1997).

The profession, however, has gradually withdrawn from using the arts, humanities, and sports as part of interventions, with schools of social work rarely preparing students for settings using these types of activities (Sanders 1998). Morrison, Alcorn, and Nelums (1997:322) comment on social work's nonpresence in the field of neighborhood-based youth development services:

> Despite social workers' professed interest in the development of youth, family, and community, they staff relatively few of the neighborhood-based youth development services. Instead, social workers are more likely to be found in treatment-oriented agencies . . . . This has not always been the case. Settlement houses and youth service agencies, like community centers, YMCAs, and Boys' and Girls' Clubs, were once extensively staffed with professionally trained social workers . . . Today, . . . they have little professional social work presence . . . Social work's training [emphasis on therapy], professional licensure, and financial arrangements have all come to support this.

Finn and Checkoway (1998 344), however, go further in their critique of the profession's lack of visibility in these and other arenas that can be classified from a youth development perspective: Social workers have an uneven record in the promotion of youth participation as competent community builders. It is time to take the capacity of young people seriously and challenge the limits of our helping paradigms in the process. This calls for a reorientation from therapeutic models of individual treatment to consciousness-raising models for group reflection and action. It demands a redirection from emphasis on social work roles of counselor, case manager, and broker to those of collaborator, mentor, and animator.

Using the arts, humanities, and sports as a means for delivering services is not out of the ordinary since numerous organizations across the United States, including schools, are doing just that. These types of activities, in addition, can also be delivered by nontraditional settings such as houses of worship, local businesses sponsoring sports leagues, domino tournaments, etc. However, regardless of the type of institution sponsoring the activity, these institutions have been successful in turning "ordinary" activities into life-altering experiences. Ball and Heath (1993) note that youth organizations based in cities have increasingly turned to the arts as viable vehicles for attracting "at-risk" youth and providing an alternative for drugs, crime, and disengagement from school. Artistic activities can successfully compete with athletics for the attention of youth. The arts can provide discipline, commitment, and a sense of group solidarity for youth.

Although schools can provide important options for youth to do art, humanities, and sports, packed curricula, tight budgets, and, in some cases, lack of an inviting and supportive environment creates a need for outside school opportunities (Caffey 1998). These new arenas not only serve to provide youth with safe and structured activities outside of school hours, but they can also serve to open up career options for those with talent and commitment (Caffey 1998). In essence, these activities must be able to accommodate everyone, from those starting out with minimal natural talents to those who with more advanced skills.

However, two words of caution are in order regarding sports, and the limited opportunities for youth to pursue this avenue into the professional ranks. Any fulfillment of the dream of prefessionally playing at any type of sport is very limited in contemporary society. Consequently, it becomes imperative for youths to seriously consider alternative careers. Second, youths' participation in competitive sports such as Little League, for example, has increasingly been the source of conflict for the parents of the children. Sporting activities are just that—sports for fun. Increased pressure placed on youths by parents and coaches may well have a detrimental affect upon them.

The increase of parental initiated violence has resulted in the National Association of Sports Officials, with approximately 19,000 members, to issue assault insurance (Dedman 1998). The increase in adult violence at children's sporting activities is probably the result of a variety of factors (Dedman 1998): (1) an overemphasis on winning at all cost; (2) parental belief that winning helps prepare children to succeed in other arenas; (3) parental fears that their children are poorly equipped to handle failure; and (4) parental suffering from what sports psychologists call "achievement proxy."

Youth-focused organized activities, even those with a perceived very narrow focus such as gymnastics, theater, basketball, dance, that tap their talents, enthusiasm, and provide potential for growth, result in youth involvement in positive actions. Involvement of youths in these and other activities will reduce the likelihood of gangs recruiting them since the primary target of gangs is unaffiliated youths (McLaughlin 1993). Offering a variety of activities within youth programs serves to not only broaden the appeal of these activities to a wide range of youth; some, for example, are only interested in sporting activities while others may be attracted to arts and crafts. However, offering a variety of activities also serves to widen program participation by youths, allowing them to explore and engage in a range of activities that they normally would not consider.

The benefits derived from participating in youth activities can be quite extensive in nature. One recent study of voluntary youth-serving organizations found that participants obtained desired benefits in six out of seven key developmental areas that were examined—leadership, social support from adults, challenging and interesting activities, belonging, input and decision making, and safety (Gambone and Arbreton 1997). Service to community was the exception and this may have been the result of limited opportunities to serve.

Consequently, it is imperative that social workers and other helping professionals not be biased against the use of activities that, on the surface, appear as narrow, with little or no educational or therapeutic value. This is particularly true for those professionally trained practitioners who were not exposed to alternative approaches as effective means for engaging and assisting youth in their educational experience, particularly those related to course work.

Organized activities such as the ones addressed in this book also bring an added dimension and benefits associated with peer group socialization. The influence of peer groups on youth, particularly adolescents, are well recognized among helping professions (Alder and Alder 1998; Frank 1996). Peer interactions with each other can reinforce behaviors that are constructive—in essence, the opposite types of behaviors associated with gangs.

A number of scholars, some of them social workers, have stressed the importance of youths having positive alternatives; these alternatives continue in importance even after youths join gangs (Fox 1990:29):

> Gang members expressed boredom and frustration about the lack of athletic facilities in the neighborhood. Consequently, one of their favorite activities was harassing employees and destroying property at a nearby hospital. With the gang's consent, the worker approached the hospital's administration to suggest that part of the hospital's large paved parking lot be equipped with backboards and basketball court markings. The administration agreed to try this in the hope that it would reduce harassment from the gang. The worker arranged a meeting between several gang members and the hospital superintendent of buildings and grounds for a semiformal presentation of the court to the gang. There was an immediate cessation of trouble from the gang, and the members expressed great satisfaction with the new facility.

It is important to pause and note that programming activities, as found in a New York City study, must take into account gender, if activities are to be relevant to youth participants. The Academy for Educational Development's (1997) survey, one of the few such studies in the country, found that girls require special strategies for outreach and engagement. Their accessing programs is enhanced when they have separate programs, forums, discussion groups, and an emphasis on personal development and issues related to girls. Further, programming targeting girls must be broad in nature and not be restricted to sexuality and pregnancy prevention.

The Academy's findings should not come as any great surprise to anyone working in the youth field. Similar conclusions can be made for sociodemographic factors such as age, socioeconomic class, documented status, and ethnicity/race. Programming, as a consequence, must take into consideration the background of youth in order to maximize the benefits from participation in activities.

THE AFTER-SCHOOL SCENE

After-School Settings

There is a growing awareness that the time spent in after-school related activities is almost as important, if not more so, than the time spent in school (Gardner 1994:ix–x):

> Delivery of services is not enough. Someone has to build community, and everyone knows, community is built by shared values. Absence of instruction in values is the least of our problems. What is a problem is that the values taught may be destructive. The young person is bombarded by value instruction, for good or evil, every waking hour—at home and in school, in Sunday school and at the movies. The playground teaches. The street corner teaches. Television teaches. . . No one escapes. . . . The environment teaches—insistently and in many voices. Where family and community have disintegrated, the likelihood of good lessons is minimal. Therein lies the problem. Both family and community have suffered devastating blows in modern society, and to be blunt about it, neither will ever be wholly reinstated in its old form. Those of us concerned for youth have focused heavily on the schools and have paid all too little attention to what happens after school. Yet that is a time of particular danger. That is when much of the trouble occurs.

However, according to a study of tenth-grade students, most are not actively engaged in after-school activities (Zill, Nord, and Loomis 1995): less than one-third attend religious services at least once a week, a fifth participate in structured recreational activities such as art, music, language, or dance at least once a week, one-eighth take weekly sporting lessons outside of school, and one in fourteen volunteer or perform community service. A recent study of television viewing habits by youths found that they spend a disproportionate amount of time engaged in this passive activity. Watching television is the most common after-school activity for children and adolescents, who on average spend 23 and 22 hours per week respectively in front of a TV set (U.S. Dept. of Education 1998). This time can be better spent in pursuit of activities that not only benefit youth in school but also in their social relations with peers and adults.

Recent national attention to the potential of after-school activities for enhancing youth skills has resulted in community-based youth agencies seeking a greater role in providing activities within school settings (Archibold 1999; Boyle and Wolfson 1998; O'Donnell, Michalak, and Ames 1999). All programs for children and youth are about education (CCNY 1994c). After-school programs must seek to achieve at least four major goals for youth: (1) development of positive relationships with adults; (2) access to enriching learning activities; (3) provision of a safe and healthy environment; and (4) creation of partnerships between family, school and community (U.S. Dept. of Education 1998). These goals are highly inter-related and stress physical, cognitive, and social aspects. Further, achievement of these goals not only results in youth participants benefiting directly, but also their families and communities.

This thrust has generally resulted in greater cooperation between youth agencies, houses of worship, and schools, ultimately benefiting all parties and the respective communities they serve (Boyle 1998d; Traver 1998; Wolfson 1998). Consequently, these new forms of partnerships have opened new possibilities for youth activities through combination of resources and increased cooperation.

Nevertheless, not every child who wishes to participate in after-school programs can do so—demand for school-based after-school programs far outpaces availability by a 2-to-1 ratio (U.S. Dept. of Education). Barriers to increasing accessibility for all youth who wish to participate fall into seven categories (Childers 1998): (1) attitudes about the need and value of school-age care—these settings must fulfill roles that go beyond custodial care, they must promote growth; (2) lack of partnerships with schools—school-age care programs cannot be "distant relatives" to schools, they must be an integral part of the activities; (3) need for flexible facilities—access to indoor and outdoor space is critical in order to run a wide range of activities; (4) burden of start-up costs—the issues associated with this phase of programming severely limit who can sponsor programs; (5) need for transportation access—programs that are nonschool based require that participants get transportation, limiting those families that cannot do so; (6) affordability—access to after-school programs is very limited for many poor and working-class families, even though their value to participants is well understood; and (7) need for training paid staff and volunteers—well-trained staff and volunteers are a key to quality school-care programs.

Limited access, however, does not have to do with bias, or lack of knowledge of existing programs. One study found that 83 percent of 50,000 school-age child care programs in the United States are dependent upon parent fees (Durrence 1998), severely limiting the number of families that can take advantage of the programs. It is estimated that there are anywhere from 1.5 million to 7 million children who are left unsupervised by an adult. The hours between when school is out to 5:30 P.M. are the most critical period of the day when children are left unsupervised (CCNY 1994c). These and other children can be prime beneficiaries of an after-school program.

After-school programs can be provided through a variety of structures: summer programs, after-school, both after-school and summer programs, evening and late-night programs. Further, programs can be based in a wide range of settings such as libraries, parks and recreation departments, museums, adult service clubs, senior citizens groups, housing sites, schools, houses of worship, among others, in addition to youth agencies (CCAD 1992). Variability in structure and setting allows communities the flexibility to design and deliver activities during times and places where they address the greatest needs.

Youth organizations rank second to schools in the number of youths they reach. It is estimated that fifteen major national organizations alone reach approximately thirty million youths per year (CCAD 1992). However, youths of color from low-income families continue to be underserved. Fees related to participation continue to be the primary barrier for these youths.

After-School in a Historical Context   After-school activities have essentially consisted of spontaneous play, initiated and supervised by and for children. These forms of play consisted of a myriad of activities that took into consideration seasonal changes, and each was created by children with appropriate sets of rules, roles, parameters, and means of integrating capable and less capable players. Many skills are learned through spontaneous play, such as negotiation, problem-solving, communication, planning, and team play, to list but a few. However, since the early 1970s there has been a systematic and broad expansion of adult-determined, staffed, and controlled after-school activities (Alder and Adler 1998).

This gradual but significant shift from youth-developed and controlled to adult-determined has been accomplished, with some exceptions, without youth playing significant roles in determining the activities. The skills and lessons learned through spontaneous play have been replaced by adult versions that may not reflect the reality of youths, particularly those who are marginalized in society. A move toward an "elite" level of competition results in a corresponding increased level of adult-control over the activity.

Alder and Alder (1998:111–112) found in their study that youths had minimal say over how the activities transpired:

> Once selected for the squad, participants soon discovered that adults treated elite activities seriously and expected that adolescents and preadolescents would impart the same degree of commitment. Practices moved from weekly or twice weekly to almost daily and required strenuous concentration. Coaches demanded strict attention and allegiance, subordinating not only participants but their families as well. Although recreational and competitive after-school activities were regarded as ends in themselves . . . , elite after-school activities incorporated a different attitude; many participants and parents regarded elite activities as a track into some future enterprise."

After-School Core Elements   After-school activities offer participants an abundance of ways of enriching their lives in the process of providing a safe area to be in. These activities offer endless possibilities for work within the community through gardening efforts, mural painting, building playgrounds, and other community-beneficial projects (Delgado, in press; Wolfson 1998). After-school activities, in turn, must be carefully crafted to take into account the community they draw from and seek to serve (National Assembly, 1998).

According to the Carnegie Council on Adolescent Development (1994), after-school programs, regardless of activity, must consist of at least eleven core elements if they to be successful . These elements, in turn, when combined with the principles outlined in chapter 3, provide important directions for social workers interested in these arenas for practice with urban youth: (1) programming must utilize the latest research findings on youth development—research that is culturally based and takes into consideration the operative reality of life in an urban area; (2) the organizational climate must be family-like and emphasize positive social relationships between participants and adults; (3) parental participation needs to be stressed; (4) youth must play an active and meaningful role in all aspects of the program and be specific to local community circumstances; (5) activities must be "fun," flexible, educational, and take into account changes in interest and community (indigenous) resources; (6) food must be provided; (7) membership roles are specific, clear, and consistently followed; (8) collaboration with local organizations (formal and informal) must be actively pursued; (9) settings must act as a sanctuary, shielding youth from the vicissitudes and dangers of urban life—both physical and psychological safety must be both a goal and reality; (10) program must stress strong and active linkages with schools and other resources; and (11) although the primary focus of activities is on recreation and enhancement of skills, other services, as needed, must be integrated as part of the service.

After-school activities, in turn, can consist of any or all of the following types: cooking, academics, arts, music, drama, sports, photography, sports, recreation. Parents, in turn, can engage in cooking, aerobics, English as a Second Language classes, job skills, citizenship classes, to list a few. The possibilities for other activities involving both adults and their children can also be offered. These activities, as a result, can encompass those that have historically been within the domain of services provided by social service organizations. In essence, both youths and adults can share activities but also benefit from individualized activities (Boyle 1998d; Boyle and Wolfson 1998).

After-School Activities and Social Work   After-school activities can consist of a multitude of types, as already discussed. These activities can have simple goals such as keeping youth off the streets to more complex social, educational, and political goals. A focus on the use of the arts, music, humanities, and sports (leisure activities) requires that the profession of social work combine theories from the social sciences, leisure fields, and social work practice (De Vincent 1996; Raimar 1995). This comprehensive view increases the likelihood that youths benefit from carefully planned programs that look at the whole youth rather than a single, and almost always narrow, perspective. The interface between social work and other professions, particularly those usually not collaborators with social workers, will necessitate the development of a dialogue between professions that, with rare exceptions, is sorely lacking.

The profession of social work has historically drawn from other professions in the development of practice, and disciplines such as anthropology, psychology, political science, and sociology. However, the fields of education and recreation, not to mention the arts, music, and humanities, have not played active roles in influencing the profession's knowledge base to the degree that it would be expected—we very often practice in the same arenas, i.e., communities, and share the same consumers—particularly youths. Interestingly enough, the existence of modern recreation centers have been traced back to the pioneering work done by Jane Addams in Chicago's Hull

House (Witt and Crompton 1996b). Thus, the fields of social work and recreation share a great deal in common.

The following mission description provided by a recreational project director sums up quite well the varied, complex, and important roles they can play—roles that, incidentally, are not dissimilar to those of social workers (Jordan 1996:99):

> The mission of the recreation field is to demonstrate that we are more than fun and games. Allowing ourselves to be relegated to just fun and games has weakened our competitive position at budget time. We are big brothers and big sisters. We are the nurses, the chauffeurs. We feed them. We pick them up. We patch them up. We are their role models; we are their friends. We play multiple roles in parks and recreation, and that is why the responsibility is so awesome. But it is also a tremendous opportunity, and we recognize that.

Staff working with youth, as a result, must be flexible in how they conceive their roles because of the complex nature of the needs youth present.

A Phoenix Parks and Recreation Department director reinforces the points made by Jordan (1996) when stating (Witt and Crompton 1996b:16–17):

> My staff say we are becoming counselors and social workers. That's fine, I believe we should be. We have always done this, but there is much more emphasis on it now than there has been in a couple of decades . . . We respond as best we can whatever they need. I would not have a problem with my Department being called a Department of Community Service. Our job is to make young people whole in any way we can, and offering wholesome recreation activities is only one aspect of that. It's a way of reaching them and gives us an opportunity to help straighten out other parts of their lives.

In essence, recreation programs, be they focused on sports or other activities, can no longer view youth from a narrow perspective—namely, leisure needs (Foley and Pick 1995). These programs, as a result, have expanded their mission to take a more holistic view of youth, and in so doing, have entered into areas that were occupied by other professions, social work being one. This "blurring" of boundaries opens up the possibilities for opportunities to collaborate across disciplines; unfortunately, it also opens opportunities for conflicts across the same disciplines.

Be cautioned, however, that after-school activities such as the arts, humanities, and sports cannot be a panacea for all of the hurdles facing marginalized urban youth (Editorial 1998a:2): Couldn't just keeping kids busy with positive, empowering and enjoyable youth development activities from 3 P.M. to 6 P.M. really eliminate drug abuse, teen pregnancy, petty crime, and worse? Of course not. But quality after-school programs certainly help build youth assets while curbing a mix of negative youth behaviors, and do so with more cost-effectiveness than does the current jumble of programs that policy makers unrealistically aim at a single "youth problem."

Self-Esteem   There is little argument that the construct of self-esteem plays an important role in helping youths develop the necessary competencies to be successful in school and in the community. Many practitioners would argue that after-school programs must actively seek to enhance youths' self-esteem if they hope to achieve any goals related to academic and social competencies.

The concept of self-esteem takes on greater prominence when applied to low-income and marginalized youths who, by the very nature of their circumstances, no doubt possess low self-esteem. However, it would be simplistic to think that the arts, music, humanities, or sports, or another other activity for that matter, can successfully achieve its potential by only stressing techniques, practice, and providing urban youth with opportunities to perform in public. The arts, music, humanities, and sports can only achieve their potential if they also successfully build up youths' self-esteem.

The concept of self-esteem is well recognized in the field of social work, and represents an important, if not the most important, anchor in helping people achieve their potential (Hamburg et al. 1993:377):

> Today our children and adolescents need to find ways to develop a positive vision of the future, to formulate an image of what adulthood offers and demands, and to work out a perception of opportunity and paths toward practical implementation of such opportunity. They also need to formulate ways to earn respect and to develop self-esteem and modes of establishing a sense of belonging in at least one highly valued group.

Cox and Powers's (1998) review of the literature noted that although it is arduous to sort out all of the causal relationships between self-esteem and the extensive number of factors correlated with it, high self-esteem is still very much associated with capacities to perform, acceptance of peers, and self-acceptance. Identity and self-esteem are two constructs that are closely linked in this society for undervalued groups such as low-income youth of color, and any effort to separate them is artificial. Thus, interventions that integrate these two constructs will have greater success than those that separate them.

According to Leadbeater and Way (1996) identity formation is the result of a dynamic process that occurs at various levels, and involves comparing oneself with the standards and ideals of others in one's community. In addition, it is influenced by the successes and failures experienced. It is very important that an individual's assets and goals must be greeted with social opportunities for their actualization.

Much of the literature examining identity for youths of color is very narrow in focus, emphasizes Eurocentric standards, and fails to take sufficient account of the role of cultural heritage in identity formation (Leadbeater and Way 1996). Thus, culturally competent social work practice with youths of color, and other marginalized groups, not only necessitates an understanding of the dynamic environmental forces experienced by this age group, it also requires an in-depth understanding of cultural factors (Greene and Barnes 1998; Van Voorhis 1998; Leffert, Saito, Blyth, and Kroenke 1996).

Thus, opportunities for self-actualization, along with a positive ethnic sense of self, play a very important role in the development of an identity. Opportunities to succeed, and a lack of barriers to achievement because of racial, gender, and ethnic background, result in high self-esteem—in essence, the individual likes who she/he is and his/her future. Low self-esteem results from belonging to an "undesirable" racial and ethnic background, and/or having a low probability of achieving success. Positive self-esteem translates into effective use of coping strategies to combat stress, and having competence and confidence in their beliefs that they can control their own destinies. Many practitioners and researchers subscribe to the belief that adolescents engage in risk-taking behavior as a means of coping with various environmental stressors, including those associated with entering adolescence, reduced coping, or both (Delgado 1997; Dryfoos 1990; Gaunti 1998; Gibbs 1996; Leadbeater and Way, 1996; McWhirter et al. 1993; Urban Institute 1993).

However, enhancement of self-esteem in urban youths of color takes on greater importance because of the dual impact of racism and classism on their lives. Media images of youths of color rarely portray them in positive roles (McLaughlin 1993). Most rarely have had an opportunity to discover who they are while in school, and even rarer have been the opportunities to understand their ethnic and racial contributions to society. Consequently, lack of positive knowledge of one's ethnic/racial background or shame can result in low self-esteem (Allen et al. 1996; De Leon 1996; Dryfoos 1990; Erkut et al. 1996; Krimsky and Golding 1992; Rotheram-Borus et al. 1996; Santiago 1995). Low self-esteem, in turn, severely limits how youths can generate the excitement and hope that are necessary to successfully negotiate major life transitions. Further, it severely impedes their creative impulses, limiting the possible contributions that they can make in the arts, humanities, and sports (Torregrosa 1998).

McLaughlin's (1993:60) conclusions based upon researching successful youth agencies stressed the importance of cultural pride related activities in these organizations:

> Many adults in these settings stressed the importance of alliance with well-grounded cultural history as a component of general self-esteem and social competence. Youth workers understood the importance of cultural awareness and pride and of youth's development of a positive sense of this aspect of their identity. Within the broader community context, there is often little with which to ascribe value or pride to African-American and Latino youths.

The increase in self-esteem becomes even more critical for youths who are living in two cultures because they must blend their traditional heritage and values with those of the dominant culture (Delgado 1997; Goplerud 1994; Phinney 1995; Saldana 1995).

Self-esteem, however, cannot be separated from the influence of peers. Those youths who have an active, supportive, and positive peer support system are more likely to also have positive self-esteem. Thus, the increase in self-esteem is closely tied to activities involving groups of peers, using the group as a powerful reinforcer of positive messages. Although this book focuses on a select number and type of activities, there are numerous others, such as wilderness experiences (Freeland 1998).

The arts, sports, and, to a much lesser extent, humanity subjects witnessed incredible budget cuts during the 1980s and 1990s in many urban school systems across the United States (Archibold 1998b). The consequences of cuts in the arts and music in New York City's school systems are quite stark (Archibold 1998:A14):

Art advocates in New York hope to erase what they consider an embarrassment: a city famous for the arts had all but excised them from its public schools during the fiscal crises of the mid-1970's and recession of the 1980's. Of the more than 14,000 teachers who lost their jobs, art and music teachers were often the first to go. Many bands and orchestras went silent . . . Before the cuts began in the 1970's, most schools had at least one art or music teacher. By 1991, two-thirds of the elementary schools had none.

Thus, countless numbers of youths, most of them being of low-income and of color, did not have an opportunity to be exposed to the arts or involvement in other youth development activities, thereby limiting the potential of these arenas for engaging and enriching their lives.

The propensity to view youth from a deficit perspective has seriously limited how most conventional types of organizations have reached out to this group (Pittman and Fleming 1991:3):

For years, Americans have accepted the notion that—with the exception of education—service for youth, particularly publicly funded services, exist to address youth problems. We have assumed that positive youth development occurs naturally in the absence of youth problems. Such thinking has created an assortment of youth services focused on "fixing" adolescents engaged in risky behaviors or preventing other youth from "getting into trouble.." . . What is needed is a massive conceptual shift—from thinking that youth problems are merely the principal barrier to youth development to thinking that youth development serves as the most effective strategy for the prevention of youth problems. Nothing short of a broad national initiative will accomplish this.

As noted earlier, new arenas have tremendous potential for exceeding the value of their practice because if properly conceptualized, they can take a holistic perspective of youth. Katz and Dickey (1995:i) sum up the importance of the arts well when stating:

The arts have always been, and always should be, valued and supported for their inherent worth. But we should not overlook their other public benefits; the arts enrich, transform, and even save lives. And in so doing they help to address some of society's greatest challenges, especially those

involving youth . . . Of course, the arts cannot by themselves address all
of the problems that affect the lives of children.

The same sentiments apply to the other arenas addressed in this book. New
arenas, and the field of youth development can be very effective in bringing social workers into new practice settings.

As organizations moved to replace and/or supplement the work of
schools in these areas, it provided opportunities for community-based organizations to expand their activities in these arenas. Unfortunately, although
a noble effort was made to fill the void created by public schools in some
communities, resources did not allow community-based efforts to com-
pletely meet all of the needs of youth (Archibold 1998b). Consequently, the
early part of the twenty-first century will represent a critical period in the
field of youth development. The social work profession can elect to continue
to stay out of that field or play an influential role in helping to shape it.

PART 2

—

REFLECTIONS FROM THE FIELD

Part 2 provides an opportunity to apply the themes reviewed in chapters 1 through 4 and apply them to individual cases. In addition to numerous case illustrations interspersed throughout chapters 5 through 7, a total of eight case studies (they differ from case illustrations because of the depth of information given) will be presented in chapter 8, and provide a more detailed glimpse into activities, planning considerations, and challenges practitioners can expect to face during practice involving the arts, humanities, and sports. These case studies were developed with a goal of covering cities with a wide range of populations, different geographic regions of the country, various types of arenas, and methods for delivering activities. Further, the use of case studies serves to provide an opportunity to witness practice in the "real world," and therefore highlight the endless number of possibilities for programming, as well as identifying, the many rewards and challenges associated with these forms of practice with urban-based youth.

CHAPTER 5

——

THE ARTS

New arenas as represented through the arts are generally not thought of as "legitimate" areas for social workers, unless they are referred to as "music therapy" or "art therapy." Although these are important dimensions to the arts and music, and there are creative examples of how they can be used (Steinhardt 1994), they are not the only perspectives on how attainment can be used to bring about change in individuals, families, and communities. The arts offer a tremendous number of approaches and activities, and appeal to a wide range of youngsters and circumstances (Hillman et al. 1991; Schinke et al. 1994).

These activities provide youth and communities with opportunities to be expressive, taking into account their cultural heritage, and issues of oppression in their lives. Music, for example, is not restricted to the classics, and in all likelihood, will encompass modern day types such as rap, whose origins are deeply rooted in the communities they speak about in the lyrics (Deyhle 1998; Hager 1984; Jones 1994; Ribadeneira 1998; Rook 1998).

THE POTENTIAL OF THE ARTS

Projects that stress youths' involvement and the shaping of their environment offer great promise (Rook 1998). The concept of community capacity enhancement, as already noted, takes on added significance when it not only enhances a participants' skills, knowledge, and attitudes, but also transforms an urban environment in the process by providing residents with an opportunity to do so (Delgado, in press). Visual art projects, for example, have the potential to do just that if they are conceptualized from an enhancement perspective, actively seek community input, and stress an asset perspective.

Whether the project involves the creation of street banners (Breitbart 1995, 1998), sculptures, or murals (Delgado and Barton 1998), or other forms of artwork, they not only beautify the community, but also serve as vehicles for youths to tell their stories to each other and to the outside world—a world, which incidentally, rarely provides them with such access. These projects, as a result, serve as testaments, or artifacts, of youths' resilience and hopes, with profound implications for an entire community. Exposure to and work with artists and performers provides youths with a unique opportunity to both develop their artistic talents, and learn to work with adults who are artists, in a supportive environment; artists, in turn, teach the aspects of their crafts, and do so within a political context that has relevance for youths (Lakes 1996).

The use of the arts as an organized activity, with multiple social purposes, has its origins during the settlement house movement in the late nineteenth century; consequently, the use of the arts in low income communities is not new in the United States. The arts were used by the earliest social workers as a means of assisting immigrants in their adjustment to the new world (Reardon 1996a). This form of intervention, however, with the possible exception of art therapy, has not been embraced by contemporary social workers.

A careful examination of urban murals, for example, will reveal a great deal about the artist and his/her community (Breitbart 1998). Murals and other forms of public art provide youths with mechanisms for exploring social problems and solutions, and concomitantly provide a means for them to share their stories with other youths and adults. Art, as a result, makes difficult circumstances more tolerable. Lakes (1996:96–97) brings another dimension to the arts, namely, connectedness with cultural identity:

The visual and performing arts . . . offer anti-elitist messages derived from the positionality of youths on the margins of society. Their creativity displays of ancestral origins, identity politics, and subcultural alliances describe both literal and figurative meanings of street life in urban America. A teenager's social imagination and utopian vision can be developed through individual artistic presentation. When provided apprenticeship settings with connections to professional artists, impoverished kids will learn that their cultural struggles can be shaped into aesthetic expressions.

It is unreasonable to expect youth to be attracted to all of these forms of expression. The arts, for example, may provide a viable alternative to sports as an activity to create a sense of connectedness for youth—group versus individual achievement as is customary in the United States (Ball and Heath 1993). The arts can also play a meaningful and active role in helping both individuals and communities, but alone cannot solve all of the problems associated with living in poor neighborhoods. However, they can play a meaningful role in helping to restore a people's spirit through promotion of cultural pride and community identity, an important initial step in helping communities address a multitude of problems (Reardon 1996).

The following comments made by an art director (East Los Angeles) concerning the potential of the arts for preparing youths of color for the twenty-first century eloquently raises their importance in helping to transform lives (Benavidez and Vozoff 1995:33):

> The point [she maintains] is to prepare young people for the challenges of the twenty-first century. "That's what this this program really offers: a vision of the future that includes these kids all grown up into creative, productive men and women." That's a tall order given the complex and competitive future that awaits them. The twenty-first century is not likely to pose easy challenges for anyone. And the inescapable disadvantages that plague poor minority kids make their chances for success that much slimmer. Still, it is worthwhile to remember that the future does not happen in large leaps and bounds. It happens one step at a time, one small decision after another until a life direction begins to emerge for a child as he or she becomes first an adolescent and later an adult. These . . . art programs certainly cannot turn life around for a whole community. They have, however, proved to be life-changing for the thousands of youngsters who have been a part of them. In a simple but very real way, that's quite an accomplishment.

Christenson and Roberts (1990) note that adolescence is a developmental period of "intense information-seeking and media use," with popular music being especially attractive to this age-group, although academics have largely ignored studying music media. Radio stations, and more specifically music stations, very often target adolescents and young adults. This group is not only highly attuned to music, but is also a big consumer of various products and merchandise related to music. The use of music as an activity holds much promise for engaging and teaching urban youths a variety of skills from production, composition, and actual performance.

It is impossible to discuss the use of music as an activity without also discussing the role and importance of "rap" in the lives of urban youths, particularly those of color (Valentine, Skelton, and Chambers 1998). "Rap is the most important music to emerge in America during the 1980s and 1990s. Yet rap is more than music or entertainment . . . The creation of young African Americans, rap reaches far beyond America's inner cities. Its booming bass and many voices resound on every continent. The sentiments expressed in many rap songs can't be dismissed as kid stuff. Politicians, clergy, journalists, and social scientists all ponder the utterances of rappers" (Jones 1994:17). "Rap music, like graffiti, can be conceptualized as a vehicle through which youth can both identify the sources of oppression and challenge them in the process" (Breitbart 1998).

Deyhle (1998) does a commendable job of summarizing the literature and highlighting the importance of music and dancing for marginalized youths, particularly those who are of color. I note that "competitive dancing" (break dancing) in New York City during the early 1970s served the purpose of providing an alternative to gang violence. Music, like dancing, must be contextualized and, in doing so, provides important clues to its form and existence among urban youths of color (Hager 1984). These two forms of expression had, and continue to have, great appeal for urban youth because of the liberating qualities they unleash; youths, as a result, can find their voices through these mediums.

The use of the arts in community development is well recognized in the field (Bowles 1995; Reardon 1996b; Rook 1998). The Ford Foundation's report on the role of the arts and community development corporations highlights how local circumstances dictate the use of the arts as a means of developing community. One corporation in Brooklyn developed youth-focused workshops for its theater, art gallery, and dance programs. In Kansas City, Missouri, another corporation actively developed partnerships to expand its jazz festival. In Chicago, an institute was created for local artists and arts organizations, in addition to broadening an arts training program for youth. In Phoenix, a Mexican-American community development corporation expanded its museum to accommodate more art exhibits and performing arts events, in addition to creating an arts education program for local schools. In Detroit, a corporation started a youth-training program to aid students to learn photojournalism, and provided space for their exhibits. Finally, in Newark, New Jersey, one corporation created a community cultural calender by training youths in the use of graphic arts, and produced a jazz series for a local public radio station (Reardon 1996b).

The arts can play an influential role in nurturing talent and free expression, as well as improve intercultural relations and foster youth enhancement through use of self-discipline that can easily be transferred to schoolwork (Reardon 1996a). The following series of quotes from various art directors across the United States highlight the multiple goals of using art as a form of intervention for urban youths and their communities:

Newport, Ore.: "Improving self-esteem and encouraging considerations of options—as to careers, health issues, choice of partners—are threads that run through most of the programs of the Family Arts Agenda" (Tilghman 1995:64);

Houston: "Transitions are achieved by the individuals who gain in self-confidence as they develop their artistic skills and who gain in pride and self-respect as they broaden their appreciation of their own and others' cultural heritage" (Goldman 1995:67);

Phoenix: "Artists also work directly with the children in workshops that don't necessarily focus on antidrug themes, but which do use the experience of making art as a vehicle for promoting cooperation, finding alternate solutions to conflicts, and increasing pride, self-esteem, and confidence (McBride 1995:18);

Los Angeles: "Art here is about what you are able to learn about yourself and your heritage. We do that through the art process" (Benavidez and Vozoff 1995:33);

Columbia, S.C.: "The arts can provide [disadvantaged] children with ways of achieving success, giving them a feeling of pride. The arts are one area in which background is not a large determinant of success" (Stucker 1995:46);

Denver: "Neighborhood Cultures of Denver is a unique collaboration that brings the arts to neighborhoods as a tool to celebrate strengths and diversity while finding solutions to community issues" (Aver 1995:50);

New Orleans: "Ya/Ya [Young Aspirations/Young Artists] is an experiment whose goal is to prove that if given the right tools and a fertile environment, motivated students can do extraordinary things" (Barker 1995:40);

Richmond: "I see the ability of a theatrical program to deliver a message of social concern, in a way that lectures and books and talks
are not able to do" (Neale 1995:75).

A number of museums across the country have created initiatives targeting youths as a means of attracting them to museums (Alexander 1998;
Graeber 1998). These initiatives have sought to make these institutions
more accessible and responsive to youths who would normally not visit
museums, and in doing so, have made a major effort to break down stereotypes. These efforts, in turn, have necessitated museums creating staff positions to specifically reach out to youths and create programming for them.
Some museums have established internships, work-study programs, and
summer employment to help staff these initiatives as well as provide youths
with on-the-job learning that could eventually lead to employment in
museums (Lurie 1991).

There are a number of museums based in cities that specifically target
low-income youths and communities of color. The Mexic-Arte Museum,
Austin, Texas, established in 1983, has a number of school- and non-
school-based programs that stress the importance of cultural pride and
knowledge of heritage. Its mission statement reads (Mexic-Arte Museum,
undated): "Mexic-Arte Museum's goal is to preserve culture and tradition
as well as to promote new and evolving contemporary art through high
quality multidisciplinary programming for primarily the Austin and
Central Texas area and beyond." Mexican-American artists, through the
Role Models in the Schools and Community Centers Program, visit
Austin public schools and give classroom presentations regarding their
work. The Family Days program sponsors activities on such topics as
papier mâché, allowing both youths and their parents to work together.
The museum also sponsors teacher-training workshops in local elementary schools.

There are other museums that have initiated special efforts at reaching
youths and communities that typically would not visit a museum (Goldberg 1999; Tucker 1999). Museums do not have to be stationary places
that very often are not geographically located within marginalized communities, requiring patrons to travel long distances. Museums can
undertake exhibitions in showplaces within communities, not only
increasing the likelihood of drawing new patrons, but also increasing the
likelihood that the exhibitions are relevant, in order to attract new
patrons.

CASE ILLUSTRATIONS

The arts, be they visual or performing, have increased potential to act as social vehicles, in a culturally-relevant way, to address a multitude of issues and needs at both an individual and community level. Further, they can do so in a manner that is nonstigmatizing and ethnically/racially affirming.

The following case illustrations show the richness of using art (visual and performing) as a form of intervention, and how it can address youth and social issues in a creative and affirming manner. The arts not only provide a viable alternative for youths in trouble with the law, but can also be an enriching experience for those who are not in trouble with various types of authorities.

Visual Arts

Painting   In Houston, a project actively combines the arts and social services (Glentzer 1996:64):

> Through the installations it commissions in the art houses [transitional housing for young single mothers], Project Row Houses connects regional and national artists with the Third Ward Community. An after-school art program enriches neighborhood children at the same time it provides a job for one of the young mothers in the residential program—which in turn employs a writer who is the woman's live-in mentor. The synergy flows full circle. Art and the social services, far from being an idealistic combination, turn out to be practical bedfellows.

Interventions utilizing young artists engaged in "unproductive" activities, such as painting graffiti in schools, have resulted in turning the lives of these individuals around through the provision of constructive alternatives (Pring 1997). Graffiti, like music, often serves as a mechanism for youths to express their anger with society, as well as provide them with a means of expressing artistic talent (Breitbart 1995, 1998; Hager 1984; White 1998; Boyle 1998c). Initially, graffiti was viewed by the community as an effort on the part of youths to express themselves, and these acts were viewed more as disrespectful and an irritant by communities. However, in some cities, graffiti went from being an irritant to being an indicator of a more serious situation—namely, a symbol of community decay.

Some organizations like New York City's Phun Phactory and Philadelphia's Mural Arts Program have specifically embraced a mission of providing constructive outlets for young graffiti artists (Boyle 1998c). Phun Phactory's mission is very simple (Boyle 1998a): "to give graffiti writers a place to paint, and maybe they won't scrawl so much on bridges, billboards and buildings." The program invites artists to paint the outside walls of the founder's Long Island City warehouse, along with other walls of participating businesses. After reviewing the proposed design (one of the requirements of participation is no gang-related art), the artist is allowed to paint a section of a wall, which can be expected to stay up for approximately three months. No "tagging" in the surrounding neighborhoods is another requirement for participation in the program.

Philadelphia's Mural Arts Program is another example of a community-wide effort at addressing graffiti. In this case, the effort was spearheaded by city government. The program was initiated in 1985 as part of the city's Anti-Graffiti Network, and combines art, teaching, and diversion toward "legitimate" art forms. Youths get involved in neighborhood clean-up projects, as well as paint murals (Boyle 1998a).

The painting of murals and other art media can have great appeal for youth, as evidenced by this case. The use of visual arts can achieve significant social goals in addition to beautifying the environment in the process. Art can also serve as a bridge for bringing together youths from different ethnic and racial backgrounds through exploration of common themes and issues in their lives. The showcasing of these artistic projects can be enhanced when placed within a prominent place in the community. The following case of Neighborhood Safe Art Spot provides an example involving a large number of Native American youths. The city of Minneapolis has a youth organization that is devoted to having youth paint murals and create other art-related projects throughout the neighborhoods (Delgado, in press).

Neighborhood Safe Art Spot was established by a mural artist named Marilyn Lindstrom who, as a result of attending a neighborhood crime watch sponsored by the Minneapolis Police Department, decided to accept the challenge of getting involved in the community. This community had the largest concentration of urban-based Native Americans in the United States. Native American youth rarely get the attention they deserve and very often get "subsumed" under "youth of color" categories without special attention being paid to their unique history and circumstances surrounding their lives in urban areas. Many of the projects initiated by Neighborhood Safe Art Spot have had a distinctive Native American perspective, and this is represented through the themes covered in the art work (Delgado, in press).

The arts, for example, can provide an important outlet for undervalued groups such as the homeless (Kenyon 1997:77): "There are a lot of talented people on the streets —a community of artists." One program, based in San Diego, provides art classes for homeless people and an opportunity for them to show their work to the public. A recent exhibition also had artists read original stores and poems (Kenyon 1997). Programs such as these serve to tap indigenous talent as well as undo stereotypes of homeless people. These individuals may be homeless, but it does not mean that they do not have stories to share and talents to use.

Video, Film, and Photography Documentaries   The use of video, film, and photography has tremendous potential for involving and reaching urban youths (Rook 1998). These media have enjoyed a prodigious amount of popularity in community-based organizations targeting youth. Visually capturing youths' experiences is not restricted to certain topics or issues. It can also serve to focus on subjects that may, on the surface, appear too sensitive. Documenting issues such as sexuality, class, and identity are not out of the realm of possibilities in video and films (Ford Foundation Report 1998). It is important to remember that in the case of video, most youths have grown up with this medium and can relate to it quite well.

The visualization of issues and challenges presented can serve as an important "product" that can be shown and shared with countless other individuals, as reflected in chapter 6. These "shows," in turn, are not restricted to other youths and can involve adults, leaders, and community stakeholders. However, the "process" used to gather input, write, and in some cases, act, is just as important for adolescents than the "finished" product at the end, although this should never be minimized. Society tends to stress the "bottom line," which often translates into some form of product, losing sight on the process that ultimately produced the product. The lessons learned in this journey must not be lost on youth.

Projects initiated and directed by youth themselves have a great potential for transforming the broader community. After all, "movie stars" do not live next door to an urban adolescent, nor do they shop in the same stores. However, an adolescent sharing her/his story on a screen or in a picture essay allows the neighborhood youngster to be able to "relate" to them, their experiences and circumstances. This ability to relate increases the significance of the central message for a community audience. Although these works can be shared with other communities across the city, state, and nation, they never fully achieve the same impact as when they are shown in the community upon which they are based. This, quite frankly, is to be expected and should not detract youth workers from showing these works within their respective communities.

Performing Arts

Choirs   Participation in choirs is not restricted to any one setting. Nevertheless, choirs are generally associated with houses of worship, particularly African-American churches in inner-city communities. Choir participation in churches is not without prestige and sacrifice (George 1992:33):

> Choir affiliation undeniably grants prestige—a bit of high-gloss glamour at the local level. . . . But for most community choirs, singing for fame (let alone money) is not the goal. If it is . . . the heart is in the wrong place and . . . choir life isn't glamorous as people might think. The robes get hot in summer; call rehearsals can be frequent; and Sunday's congregation can present a sea of confrontational faces. Participation in choirs is about belonging to a group of similar minded individuals who also share a desire to contribute to the well-being of the organization and community. In addition, it provides an outlet for youngsters who have a talent and interest in singing that goes beyond the usual interests related to a singing group.

The Boys Choir of Harlem is arguably one of the most well-known and respected groups in the United States. There are probably few choral organizations in this country that have enjoyed a greater reputation than the Harlem Boys Choir of New York City. This organization has not only toured throughout the country, but has also performed in numerous cities throughout the world. Since its founding in 1968 by Dr. Walter Yurnbull, it has grown from a relatively small community choir to a 500 member performing arts institution with a national and international following and reputation. The Harlem Boys Choir accepts youths ages 8 through 18. Its musical repertoire covers a tremendous range from classical music to jazz, gospel and spirituals, to contemporary songs.

The following description of the "typical" boy involved in the Boys Choir of Harlem highlights this point (Kennedy 1997:A24): "The Boys' Choir has long served as an inner-city lifeboat for its young members, about seventy-five percent of whom come from single-parent households headed by women, many with incomes below the poverty level." The Girls Choir of Harlem may not have achieved the same acclaim as their male counterparts. However, the goals and importance of the choir will be measured by "whether their choir can also be used to lift girls out of cycles of poverty" (Kennedy 1997:A24). The social impact of the Harlem Boys and Girls Choirs is generally unknown, yet it is quite significant, impacting on youth and their families.

Dance   Dance not only provides youths with an opportunity to express themselves, but also an opportunity through which to exercise and develop their bodies as well as their minds (Rook 1998). Attracting boys to dance may prove a challenge for many programs, but it is still possible to do so if one is creative. One program based in Cleveland managed to attract boys by calling a course called "Body Conditioning" (Rook 1998). After the course began, "dance" was a natural progression for the participants. Consequently, dance as an activity can have appeal to youths, regardless of gender, if this factor is taken into account in the planning of the activity.

Probably no form of dance is less associated with low-income youths of color than ballet. However, ballet has tremendous potential for reaching these youths. Ballet requires great discipline, mental and physical, and commitment from its dancers, as evidenced by the amount of time that must be devoted to practice and studying this dance form. Although ballet has not made significant inroads into low-income urban areas across the country, it still has the potential to reach youth.

The case of the St. Joseph Ballet Company of Santa Ana, California, illustrates the potential of this dance form for reaching urban youths of color. The company has maintained an active ballet program since 1983 that seeks to provide low-income youths ages 9 to 18 with a "sense of purpose and accomplishment" by teaching them to dance. An evaluation of the program conducted by researchers from the University of California, Irvine, concluded that high-school age, long-term participants in the program were less likely than their nonparticipant counterparts to use alcohol or drugs or to engage in sexual activities. In addition, they were more likely to use their free time more constructively. The results are increased for participants who stay in the program for more than one year.

Music   The study and performance of music requires a tremendous amount of discipline in order to achieve success (Archibold 1998). Music, however, must be viewed very broadly, encompassing a variety of forms, instruments, and vocals. Consequently, urban-based music programs must be sufficiently broad in conceptualization to incorporate various types of music to interest youths with a variety of abilities, desires, and financial resources—expensive instruments that also require constant calibrations, for example, may be beyond the economic means of many inner-city youths and the organizations they participate in.

One summer camp program, based in Boston, seeks to engage youths through their involvement in the production of music. Thirty-two youngsters from throughout the country are recruited and exposed to to the "nuts-and-bolts" of the music industry. The program utilizes rap music as a vehicle that can be used for positive, rather than negative, purposes (Ribadeneira 1998) by using adolescents' interest as a vehicle for teaching them life skills, morals, and conflict resolution. Further, the establishment of multimedia studios in the nation's most blighted neighborhoods also serves to generate jobs for residents and attract other businesses into the community. Thus, music becomes the vehicle for engaging and teaching urban youths skills that can be used in helping them pursue careers in the industry. When they leave the camp, participants are also given a compact disk of the songs they created.

Numerous types of services can be effectively integrated into programming involving new arenas if done in a creative and nonstigmatizing manner. The following is one example of how conventional types of social services can be delivered in innovative and highly effective ways within a school setting. In Miami, a local high school (Miami Senior High School) has effectively used a jazz band as a mechanism for reaching out to newcomers (documented and undocumented), and getting them to graduate from school and pursue higher education or careers in the music industry (Mears 1997).

Theater   Theater as a medium provides youths with an opportunity to combine a variety of activities and skills in bringing to life stories and experiences before an audience, an audience that can consist of internal and external community members. Theater, however, is not possible without the other arts playing important roles such as in set and costume design, music, writing, and directorship. Consequently, this medium provides a wealth of opportunity for youths who are not particularly interested in being on stage.

The development of a play written, directed, and acted by inner-city youths can help them find expression and validity through theater. Ball and Heath's (1993) description of a play created by young people is an excellent example of the potential of this medium.

The script focused on a theme not uncommon among youths who reside in inner-cities across the nation—namely, the death of a young male (11 years old) as a result of a random shooting. The play's settings shift as the story progresses, from the shooting in the projects, to the news reporting of the crime, and to the funeral of the child. Each scene, in turn, captures for the audiences the pain, confusion, anger, and depression for the family and friends of the dead child. Although the theme of the play is very sad, it is not outside of the experiences of the writers and actors.

The following case illustration, based in Chicago, has a primary focus on acting and activities related to this form of art. Further, it provides a very visual illustration of the empowering aspects of drama. The power of drama has usually been cast as "therapeutic" in nature. However, this form of expression can have sociopolitical benefits for youth as well. The empowering nature of drama, as a result, is very often an integral part of youth development in all of its many manifestations. Drama is just one form of this manifestation.

Chicago's Free Street Theater is a good example of how theater can play a transformational role in a participant's life and offers tremendous potential for youths not only to enhance their expressive abilities through acting, but writing, set design and construction, and leadership (Rook 1998). The acquisition of these skills, in turn, can lead to employment in theater. Nearly 200 teens have been a part of the jobs program during its first five years of existence. This program consists of an 8-week summer schedule, and has approximately 30 participants per year. The touring company, in turn, employs anywhere between 15 and 20 participants, and is a 7-month-long program.

Chicago's Free Street Theater's (FST) "TeenStreet" merges together both vocational and career development perspectives, as well as community education, entertainment, and youth skill enhancement. Its mission and history reflect a commitment to reaching youth through the use of cultural programming (Free Street 1998:1):

Free Street Theater was one of the first arts organizations in Chicago dedicated to community arts. Its mission is to provide cultural programming for and with disadvantaged populations in Chicago. Founded

in 1969 by Goodman director Patrick Henry, Free Street over the years
has linked quality programs in the performing arts with effective social
service, creating diverse programs to fit the changing needs of the community. In doing so, it has created shows and programs with the physically challenged, seniors, prisoners, hospitalized children, parenting and
pregnant teens, and inner-city youth and teens . . . . In 1991 when David
Schein became Artistic Director, Free Street Theater changed its name
to Free Street Programs, and targeted low-income and special populations of Chicago youth and teens with new programs designed to allow
children to step up from workshops in schools and parks into employment in teen theater companies.

Free Street can probably best be conceptualized as a program that utilizes the arts as a vehicle for increasing youths' skills, knowledge, self-confidence, and employment opportunities in the arts field; it does so by systematically providing arts opportunities across the lifespan of youth
(Schein 1997–1998:9):

> So when you think of Free Street, think of a pyramid of programs. At the
> base of the pyramid a child or teen in an Arts Literacy, Parenteen of Arts
> Connect program develops their basic communication skills and cre-
> ativity. In the second stage they step up into a summer jobs program
> receiving employment training and building children's shows for kids in
> the Chicago Parks Daycamp. Then, if they are talented and motivated,
> they can ascend to the summit of the Free Street experience and be cho-
> sen to join the year-round TeenStreet company, where they will tour
> Europe and perform at the best of Chicago Theaters.

The multifaceted role of Free Street facilitates reaching youth across the
lifespan and does so by integrating social and educational services, and
instilling job-readiness skills in the process (Lakes 1996:96):

> TeenStreet prepares youth in the performance arts with a heavy empha-
> sis upon the development of job skills such as self-discipline, self-esteem,
> punctuality, taking direction, focus, and team work, leading to career
> successes. Each applicant's creativity is tapped in the writing of twenty-
> minute ensemble pieces during the summer program, an authentic
> learning outcome that advances their literacy and communication levels
> as well.

Membership in TeenStreet is highly competitive with prospective members required to audition for a spot in the troupe. Youths create the plays and perform them throughout the city in parks and neighborhood events. Performances, in turn, are based upon the operative reality of urban life for youth (Lakes 1996:96):

> This performance company engaged in shows that resonate with the lived experiences—and raw emotions—of urban kids exposed to violence, drugs, unemployment, and poverty in their gang-infested residential and housing project communities throughout the city. . . .their dramatic productions underscore the pain as well as the pleasure—and a wide range of human emotions in between—of the harsh and inhospitable world they inhabit . . . , yet the shows succeed in turning agit-prop theatre into performance art by "marrying plaintive tales of life in the ghetto and an avant-garde formal structure."

Among many subjects, participants are required to take workshops on poetry and writing, in order to be exposed to writing for the purposes of self-expression (Bernardi-Reis 1996:13): "[The teens] are people who were writing as response for their lives. . . . Writing is an action of purging. A lot of people's writing was infected by their distrust of how to express themselves." Participants are exposed to writers and poets, and are provided with an opportunity to question them about the use of this medium as a means of reflection, communication, and use of words. This experience, in turn, serves as an important foundation for the creation of original dramas, books, and videos. Drama, incidentally, is based upon their life experiences and those of their loved ones. The realism associated with their production not only serves to inform their audiences, but also allows participants to find a productive outlet for their stories.

An interview with Teen Street's director (David Schein) reflects on the importance of integrating performing and job-related skills (Bernardi-Reis 1996:13):

> I wanted to start a jobs program—offer an economic incentive. Then we wouldn't be competing with the drug dealers and other things . . . We would be getting consistent work. . . . The program uses the arts to develop practical skills, such as those needed for interviews, resumes and other pre-job skills, such as writing and speaking extemporaneously. And they do all of this while creating amazing art."

Thus, theater represents an excellent vehicle for accomplishing multiple goals related to youth development, and does so in a way that is fun, intellectually challenging, and practical.

The arts do not necessarily have to be considered academic subjects that can only be taught in school-based curricula. These subjects can be used by almost any organization and community as an effective means of providing urban youths with an awareness of their ethnic/racial heritage, as a means of transforming their environments, and as a means of teaching them skills that can easily be translated into other arenas such as education and work. These arenas, in turn, do not have to be costly and result in the purchase of supplies and instruments, placing them well within the reach of community-based organizations. Further, getting artists and musicians to play the role of teachers provides communities with an opportunity to tap their own residents, enhancing the appeal of the arts and music by increasing the degree of relevance of the experience.

The appeal of the arts to youth goes far beyond the conventional satisfaction of mastering an instrument or activity, or the thrill of performing or exhibiting before a public gathering. It has the potential to transform lives and influence career paths in the process. Participation in these forms of activities not only keeps youngsters "off the street" and "out of trouble," but also serves to provide an artistic, or creative, outlet for youths. This outlet, in turn, may very well represent one of the few times youths have to enjoy the fruits of their labor in a way that is both affirming and a testament to their creative abilities.

The need for an outlet for creativity, however, is not restricted to youths. Youth workers and organizations must endeavor to find new ways of providing opportunities for youths to participate and use the arts as an effective vehicle for meeting their needs, but also tapping their potential. Adults, as a result, must be very attuned to what youths are interested and engaged by in order to create a program that maximizes this interest in pursuit of youth and community development.

The arts are very important to all human beings. However, they take on particular meaning in the lives of low-income urban youths of color. Lakes (1996:81) summarizes quite well this importance when stating:

> The visual and performing arts for inner-city youths are democratizing influences reaching outward to new communities of individuals engaged in the creative process and to new venues for attracting audiences inter-

ested in these forms of cultural expression. Kids react positively when they realize that their works are legitimized in public spaces as mural designs on street-corner buildings, as sculpture in transportation centers, or as theatrical performances in park district buildings.

Our tasks as social workers is to tap this arena in the development of youth initiatives!

CHAPTER 6

—

THE HUMANITIES

The term "humanity," according to Webster's Dictionary, can be defined as "The fact or quality of being human." The subject of the humanities, as a result, usually encompass languages and literature, and the branches of learning associated with human relations and thought. Some scholars would argue that the arts are part of the humanities. For the purposes of this book, however, I have separated out the arts (visual and performing) and focused this subject of the humanities as preparation of youth for citizenship and participation in public affairs.

The use of the humanities provides practitioners with a wonderful opportunity to reach out to urban youths in an effort to provide a foundation from which to have them examine their experiences and direct them in constructive manners in search of a brighter future. The use of literature, history, philosophy, to list but three subjects, can provide the necessary context to better understand an individual's place in society. However, just as importantly, they can help youths develop a better sense of who they are at a development time period when identity is an important factor.

THE POTENTIAL OF THE HUMANITIES

A grounding in the humanities not only serves to better inform youths about their role in society, but also helps them develop a greater appreciation and understanding of their place in history. Knowledge of history, for example, particularly when related to cultural heritage and the local community, serves to ground youths in their social, economic, and political circumstances. For many Latinos, for example, the extent of their cultural history covered in secondary schools is very limited and generally relates to three historical periods—"the discovery of the new world," the Mexican War of 1846–1848, and the Spanish-American War of 1898. Rarely is history used to inculcate in Latino youths the contributions their ancestors have made in the world, much less in our society. Consequently, the history these youths have been exposed to in school has generally served to undermine their self-esteem. Making history relevant to urban youths, as a result, serves to help them make important connections to their past, present, and future.

Shorris (1997:53), in describing the rationale for using the humanities to teach/reach urban based students, notes:

You've been cheated . . . Rich people learn the humanities; you didn't. The humanities are a foundation for getting along in the world, for thinking, for learning to reflect on the world instead of just reacting to whatever force is turned against you. I think humanities are one of the ways to become political, and I don't mean political in the sense of voting in an election but in the broad sense."

Shorris has inspired a number of institutions to establish courses targeting the "nontraditional student" such as the homeless (Bronner 1999). The University of Notre Dame and Bard College, for example, have established humanities courses targeting former and current homeless men and women. Community agencies such as the Roberto Clemente Family Guidance Center in New York City have also established such courses and achieved considerable success in channeling graduates into college.

Traditionally, the humanities have usually been referred to such topics as history and philosophy. The humanities, in essence, provide a context for learning that results in a better understanding of the world. In so doing, they serve to help learners learn more about themselves in the process, and better appreciate the context in which they find themselves—a necessary element of development in helping youths create a sense of self in an adult-dominated world.

Where "education" starts for youngsters is always a matter of debate. Some scholars would argue that learning starts the minute after one is born and that it takes place all of the time, and not just in a formalized and structured setting. If learning is contextual in nature, namely, it is just as likely to occur within a classroom as outside of the classroom, then the time spent outside of the classroom takes on greater meaning for youth. This is particularly true in circumstances where school is associated with poor self-image and lack of achievement. Consequently, a search for settings that are conducive for learning must be undertaken and, when found, supported and encouraged. When these settings are located within the community in which youths live, then they take on added meaning and significance. Libraries, houses of worship, community-based organizations, for example, can fulfill this key role in helping youths reclaim their past.

Achievement of cultural literacy, according to the President's Committee on the Arts and Humanities, is an important goal in any form of formal education (1996:19):

> Developing cultural literacy in children and youth gives them a sense of perspective in traditions of expression from which they learn and to which they can contribute. As humanist John William Ward writes: "Humanistic learning is centered on the individual who has important questions about self and society. To learn some of the answers to those questions means the fullest and richest and most imaginative development of every single self."

Unfortunately, most educational programs in elementary and secondary schools rarely address the histories of communities of color in the United States. When they do, the time period covered seems very arbitrary and not reflective of reality. For example, African-American history usually covers the period of 1619 to the present; another perspective on this time period is plantation to ghetto life (George 1992). The development of a historical account of African-Americans, Latinos, Native Americans, and Asians in the United States must be placed within a context that traces these groups back to their home countries, with the exception of Native Americans, since they were the original "Americans." Doing this, in turn, requires us to be better informed about their contributions and the circumstances that lead them to leave their native countries. "Multicultural" education represents an attempt to "undo" historical misinformation about people of color, their attributes, and the circumstances surrounding their arrival here. It is possible, for example, to teach African-American youths about their history, and also teach study skills, writing, comprehension, etc. In essence, when history is relevant, it can be a superb mechanism for teaching other academic subjects and skills (Coleman 1994).

Case Illustrations

The media, unfortunately, have had a disproportionate influence in shaping this country's images of people of color (George 1992). The humanities can play a significant role in helping youths of color reclaim what was rightfully theirs—namely, an understanding of their history in this world, and their influence on all sectors of society (PCAH 1996:19): "For some children, the exploration of their unique cultural histories can be critical to their sense of themselves and to others' images of them. This knowledge can help bind them more fully to the larger society of which they are a part." Failure to reclaim a history severely limits a group's ability to strike a claim for a future. Any mechanism that can facilitate the capture of this past will have profound impact on all sectors of a community, from its most senior members to its most junior in age. Ethnic pride can serve to unite all age groups.

Video   As already noted, the opportunities that videotaping offer youths has not fully been appreciated by practitioners. This method for engaging youths offers much promise for taking their stories to countless other youths and communities across the United States because of low cost, once produced, accessibility of communities to the equipment to show the video, and the ease in which this medium can be utilized (Educational Video Center 1994; Fishman 1998). The use of video can be approached from a strictly vocational perspective, namely, learning the trade as a means of obtaining future employment in this business.

However, video also offers another perspective that can be complementary of a vocational approach—the use of this medium as an empowering mechanism (Educational Development Center 1994:2):

> While empowerment approaches differ, they tend to share a view of video production as subjective expression, reflected in goals like "putting the camera into the hands of kids so they can tell their own stories" or "giving voice to young people." Much student work in this mode is powerful personal testimony: students celebrating an aspect of their lives or bearing witness to oppressive circumstances. But media-arts based, youth-empowerment approaches often lack concrete methods for helping students reflect on, revise, and deepen their thinking throughout the production process." Thus, there is a need to incorporate skills related to video, as well as the more reflective and critical thinking aspects of empowerment.

The case illustrations in this chapter highlight the role and potential of video for use with urban youth. The effective use of video is very much dependent upon carefully planning, script development, scene setting, and execution. Consequently, each of these aspects offers opportunities to teach and engage youths. This method for presentation, in turn, can also serve as an excellent organizing tool for communities. The power of video has generally been untapped in the arena of organizing undervalued communities. When the videos are developed by youths, this vehicle serves to reinforce the value of youths and their communities coming together in search positive planned change.

The use of poetry and videotaping, for example, as interventions raises another dimension to the arts and humanities (Curry 1997:88):

> For those of us on the outside, the life of an inner-city twelve-year-old is often hard to imagine . . . . Gabriel and nine of his peers spent last summer writing poems on the subject of police harassment and excessive force—as they see it—and then scripting their works for a collaborative cinema-verite-style video called "Around My Block." . . . As they learn skills ranging from basic grammar to video production to teamwork, they are gaining a sense of self-worth and mastery that many of them have not been able to find in a traditional classroom.

Another program called River of Words combines poetry and science as a means of exposing youths to their environment and providing them with a voice to express their feelings about this experience (Stover 1998).

The combination of using video with other media provides practitioners with an endless number of possibilities for using these new arenas with youths, involving communities, and showing the external community perspectives that are generally not provided by the media—namely, the possibility of youths projecting positive aspects of their lives and communities, in addition to telling their stories in their own words, without the benefit of an outsider filtering their messages. One of the major challenges facing urban-based communities that are low-income and primarily of color is the negative image that is often projected by print and visual media. Any opportunity that can be exercised to counter these deficit images will go a long way toward allowing these communities to share their stories and perspectives.

The use of videos to capture and tell stories is the primary medium of the Educational and Video Center (EVC) in New York City. EVC is a community-based media center that teaches youths and adults who work with youths how to create videos and do media analysis (EVC 1998:2):

> Since 1984, EVC has provided training and support services in documentary video production and media literacy to high school students and their teachers. Through the process of creating documentaries on youth and community issues, EVC students learn valuable research, reporting, editing and critical media viewing skills. The results are high quality educational materials produced by young people that speak directly to their peers . . . Their tapes are powerful expressions of the problems young people face every day at home, in school, and on the streets of their communities. They explore the causes and possible solutions for critical issues specific to their lives in the inner city, and common to many young people growing up throughout America. Through the production of video documentaries based in their communities, students gain a more profound understanding of their abilities to shape their own lives and positively impact the world around them.

EVC participants are students enrolled in the public school system, range in age from 15 to 20, and represent the diverse ethnic/racial, economic, and cultural backgrounds of the school system. A total of sixty youngsters each year participate in a semester-long internship during which they receive high school credit and learn such production skills as scriptwriting, interviewing, camera work, and film editing. At the end of their internship, students are required to present their work in public screenings and have their work reviewed in portfolio round tables. The portfolio assessment addresses four goals (Goodman and Tally 1993:31): "To provide students with the skills, knowledge, and confidence necessary to become independent thinkers and creative media artists. To document students' performance on multiple tasks over time. To integrate performance assessment with classroom instruction. To provide information on which to base on-going development of curriculum that is responsive to student needs." Each goal, in turn, is evaluated through use of products developed by the student and a journal (The Production Notebook) kept during the semester.

A total of six different portfolios are created by students for evaluation (Educational Development Center 1994b): (1) technical arts (camera work, lighting, and sound); (2) research; (3) writing; (4) editing; (5) critical viewing; and (6) public speaking. The qualities of final documentaries involve the following four dimensions: (1) technical proficiency (image, audio, editing, and special effects); (2) story structure (compelling storyline, visual storytelling, visual genres and conventions); (3) content (argument developed, depth, multiple angles, and critical perspective); (4) student voice (youth perspective, personal voice, and uniqueness). The final assessment takes into account the panel's, students' own assessments, and the instructor's; all three are then summarized and ranked as either nonproficient, proficient, or masterful.

In Somerville, Massachusetts, a project titled "Somerville's Mirror Project," uses video production as a means for youths to tell their stories to the outside world (Duehr 1998:L1): 'When young people see their everyday experiences on video, they begin to reflect on who they are . . . What could speak to them more than videos created in their own community?" The project has been in existence for six years (established in 1992) and has been responsible for creating more than 90 videos. The project is carried out through a local community access television station and is almost totally shoot on location in the community. The focus of the videos, quite simply, is to allow youth to examine their lives and tell the audience what they do, think, and how they define themselves. As noted by the project director (Fishman 1998:12 City): "It's being able to educate people outside of our community . . . It's representing points of view not seen in mainstream media in which inner-city kids are stereotypes. You're not looking at kids who are in a housing project, but at a girl who's singing a song or wants to be a doctor."

The Mirror Project videos have been shown in many different settings within and outside of the community, including museums such as the DeCordova, the Boston Museum of Fine Arts, New York's New Museum of Contemporary Art, and at the International Women in the Director's Chair Festival in Chicago (Duehr 1998). This external exposure serves to broaden youths' perspective on the world and allows the external world to develop a deeper understanding of life for an adolescent living in an urban area of the country.

Photography   Photography represents a different dimension from that of videos, and is no less powerful as a means of helping youths better understand their environment and their place within it, as well as a means of communicating with the outside world. Photography, according to an organization named "To Make the World a Better Place" (TMTW), based in New York City, when combined with words, becomes a very powerful medium for empowering urban youths (Lefkowitz 1998). They learn to express themselves, engage in critical thinking, increase their self-confidence, and engage in the larger would.

The process of integrating art into education and youth services is not as arduous as most practitioners would think. In fact, "enhancement and encouraging of thinking" takes on added meaning and significance if multiple activities are coordinated, with each activity drawing upon separate skills (Lefkowitz 1998). The final "product" consists of photography, accompanied by the student's own description of the photo and the reasons for taking the picture. The dialogue that ensues helps bridge the communication gap between youths and adults and serves to ground the student in his community.

TMTW also has a mentorship component that brings together professional photographers, painters, and other artists with adolescents. The program consists of a total of twelve sessions, three or more of which involve mentors. Mentors, in the spirit of mentorship, not only provide technical and artistic advice to participants, but also share advice about "life," and in so doing, increase the mentee's self-confidence.

An activity such as photography, like video production, can have value onto itself. However, it can also be a mechanism for bringing other services to work and help youth (Lefkowitz 1998:68): "For teenagers . . . this often means getting their GED, joining an entrepreneurship program, or enrolling in college. When you attend to what someone is saying, when you find out what is really important to them . . . it's much easier to help them. It's much easier for them to help themselves."

Writing   The use of writing and journalism can also be effective tools to help urban youth express their sentiments, experiences, fears, and hopes in a manner that can be shared with family, friends, and the outside world. Youth Communication is an organization based in New York City that has the teaching writing, journalism, and leadership skills. This youth organization produces two teen-written publications that provide an active outlet for writers. New Youth Connections is a general-interest youth magazine that addresses topics such as violence, drugs, sexuality, among other topics of particular interest to urban adolescents. The other publication is entitled Foster Care Youth United, and targets youth in foster care. Youth Communication also has published several books of writings.

The enhancement of writing skills does not have to be dry or boring, as is often thought. When the activity is directly tied to a youngster's life circumstances, and it becomes a liberating tool, then the learning process takes on added significance (Kay, Estepa, and Desetta 1998:279):

> Many of the students who walk through our doors have uneven skills, as a result of poor education, living under extremely stressful conditions, or coming from homes where English is a second language. Yet, to complete their stories, students must successfully perform a wide range of activities, including writing and rewriting, reading, discussion, reflection, research, interviewing, and typing. They must work as members of a team and they must accept a great deal of individual responsibility. They learn to verify facts and cope with rejection. They engage in explorations of truthfulness and fairness. They meet deadlines. They must develop the audacity to believe that they have something important to say and the humility to recognize that saying it well is not a process of instant gratification, but usually requires a long, hard struggle through many discussions and much rewriting.

The general availability of video that emerged in the 1990s, and its popularity among youths as evidenced with its use in the music industry, lends itself well to use in activities involving drama, music, poetry, dance, and the humanities The techniques involved in producing high quality videos lend themselves to teaching youths many academic and life skills that can easily be transferred over to their daily life. For those youths who have an affinity for and a capacity for this medium, it can also lead to future employment in this area. Photography, too, offers much promise for reaching urban youths and increasing their understanding of their place in today's world. The teaching of humanities, as a result, can be achieved through a variety of means and using the arts can be an effective way to do so (PCAH 1996:19): "Because dance, music, photography and other visual arts transcend language, they can bridge barriers among cultural, racial and ethnic groups. The arts also can provide a deeper understanding of similarities and differences among religious, races and cultural traditions."

The case illustrations used here provide wonderful examples of youths working together, and with adults, in search of creating common goals, and producing constructive activities to achieve these goals. Further, these case illustrations highlight the importance of collaborative approaches for involving other service-oriented organizations, key stakeholders, and communities. These efforts not only maximize available resources, but do so in a way that affirms the community's assets, an important dimension of community-focused endeavors. Collaboration is not only necessary, but an essential aspect of work in new arenas.

The study of humanities, in and by itself, may be insufficient to reach and actively engage urban youths who are struggling with a multitude of stressors. However, using a multimodality approach, including the production of videos and other "products," will serve to both facilitate the introduce humanities-related subjects, as well as teach youths skills related to product production. The process of learning "academic" subjects takes on added significance when they are grounded in the life of the youngster. Allowing for flexibility in carrying out this search for meaning and understanding also increases the likelihood of playing into a participants' strengths and likes. However, creativity in "packaging" these subjects will go a long way towards making them relevant, accessible, and practical for urban youths.

CHAPTER 7

——

SPORTS

The professional literature on the use of sports with youth is severely limited, particularly when compared with the literature on youth and families, schools, and peers (Reppucci 1987). The field of sports has long been recognized as having tremendous potential for involving youths and teaching them skills and principles that would serve them well in life. Youths involved in organized physical activities as represented through sports have been shown to do better academically, interpersonally, and healthwise than their counterparts who are not involved (Poinsett 1996). Participation in sports, however, does not have to be in an organized capacity; youths can enjoy many of the benefits associated with sports without engaging in systematic programming. Nevertheless, organized sports provide youths with the structure and support that can be very beneficial to them.

THE POTENTIAL OF SPORTS

Sports activities not only have the potential to reach youths and unite them at the community level, but can also serve to unite them across communities, and at a national level. The following examples illustrate this latter goal—one based out of Los Angeles and the other out of Atlanta.

The Inner-City Games of Los Angeles were established in 1991 by Daniel Hernandez as an effort to stem youth violence, drug, and gang involvement in Los Angeles and, more specifically, East Los Angeles. The Games also involve youth participation in academic projects such as writing essays and artwork competition. The founder saw the Games as a way for youths to combine sports and education (Hollenbeck Youth Center 1998). Initially, the Games attracted 40,000 youths from East Los Angeles.

However, the Games have since expanded to include over 100,000 youths from Southern California. In 1998, the Games spread to thirteen cities across the United States (Atlanta, Chicago, Houston, Philadelphia, Las Vegas, Oakland, Los Angeles, Miami, New York City, Orlando, San Antonio, San Diego, and San José). These games involve youths in competitions in an assortment of activities—basketball, boxing, fitness and body-building, softball, volleyball, flag football, soccer, baseball, track and field, dance and drill, tennis, fencing, gymnastics, and roller hockey among others.

Soccer in the Streets, Jonesboro, Georgia, is another organization that is nationwide and seeks to use sports, in this case soccer, as a vehicle for reaching urban youth.

The benefits of sports can also extend themselves to promoting intercultural contact and tolerance among youths, particularly in situations where contact is very limited or unstructured (Braddock, Dawkins, and Wilson 1995; Chantelat and Fodimbi 1994). Sports activity can serve as a communication vehicle for groups that do not necessarily share similar backgrounds. The participation in a common activity such as sports may be one of the few opportunities for groups of different backgrounds to come together. Thus, the use of organized sports can be an effective vehicle for promoting intergroup harmony through the emphasis on equal-status cooperation and communication (MacKenzie 1998a).

Organized sports, for the purposes of this book, can be conceptualized as falling into six major categories: (1) agency-sponsored programs; (2) national youth service organizations; (3) club sports; (4) recreation programs; (5) intramural programs; and (6) interscholastic programs (Seefeldt, Ewing, and Walk 1991). Youths, as a result, are not limited to participating in any one type of category, and can participate in multiple categories, although difficult to achieve because of practice demands and possible scheduling conflicts. These organized outlets allow youths to participate based upon their own goals, abilities, and time demands.

Although it has been estimated that 35 million children and adolescents ages 6 to 18 participate in youth sports programs each year, most sports programs rarely make special provisions for youth in low-income or high-risk environments (CCAD 1992). Economic and geographical barriers are widely cited for nonparticipation—program fees, equipment costs, and lack of transportation to site of programs. Further, it is estimated that most youths drop out of athletics and other physical activities by age 13 (Collingwood 1997).

Benefits of Sports

The role of sports in the life of communities speak to the potential benefits of this type of participatory activities. Sorin's (1990:84–88) account of the role of organized sports in a Jewish neighborhood in Brooklyn during the 1930s and 1940s illustrates the importance of youths having alternatives to choose from in determining how they use their free time, and a similar argument has been made over half a century later:

> Before their Brownsville neighborhood had well-organized athletic competition, it had been marked, they say, by fights between street gangs since at least as early as the 1920s . . . . The belief grew that sports helped some boys avoid "going bad." Boys had formed the Brownsville Boys Club in order to keep on playing ball, and in the process thought they saw in sports the power to control gang fights and juvenile delinquency.

Structuring of leisure time must also be considered a benefit of participation in organized sports.

Sports, according to the Carnegie Corporation, is an effective vehicle for helping youth meet the goals necessary for effective transition to adulthood (Poinsett 1996:4): "With sports acting as a powerful attractant, youth organizations must be helped to expand their reach in all communities, conveying information about life chances, careers, and places beyond the neighborhood and engaging young people in community and other constructive pursuits that foster education and health." Thus, participation in organized sports can be both a means to an end and an end itself. However, maximum participation is dependent upon available transportation, funding, safety, and proper leadership.

The introduction of sports early on in a youngster's life not only serves to help him/her develop physically, but also serves to help develop habits that can be carried out in adult life, in addition to providing a structured activity (Damon 1997:118): "Sports are a valuable resource that can teach children both physical skills and enduring character lessons. Regrettably, participatory sports has become a dwindling resource for young people. It also has become a misunderstood and unappreciated resource, because of highly publicized abuses." However, the use of organized sports for reaching and teaching youth is not without its critics. In fact, there is a trend in the United States to end recess periods in schools, and indirectly eliminate unorganized child's play in the process (Johnson 1998).

Prevailing thought on when to start organized sports has steadily stressed the importance of youths starting at an earlier and earlier age over the past two decades, with the age going down to 4, 5, and 6 years of age (Seefeldt, Ewing, and Walk 1991:9):

> The assumption underlying the trend toward decreasing age of eligibility for competition while concomitantly increasing the length of the sports season is that the fundamental elements of complex sports must be introduced and perfected prior to adolescence. Consequently, adolescents who have not developed the prerequisite motor skills are not likely to be selected to receive the kind of instruction that is needed for them to be competitive with their age peers. Thus, the prevailing opinion of coaches is that opportunities for successful experiences in athletics during the adolescent years are dependent upon a foundation that must be built from the experiences in childhood.

Consequently, the importance of starting at an early age takes on greater significance if organized sports programs wish to appeal to adolescents.

Exercise, as a result, be it accomplished through organized sports, or through activities undertaken during free time or after school, represents an important dimension to development (Egoscue 1998:8):

> Youth has a purpose. From a muscular-skeletal standpoint, the years between birth and the early 20's are important for building a solid foundation that insures muscles and joints will operate properly for the rest of life. This happens only one way: unstructured, spontaneous movement. As children, we are programmed by nature to be little whirling dervishes. Crawling, rolling over, walking, running, skipping, throwing and the like are all intended to form vital physical functions. Moreover, healthy development of the brain stem is directly linked to movement, starting in a mother's womb and continuing for at least the first 10 years of life . . . Children whose movements are limited because they're spending their time in front of computers or televisions, or being chauffeured to the next appointment are at risk of never achieving their full potential.

Damon (1997), in the challenge posed to communities in creating youth charters, places sports in a prominent position for achieving a society that fosters youth development. He outlines four guidelines for achieving this goal: (1) communities must make sports a priority for public funding and other forms of community support such as space, facilitates, volunteer coaches; (2) parents and coaches must place standards of conduct as a primary goal of youth sports, rather than winning; (3) youth should be provided an opportunity to participate in both individual and team sports; and (4) sports programs must seek to encourage participation regardless of athletic abilities—not everyone has to be a star.

Barriers to Participation

Although there are many institutions, researchers, and leaders who champion the importance of participation in organized sports, there are significant barriers to achieving maximum participation by all youths, and particularly youths of color in urban areas. Starting at a very early age increases the importance of having coaches who are well qualified for the challenges involved in engaging very young children. Consequently, for organized sports to achieve their maximum impact, they must be lead by well-qualified coaches and other personnel. Premature dropout of organized sports activities can be quite high with estimates ranging as high as 75 percent (Poinsett 1996).

In addition, poor coaching can result in high rates of physical injuries that can discourage youths from pursuing organized sports activities (Hingson and Howland 1993; Sallis 1993). In essence, lack of qualified leadership is considered the most significant factor in premature termination. Sports, as a result, is much more than an activity that can be used to "occupy" a youngster's time—sports can achieve this goal. However, it can also achieve much more ambitious goals related to character development and acquisition of skills if the leadership is properly trained and supervised. Otherwise, sports participation can become another entry in a long list of failed efforts for youth.

The emergence of soccer, and the continued popularity of basketball, softball, lacrosse, football, and track and field, provide ample avenues for reaching out to youths during their nonschool hours; a period of time that offers great potential for "good" and "bad," depending upon which fork in the road youths take, the former if available and the latter if not available. Although some of these sports do not require extensive use of land, a rare commodity in urban areas, the popularity of soccer has necessitated that some youth-focused agencies develop playing fields to accommodate the number of youth interested in this sport (Ribadeneira 1998). The increased popularity of softball among girls, for example, has resulted in an increased demand for time on playing fields; time, which incidentally, has resulted in tensions with boys for the same fields, necessitating development of methods for allocating equitable playing time for both sexes (New York Times 1998a).

Many sports do not require highly specialized equipment such as necessary in football, or large and well-maintained playing fields. Organized sports, however, do need dedicated coaches who are willing to not only provide guidance for youths, but can also serve as mentors and role models for them. Proper coaching, as a result, takes on greater importance than having the latest equipment. The role of the coach goes far beyond that of being the prime team motivator or leader. The lessons coaches impart can well last a lifetime.

Historically, boys had much more opportunity to engage in organized sports. However, with the advent of recent legislation, girls, too, have an opportunity to benefit from organized sports activities (Conniff 1998). Passage of Title IX of the Education Amendments Act passed in 1972 provided an impetus for sports activities to be opened up to women. Increased opportunity has manifested itself in many schools and communities having almost as many sports opportunities for females as they offer males. These increased opportunities, as already noted, have created tensions in many school systems by requiring authorities to use funds normally allocated for boys to be used for girls.

Cutbacks in after-school sports activities, combined with a shortage of land for team sports such as soccer and cricket, have had disastrous consequences for youths (Johnson 1999a; Martin 1998). Sports in New York City public schools historically enjoyed a tremendous amount of support. However, in the last twenty-five years, they have been devalued, and not budget-supported (Johnson 1999a, b; Johnson and Curry 1999; Williams 1999). These consequences must be looked at from both a short- and long-term perspectives (Taylor 1990:342):

In the 1990s, America, and in particular, industrial centers began to see the results of cutting programs for sports and recreation. Such reductions, although often seen as financially necessary, have left a void that handicaps many communities and neighborhoods in their attempt to provide experiences to their youth that provide positive developments.

The need for playing space in highly populated areas of a city severely limits the number and types of sports that can be played. Limited space, in turn, is further compounded by an increased number of adults involved in organized teams sports (Martin 1998). The need for local governments to balance their budgets through cutbacks of youth-focused activities and the converting of public land for housing or commercial development may be politically feasible, but it results in increases on other budget items, most notably juvenile arrests, treatment, special school-related programs, etc. In essence, in the short term it may be politically expedient to cut sports but in the long term it will have severe consequences for communities.

Origin of Organized Sports

The origin of organized sports in the United States has been traced back to the nineteenth century, and the work accomplished by the pioneers of the social work profession and their work with boys' work groups (Berryman 1978; Reppucci 1987). Those initial efforts at using organized groups sought to use sports as a means of engaging boys in order to prevent the onset of risk-taking behaviors. It was not until the early twentieth century that voluntary organizations adopted sports as activities for engaging and serving youths, particularly boys. In 1939 Little League was established and further expanded the use of organized sports. Interestingly, schools throughout this period reluctantly embraced sports as part of their mission; this reluctance was due in large part to the concerns of educators about the impact of highly competitive sports on youth development (Berryman 1978).

Numerous authors have argued that sports can play a significant role in helping youth develop important social and psychological capacities (Damon 1997:119):

> When children and coaches conduct sports in the right way, children learn discipline, persistence, and cooperation. They also learn good sportsmanship: that is, fair play, how to win and how to lose gracefully, how to manage competition, how to take initiate while staying within a common set of rules, and how to balance the desire to win with the need to maintain good working relationships with opponents who also want to win. These lessons in good sportsmanship have enduring significance for a child's later relationships and engagements.

Damon (1997) identified the importance of sports in the development of community and listed five principles that should guide organized sports: (1) youth sports must be prioritized and receive requisite funding; (2) standards of conduct must be the primary goal of youth sports and not winning; (3) individual as well as team sports must be provided; (4) sports must accommodate the needs of ordinary as well as talented youth; and (5) sports programs must be an integral component of a coordinated community campaign to reach youth. Sports, as a result, have a potential to reach beyond the immediate participants.

In urban areas of the United States, the general absence of accessible parks increases the importance playgrounds for youth. The playground is to the inner city what a tennis court or a golf course is to an upper-middle-class community. The playground is not only the setting for a sports activity for youth, it is also the center for social relations. A playground, however, encompasses much more than just a geographical area that bears the "official" label. A playground in many urban areas can also refer to the sidewalk or street. I myself have spent many happy hours playing handball and stick ball in such settings.

Telander's (1995) vivid description of life in a New York City basketball court (Flatbush, Brooklyn), illustrates how these settings represent the microcosm of life in a low-income community of color. The hopes, dreams, and despair of youths in their search for recreation, companionship, and a better life through basketball, all play out in these types of settings. The role and importance of sports in urban areas differs considerably from that found in the suburbs and rural areas of the United States. Although inner-city basketball courts are frequently places where there is a high crime rate, they are still accessible to community youths, and provide them with an opportunity to interact without close supervision by authority figures of various kinds. Very often, there are no other settings that are a viable alternatives, unsafe as they may be.

Professional Sports and Youths of Color—African-American Men as a Case in Point

The importance attached to sports for youths of color may sometimes overshadow the life-long benefits that can be derived from this focus. Early (1998), in his article on sports in The Nation, summarized both the rewards and consequences of participation in sports at the college and professional level, particularly for African-American athletes. Tremendous riches and recognition accompany athletes who are successful at major colleges and universities across the country. Those who eventually make it to a professional level will be rewarded with lucrative contracts and endorsements.

The case of African-American men does an excellent job of illustrating the tremendous odds these youngsters face in seeking the fame and fortune associated with professional sports (Harris 1996–1997; Sailes 1996–1997a). The statistics of youth making it all the way to professional level sports such as football and basketball are very dismal (Sailes 1996–1997b:17):

> According to the NCAA, there are approximately one million high school football players and 500,000 high school basketball players in the United States . . . Of that number, about 150 make it to the National football League (NFL) and approximately 50 will sign a contract with the National Basketball Association (NBA) team. The odds of a high school football player making it to the NFL are about 6,000 to 1. The odds of a high school player making it to the NBA are approximately 10,000 to 1.

These odds, however, are rarely discussed in the public media. There are coaches who argue that playing an elite level of game may not get an athlete a professional sports contract, but can still get him a college education through an athletic scholarship. Unfortunately, this is not necessarily the case with African-American men (Sailes 1996–1997a: 7):

> If the African-American male is successful in sports, particularly if he becomes a sports star, the rewards are social prestige, recognition, and status. College scholarship offers usually find the most talented (gifted) African-American athletes. Unfortunately, over 75% of black athletes playing NCAA Division 1 basketball and football never graduate, and fewer than 1% ever sign a professional sports contract.

Unfortunately, African-American youths, and other youths of color for that matter, are confronted with very persuasive images of African-American professional athletes (80% of the NBA, 60% of the NFL, and 25% of major league baseball) are of this racial group. Thus, images of African-American athletes on television and in the print media are quite prevalent, lending credence to the possibility of actually making it to the professional level. For example, it has been estimated that over the past twenty-five years, African-Americans have won 41 percent of the Most Valuable Player awards in baseball (Early 1998).

However, the odds of making it to the professional level for youths of color are even more daunting than the ones presented for all youth. The odds of a 20-to-39-year-old African-American playing professional football in the NFL are 1:47,600; an 18-to-39-year-old playing major league baseball is 1:333,000, and a 20-to-39-year-old playing in the NBA is 1:153,800 (Melnick and Sabo 1994). For Latino males the odds are even greater in the same age cohorts: 1:2,500,000 in the NFL, 1:500,000 in major league baseball, and 1:33,300,000 in the NBA (Melnick and Sabo 1994). For a numerical standpoint, in 1994 there were only 1,200 African-American and 150 Latino males playing professional sports.

If an athlete is fortunate enough to beat the odds and make it to the professional level, he can easily have his career cut short by accidents. Injuries resulting from professional sports are not unusual in an athlete's life. However, when the athlete is of color, his injuries may severely limit employment possibilities post-competition. Coaching opportunities, for example, are not as plentiful for athletes of color when compared to their white counterparts. Life after professional sports often shows former athletes losing their social status and economic gains, not to mention facing severe limitations related to injuries sustained during their playing days.

Of those African-American athletes who cannot make it as professionals, many may wish to turn their attention to coaching. However, just like the odds associated with professional athletes, chances are not good that they, too, would be coaching. Between 1991 to 1993 there were almost 1,100 new coaches hired at American colleges, only 143, or 12.9 percent, were African American. Their fate was even worse at the assistant coach level during that time period as well with 9 percent (Brooks, Althouse, and Tucker 1996). The statistics among professional coaches is just as startling. In 1991–92, African Americans represented 7 (2 out of 27) percent of the NBA head coaches, 7 percent (3 out of 28) of the NFL head coaches, 14 percent of the NBA front office personnel, 8 percent of the NFL front office personnel, and in 1992, they were 9 percent of major league baseball management and support staff, with Latinos accounting for 7 percent (Melnick and Sabo 1994).

The Carnegie Corporation has identified the need for an active, and well-funded research agenda to both identify and synthesize what is already known about participation in organized sports, and systematically map out the benefits of sports for youths, their families, and communities (Poinsett 1996). Nevertheless, a number of studies have highlighted the importance of organized sports on the physical, emotional, and cognitive development of youths. Seidel and Reppucci's (1993) study of nine-year-olds before and after participation in organized youth sports found that participants were more likely to achieve an increased self-perception of self-worth, athletic and scholastic competence, and attention to physical appearance, before and after a season of participation.

Sports and Special Populations

Sports have the potential to reach special populations such as youths who are homeless. Homeless children face innumerable challenges at a time in their lives when they should not be worried about basic human needs like shelter. These children, in turn, have very few positive outlets that allow them to have fun and grow physical, socially, and cognitively. Their lives are often unpredictable, with multiple experiences with trauma.

Children who are homeless, usually in some form of shelter or temporary housing, are no different from their counterparts who enjoy a home; sports, however, are very much a part of growing up in the United States, whether they are organized or informal in nature. However, when organized sports target homeless children, they must take into account numerous factors that are usually taken for granted when addressing children with permanent homes. These factors, in turn, increase the challenge of providing a "normalizing" experience for homeless youths. There are many lessons learned from using sports to engage homeless children. First, homeless children enjoy sports just as much as children who not homeless. They possess a tremendous amount of energy and benefit from finding constructive ways to direct it. Team participation provides them with an opportunity to be a part of a group with peers who may not be gang related. Parents, in turn, welcome having their children engaged in a safe and nurturing environment, not having to fear for their safety is a great relief.

The case of the Mecklenburg County Park and Recreation Department in Charlotte, North Carolina, is unique because of its focus on engaging the children of homeless families in sports activities. These children, most of whom were newcomers to the community, have suffered many of the problems associated with dislocation and relocation—uprooting, hunger, witness to violence, and the other dimensions associated with poverty. The goals of the homeless youth program were fourfold: (1) reduce the social isolation of youth; (2) promote self-esteem; (3) relieve daily stress associated with homelessness; and (4) provide an avenue for fun at a time when having fun is a challenge for program participants. These goals, as a result, not only seek to provide healthy alternatives to youths, but also seek to actively engage them during a period in their lives when they should be having fun being kids.

Although the project is primarily a one-person operation, it has successfully engaged a number of volunteers and service and professional sports organizations (National Conference on Christians and Jews, the Charlotte Hornets basketball team, the Community School for the Arts, the Carolina Vipers soccer team, and the Charlotte Checkers hockey team). Consequently, its success is directly related to the involvement of countless other individuals and organizations, public and private.

CASE ILLUSTRATIONS

Although sports related to urban areas are usually thought of as being based on streets and playgrounds, otherwise known as "land-based," it will be noted later in this section that water-related sports, too, have potential for reaching urban youth. A number of relatively new sports have found their way into urban communities. Although basketball is usually associated with urban sports, other sports activities also have potential for reaching youth. Sports such as boxing (Kawakami 1996; MacGregor 1998; Schultz 1998; Smith 1998; *Los Angeles Times* 1998; Tobar 1996) and martial arts (Boyer 1996; Cimons 1995; Eckolm 1998; Willingham 1993), for example, have found great appeal to youth. These sports can be played at virtually any age-level and allow for systematic progression from one level to the next based on weight and achievement. One sport that has particular appeal to younger-age groups, and is not usually thought of as having appeal to urban youths, is the soapbox derby. One program in Southern California sponsored by the police department uses soapbox cars as a means of reaching out to urban youths (Leeds 1997).

Basketball   Probably no organized sports activity is more associated with urban youth than basketball (Waldman 1998), and no program more well-known than midnight basketball (Curry 1990; Farrell et al. 1996; Freking 1992; Tennille 1994; *New York Times* 1989; Walker 1991a, b; Will 1990). There are few urban communities in this nation that do not have basketball hoops. In fact, communities where there are "official" basketball courts, there are "unofficial" courts constructed by youths with baskets made of a variety of materials.

The success of "Midnight Basketball" epitomizes the importance of sports for youth and communities (Trust for the Public Land 1994:6): "Newark, New jersey, is also beginning to see results from an aggressively expanded recreational program. The abandoned JFK recreation center has been a magnet for vandalism and other crimes until the city invested $1.2 million in renovation. Now the center is used by 5,000 young people every month, and crime in the area has decreased. Hundreds of inner-city children are learning to ice skate, and midnight basketball is available in the summer, when criminal activity usually escalates.

The success of night basketball has resulted in the development of leagues for women, as the case in Cleveland (*New York Times* 1998b). The league is sponsored by the Cleveland Rockers of the Women's National Basketball Association and Nike. The league consists of six teams, each with ten players. There is a 55-person waiting list. Like their male counterparts, women players are required to attend job-related workshops and are expected to adhere to strict out-of-play conduct in order to be eligible to play. The Kansas City, Missouri, program reported on earlier, not only experienced a decrease in crime rates but also served to identify potential players who could be trained as referees for league games within and outside of the program. These players received the requisite training to become basketball referees (Wilkins 1996).

Although the requirements for participation in midnight basketball vary according to site by taking into account location circumstances, they usually entail any one or all of the following: (1) attendance in drug education workshops and vocational counseling; (2) attendance at practice—a missed practice results in a player not being eligible to play in the following game; (3) no gang "colors" allowed on the court; and (4) sportsmanlike behavior on the court and during practice (no drugs or fighting allowed). In essence, attendance in educational and entrepreneurial workshops and lectures brings an important dimension to this sports activity (Witt and Crompton 1996b).

As an arena, the basketball court also facilitates the delivery of a wide range of social and educational services (Farrell et al. 1996:92):

> There is a contemporary trend in U.S. cities in which a recreational activity, "mid-night basketball," is captivating inner-city youth . . . . the purpose of the program, as envisioned by its founder, was not simply to teach youths how to play basketball. Rather, by scheduling the games between 12 A.M. and 3 A.M., when many gang- and drug-related crimes occur, a major goal was to reduce the incidence of lethal violence in inner-city communities. The program included activities designed to foster responsibility in all walks of adult life. For example, the program

encouraged those males who had fathered children outside of marriage to assume responsibility for their offspring.

Basketball, in essence, is not an end in itself, as eloquently stated by one basketball league commissioner (Curry 1990:D28): "Basketball is just the hook . . . Through basketball we can expose them to everything else, like getting a job, getting a diploma or helping them get milk for their baby."

One mid-night basketball program in Kansas City, Missouri, witnessed a 25 percent decrease in violent crimes and property-related offenses in the major areas in which the program operated (Wilkins 1996). (See chapter 8 for a case study on this organization). Ferrell et al. 1996, in probably the most thorough evaluation of a midnight basketball program, found that this form of sports activity can be very effective in reducing crime. The authors estimated that the creation of a midnight basketball league served to reduced crime by 30 percent, in addition to creating positive friendships, trust, and respect among their coaches and teammates, and improving the educational and career aspirations of program participants. In one Maryland community (Glenarden), a basketball program was established during the 10 P.M. to 2 A.M. period because most drug-related crimes occurred during that those hours (*New York Times* 1989). A similar time period was used in Chicago (Curry 1990).

Boxing   The subject of boxing is not without controversy in the sports world. Boxing has a long and, some would argue, tarnished image in our society. Its violent nature, and the notoriety, have shaped the public's image of this sport. Sayings such as "The more you sweat, the less you bleed" and "No pain, no gain" do little to quell the concerns of parents. However, there is little debate that boxing has been viewed as as vehicle for youths of color to "escape" their surroundings (Jacobs 1999:E-1): "At a time when boxing is dismissed as damaging and destructive, many boxers come to the gym specifically to avoid the dangers of the street. At a time when youth sports are exploding and children routinely shuttled from one playing field to another, boxers . . . train in isolation and far from the public and parental eye."

Boxing as a youth sports activity is not for every boy and girl. However, like other sports activities, it requires participants to make a commitment, attend training sessions, follow discipline—no drugs and smoking, and in boxing teams, builds teamwork and self-confidence. The coach/trainer, too, is as influential as in other sports. The coach/trainer plays the role of

mentor, counselor, cheerleader, and friend. Consequently, boxing's potential for reaching youths is considerable, youths who, incidentally, may not
"fit" into other sports activities but who could benefit from participation
in a structured program. Most boxers will never get to the professional
ranks or be world champions. However, with the proper guidance, the benefits to be derived from boxing can be life-changing in a positive manner.

Running   Track and field and cross-country running have enjoyed
tremendous success in urban areas of the country. The sport of running,
however, can also enjoy a rich cultural tradition, as is the case with Native
Americans (Brooke 1998:20): "Running has its roots in the spiritual tradition . . . Running increases pride, self-esteem, cultural identity. It brings
people together in a healthy life style."

An organization based in New Mexico (Wings) draws upon a rich
Navajo tradition of running and seeks to provide positive alternatives to
Navajo youth, as noted by the response of one Navajo running (Brooks
1998: 20): "You can go with alcohol and sex—or you can go with running
. . . If you are serious about high school athletics, you are less likely to go
out drinking every weekend, you are less likely to get pregnant and more
likely to go to college."

Squash   Squash, like its tennis and golf counterparts, is a sports activity
that has historically been associated with the privileged classes. However,
SquashBusters, a youth-development program based in Boston, and billing
itself as the "country's first squash, academic and community service team
for urban public-school kids," seeks to open up this arena for urban youth.
The program covers a three-year regimen that uses squash instruction and
competition as a mechanism for not only teaching a sport but also teaching academics and involvement in community service. SquashBusters seeks
to accomplish four major goals: (1) instill in participants the importance of
hard work, discipline, concentration, and promote the values of respect,
humility, and honesty; (2) enhance self-esteem and social awareness; (3)
using natural interest in sports to further involve youth in education; and
(4) break down barriers of race and socioeconomic class through provision
of equal opportunity for participation and fair competition.

Tennis   Tennis as a sports activity is usually not associated with urban
youths, particularly those residing in economically-depressed communities.
This type of sport is usually synonymous with court fees, lessons, and all-
white apparel—in essence, not a sport that the typical youths of color would

aspire to play. However, the success of Arthur Ashe played a pivotal role in opening upon the world of tennis to youths of color across the United States. The success of Tiger Woods, in another sport usually associated with privilege, may also be a catalyst in the world of golf. Only time will tell. Arthur Ashe's racial background and his diligent promotion of tennis for youths of all backgrounds served as an inspiration for countless numbers of youths who would normally not think of themselves as tennis players.

Tennis clubs do not have to be associated with wealth and suburban living; they can also serve as vehicles for reaching out to urban communities. In a working-class community of Boston (Dorchester), a tennis club that serves urban youth just recently celebrated its twenty-fifth anniversary in its current location, although its history dates back to 1961. The Sportsmen's Tennis Club (is open to both boys and girls) was the first such facility in the country with the purpose of reaching "disadvantaged youth." Tennis is used as a mechanism to engage youths, but also prepare them for the challenges they will face inside and outside of tennis (Coleman 1998b: 14City): "The club has helped 400 young people attain local, regional and national tennis association rankings. Also, more than 500 youths have attended college on full or partial tennis scholarships."

The success of such African-American athletes as Arthur Ashe and Tiger Woods has opened up sports activities that have historically not been considered by urban youths. These activities, like those of more popular sports, represent important opportunities for intervention (Heller 1996; Smith 1997). Recreational activities, in essence, are much more than fun and sports! These activities open doors that normally would not be open for urban youths to achieve their potential and make important contributions to their communities and society.

Golf   Golf has historically enjoyed a privileged position among all sports in the United States. It is a game that requires a tremendous amount of land in order for it to be played. Maintenance related to keeping the grounds playable also makes golf expensive, even if a player can borrow the necessary equipment. However, the popularity of the sport among youths of color has at best been limited. They have had very few professional golfers of color to follow. The emergence of Tiger Woods, as already noted, may be a stimulus for greater interest on the part of youths of color.

The potential benefits of the sports covered in this chapter are applicable to the game of golf. Boston's Caddie Scholar Program recruits sixty-five city youths, ages 14 to 17, and pays them ($5.25 per hour) to undertake maintenance, study math and English, and learn to play golf. Participants spend one hour a day receiving tutoring in academic subjects using the measurements and the language of golf, one hour caddying and playing the game, and three hours cleaning up golf courses throughout the city. Participants are encouraged to enroll in the program for three summers. The nature of this program—play, learn, and earn—makes it very attractive to youths, and highlights the potential of integrating learning and playing, even though it involves a sport that has historically not enjoyed popularity in urban communities (Kahn 1998).

Water-Related Sports

It is not unusual not to to think about water-related sports when discussing sports activities and urban-based youth. Invariably, discussions usually focus on street-related activities. However, water-related sports can achieve many, if not all, of the goals that land-related activities address (Humke 1996). Although there is no denying that cities located on the east and west coasts have a distinct advantage in using water as a setting for sports activities, most cities, even those inland, have access to some large body of water. Thus, water-related sports should not be thought as limited to the coasts of the United States. Two water activities, sailing and scuba diving, have been given extra attention here because of the potential they have for developing teamwork and maximizing the mentor-mentee relationship.

Fishing   Fishing, for example, can be a sports activity that is not a "contact" sport, and thus is accessible to youths of all kinds of physical abilities. Yet, for fishing to have meaning for urban youth, much instruction must be given concerning ecology, types of fish, patience, development of an understanding of the nutrition that fish provide, and the importance of proper equipment, which does not have to be expensive (Radin 1998a).

Sailing   The experiences learned in sailing and ship-related activities are not limited for use only in these activities. A program based in Boston (Hull Lifelong Museum), for example, provides summer employment for fifteen teenage boys ages 14 to 18. This program has a contract with the Massachusetts Department of Youth Services to provide participants with job-readiness skills, and in so doing, has exposed them to history lessons and what it means to be associated with the sea (MacKenzie 1998a). Further, a number of youth-oriented organizations have developed sailing programs targeting inner-city youth. A program titled Courageous Sailing Center based in a neighborhood of Boston (Charlestown) actively targets youth. The Center is funded through a public charity established by Harry McDonough, a three-time America's Cup winner and named after his sailboat, Courageous. The goals for teaching sailing go far beyond the mastering of the actual activity, as noted by one of the instructors (Fishman 1998:16): "It's not only to teach kids sailing, but to teach them other skills such as communication, responsibility, self-assurance . . . They can learn all of that here."

The program consists of a five-step process. The first two steps involve a half-day week-long beginner program that exposes youths to sailing; most of the instruction takes place on boats and every effort is made to get them out to sea as quickly as possible. There is an intermediate session for the more advanced sailers, and it covers an entire summer. For those wishing even more advanced training there is a junior- and senior-instructor program (MacKenzie 1998). Many of the instructors are themselves graduates of the program and are only a few years older than the participants and thus can serve as both mentors and teachers.

Scuba Diving   A six-week summer program based at the Boston-Roxbury YMCA focuses on preparing city youths to get their diver certification (Coleman 1998a). The program recruits twenty-two boys and girls (ages 12 to 17) from local social service agencies and the Big Brother program. Special effort is made to recruit youths who have no "positive" male role models in their lives. The program's goal is ambitious, yet simple (Coleman 1998a:11): "By exposing young people to a sport that demands accountability and self-confidence . . . [it] is trying to offer skills and build relationships that can help keep them on the right path of life." When asked what the key quality the program wishes to enhance, the project director noted persistence: "I think they get out of it [what works] for people who make it in life, the key quality you have to have is being persistent . . . Persistent people will always prevail. They have this fire."

The mentor relationship is considered the most important aspect of the program and is the result of the director's experience with mentors growing up: (Coleman 1998a:11): "When you dive, you develop a very unusual intimacy with that person. We hope the relationship with the mentor will transcend the water. I had very good mentors all of my life. I was monitored by people from primary school to graduate school. They did have an effect on me. Those people just showed up at the right time."

Teamwork results from the training by having youths take classes together, practice shared breathing underwater, and practice together.

There is much academic learning that takes place during the lessons—participants need to know chemistry, math, and physiology (the impact of water pressure on the human body). An effort is also made to teach youths underwater photography as a means of increasing their interest in science.

The examples of sports activities presented here have, with the exception of basketball, avoided the usual types associated with urban youth. It was the goal of this chapter to expand the imagination of practitioners in thinking about sports and urban youth. The more options youths have in selecting sports activities, the higher the likelihood that they can find a "place" where they feel comfortable and challenged. It would certainly be sad for youths to be given just one or two selections for participation—basketball or football, just as it would be sad for adults. The same principle can be applied to music, arts, and humanities-related activities.

The topic of sports in the United States has taken on added significance due to the publicity that professional and collegiate teams receive in the media, the astronomical salaries that players receive, and the importance of franchises to a city's national reputation. The other side of sports, particularly for youngsters, is often lost in the the debate about the importance of sports in this society. Sports, nevertheless, can play an influential role in the physical, emotional, and character development of youth in urban areas. However, it would be unrealistic for most youths to think that the pursuit of sports will result in at least a college education, if not a professional contract (Harris 1996–1997).

After-school sports, however, is not a panacea for all of the struggles involved with living in urban economic distressed areas. A recent incident in Brooklyn resulted in one youth being killed after a basketball game involving youths in a program that required after-school attendance in weekly math (three hours) and counseling (one hour) to qualify for participation (Wilgoren 1999).

Sports activities may enjoy a rich tradition among certain ethnic and racial groups, further enhancing their appeal. This tradition, as the case with Navajo Indians and running, can serve as a mechanism for instilling cultural pride and enhancing ethnic-self pride in youngsters. Sports, too, have played such a role for African Americans (Wiggins 1994:153):

> From the moment they were first allowed into organized sport, then, black athletes were involved in a continually changing and sometimes ambivalent relationship with white athletes and Americans. The

achievements of black athletes . . . did serve, ironically enough, as symbols of possibility for members of the black community who strive for recognition with the same earnestness as their white counterparts and who attempted to forge their own identities in an America that held fast to racial stereotypes and refused always to honor its own precepts.

Sports are an integral part of our cultural heritage and have fulfilled important social and political agendas in numerous societies across the world.

It is hoped that this chapter has helped practitioners to develope a new, or rediscover, the importance of sports in the lives of youths, regardless of whether they are urban, suburban, or rural-based. The use of organized sports, however, must not be narrowly conceptualized as only that activity that takes place within a sanctioned setting. Many sports activities take place in city streets, etc. Consequently, an expanded vision is necessary because of the limited public space that is available for youths in most urban areas of the United States. Further, there must be a differentiation between playing organized sports as a means of recreation and integration of services, and organized sports targeting "elite" players who will use this vehicle to further their careers, or get into college through an athletic scholarship. The answer to this question will determine the focus of the sports activity, and who it will ultimately benefit.

Last, practitioners should have an expanded view of sports activities for urban-based youth. Sports activities should never be narrowly defined, nor should they be based upon what adults think urban youths would like to engage in; sports activities such as scuba diving, sailing, fishing, and tennis, for example, may have appeal beyond the socioeconomic groups usually associated with these activities. Activities, in turn, do not have to be "competitive" driven in order to have appeal and teach valuable lessons for participants.

CHAPTER 8

——

QUALITIES DEFINING AN EXEMPLARY
ORGANIZATION: CASE STUDIES OF NEW ARENAS

It is important to stop and examine what makes an organization exemplary in the field of youth development. This chapter provides a brief, but nonetheless valuable, profile of an "ideal" organization structure and process and serves as a foundation for examining the case studies presented. This profile, when placed within the context of the case studies, allows us to compare organizations highlighted in the cases with their own organization. This process of comparison will aid in better determining the generalizability of the "ideal" organization to one's own, thus facilitating a more relevant application that takes into account local circumstances. Needless to say, there is no such thing as a perfect youth-serving organization, or, for that matter, any organization regardless of the group it targets. Nevertheless, exemplary organizations do exist in this country. However, prior to focusing on a series of case studies that highlight the rewards of youth practice within new arenas, it is necessary to pause and examine what factors make organizations exemplary.

Organizations wishing to initiate youth development programs, or those that already provide them but wish to maximize their resources, must seriously determine what structure and operating processes facilitate the achievement of their goals. Gambone (1993) notes that there are three organizational features that make for an effective organization: (1) a clear and strong mission statement; (2) the leadership; and (3) the organizational climate and culture.

Networks for Youth Development (1998c) has developed a profile of the "ideal" organizational structure and operating processes based upon field-tested "best" practices. Philadelphia's PublicPrivate Ventures organization has developed an approach for determining how well voluntary youth service organizations are addressing seven program areas: (1) leadership opportunities for youth; (2) social support from adult staff; (3) development of a sense of inclusion; (4) provision of challenging and interesting activities; (5) youth input and decision making in programs; (6) community service; and (7) safety (Gambone 1993; Howard 1997b).

ESSENTIAL QUALITIES

Organizational process and structure cannot be separated from each other. However, for the purposes of facilitating discussion here, these two dimensions will be separated. These dimensions, particularly those related to organizational process, complement the staff competencies that are necessary for successful youth development work addressed in chapter 2.

Organizational Structure

The structure of the organization must be supportive of a mission that actively embraces youth development. This mission, as a result, requires having leadership with vision and a communication system that actively conveys the message of youths' assets and potential. The organization must place a high value on enhancing staff capacities through appropriate training, supervision, and consultation. In addition, it must seek to be integrally related to the community it seeks to serve and its vital institutions, both formal and informal.

The organization must be a sanctuary for youths by providing an environment that ensures physical and psychological safety as well as comfort. The physical structure of the organization, as a result, must be inviting to youths but also provide physical shelter to prevent injuries to participants as a result of acts of violence, e.g., drive-by shootings. Some organizations have commissioned youths to paint murals on the exterior walls as a means of having the organization reflect local themes, for example. This action serves to reaffirm the organization's commitment to serving local youths, and sends a similar message to the greater community.

There are a variety of activities that can be used to more firmly ground youths within the organizations serving them. This grounding can be achieved with minimal expenditure of funds and time. Young participants and their caretakers, for example, can be provided with an orientation to the agency, its mission, and the range of services that are available. This orientation serves to assist youths in developing a better understanding and appreciation for what an organization has to offer that goes beyond what is part of a particular program or activity. Further, each participant can play an active role in helping to create goals for himself/herself in order to maximize his/her potential.

Organizations have to be keenly aware of what youths are experiencing in their daily lives, within the home, family, and community. This very often necessitates that agency staff and administrators make it a point to be actively involved on the boards and advisory committees of other youth-serving organizations, as well as involved in community-sponsored activities and celebrations. Such participation increases the likelihood that they will be in positions to hear of concerns that impact on youth. The Boys and Girls Clubs of America have specifically set aside four positions out of twenty-eight on the board for young members. These members, incidentally, have all of their expenses paid for them to attend national board meetings (Boyle 1998c).

Hiring staff who live in the community also increases the likelihood that the organization will be responsive to local issues and needs. Further, it increases the likelihood of staff and administrators identifying community assets and integrating them within youth programming, and helps keep the money that is paid to them within the community. This point, as will be addressed later, serves to recirculate an important source of money. Hiring local residents, training them, and supporting them in the position ensures that the community will have another source of role models for youths. Role-model individuals who probably faced many of the same challenges as current youth, but were to able to successfully meet the challenge, are very important in youth work. Unfortunately, many urban youths have negative role-model individuals who were unable to meet the challenges, and as a result, either died or served time in prison.

Youth organizations, in addition, must seek to enhance the cultural pride of participants. Youths of color, as already noted, very often are bombarded with negative views of their ethnic and racial backgrounds. Youth organizations, as a result, must actively combat these messages. The latter is not only reflected in programming, but also in the symbols used throughout the organization and the celebrations it sponsors, hiring staff that reflect the ethnic/racial, socioeconomic class backgrounds of the youths in the program. This action, in addition, also serves to increase the pool of potential residents who can consider this line of work as a possibility in the future.

Quality of *Program Implementation*

The saying "To plan is human: To implement is divine" captures the challenge of translating plans into action. Planning is always a dynamic process that must respond to local circumstances and issues. Consequently, the ability to build in the necessary flexibility into plans to allow local circumstances to influence the ultimate outcome, is essential in youth-work field. This goal necessitates hiring staff who can quickly respond to changing conditions or crises that may occur in the community.

Smith (1997:xi), based upon an extensive evaluation of youth programs, highlights the important role implementation plays in generating positive outcomes:

The quality of program implementation matters, as we know from experience in every social field. In the studies, especially in demonstration programs, it was usually the case that those sites that most faithfully executed the intended program design showed the best results . . . High quality implementation is thoughtful and well-managed, incorporating evaluation and continuous improvement into design, fostering communication within the program and among all partners and levels of government." Consequently, implementation quality is only as good as the quality of the planning process used. These two aspects of programming are very interrelated and program staff must never lose sight of this dimension.

Responsiveness to Environmental Forces

Urban youths are in desperate need of finding places within the community that offer them a sanctuary from physical and psychological harm. Consequently, effective youth organizations take this fact into account in the physical structures and programming. Structurally, these organizations need to maintain systems of accountability pertaining to who "belongs" and who is "visiting" the program. This goal can be achieved through a variety of means from issuing youth identification cards to requiring signing in and out of the program. These actions can play an important role in minimizing who enters the premises, but also conveys to young participants the seriousness of maintaining a "safe-environment" by restricting access.

Some youths may react negatively to this restriction, particularly in cases where they wish to have nonmember friends attend. However, restrictions do not necessarily limit who can attend, they just increase accountability.

Youths who wish to have a friend attend, for example, must ultimately be responsible for that guest's actions. If the actions are detrimental to the program and its participants, then the member who signed in the guest will have to face some discipline as a result.

Programming and organizational operations must also be responsive to the environmental stressors youths face. The creation of midnight basketball serves as an excellent example of how staff can be creative in developing activities that are attractive to youths, and offering them during time periods when they are most in need of alternatives to street life. Organizations must be sufficiently flexible concerning hours and days of operation to allow programs like midnight basketball to exist. There may be particular periods in the year, like summer, when programming may extend far beyond the usual time periods in order to minimize youths engaging in risk-taking behaviors.

Explicit Mission Statements Stressing Youth Development

All human service organizations have mission statements, regardless of whether they are public or private in nature. These statements, in turn, reflect the priorities of organizations and serve to guide them in search of means for achieving their goals. Mission statements, as a result, can play a critical role in helping organizations focus their attention on particular goals. Unfortunately, in working with many human service organizations across the United States, I have found that mission statements have very little meaning or influence in the setting of programmatic priorities. It seems like few organizations really understand their mission statements and why they are important.

A mission statement that specifically embraces a youth development perspective based on assets is of tremendous importance in helping the organization plan services, hire staff, and recruit youths. This mission statement represents the "heart and soul" of an organization and will help it steer its way through the turbulent waters inherent in human service work. Thus, a mission statement is much more than a set of words organized into a series of sentences. It represents the "genetic blueprint" to all current and future activities related to youth.

A Holistic Perspective on Youth

Organizations must be able to engage youths and make them feel that they belong (Gambone and Arbreton 1997). This can be accomplished by providing youths with an agency-wide orientation, developing individual plans with mutually arrived-at goals, possessing an awareness of what youths are experiencing, and promoting multicultural understanding and validation. Integration of youths into an organization represents one of the ultimate goals of participation.

A holistic perspective toward youths' requires that staff have an understanding of the unique set of issues confronting urban youths in the United States. This perspective, as a result, requires an understanding of the peer pressures that they confront daily and the impact of risk-taking behavior in their lives. Youths have multifaceted aspects that must be acknowledged and addressed by program staff. Pressures to engage in early sexual activity and educational and career decisions are arduous enough for any youth. However, when these decisions are filtered through issues related to oppression because of skin color, gender, or income, the challenge of successfully addressing youth becomes even greater. However, taking a holistic perspective through programming increases the likelihood that youths will be understood, and thereby better served.

Opportunities for Contributions

Although service opportunities for youths have historically been very limited, the research literature on youth service has clearly pointed out the important role of service to community in enhancing the lives of youths (Smith and Jucovy 1996). Service, as a key component of any youth programming, has started to get the attention and recognition that it deserves. Thus, organizations must seek to ensure youths participation in the organization, provide community service opportunities, maintain an active participant feedback mechanism, provide opportunities for youth leadership, involve youths in community development, and create youth ownership of programs.

Until recently, the concept of youth service to the community has not received the attention it deserves, although the literature on the topic highlights its importance for both youths and their community. Further, an opportunity to serve in a structured and monitored way, with appropriate supports and supervision, can open up possibilities for careers. I remember conducting a series of needs assessments in a Latino community in a large New England city, with several of the young participants who were interviewers deciding to enter a human service career as a result. This exposure would not have been possible if they had not been given an opportunity to be community researchers.

Creation of Caring and Trusting Relationships

It seems very easy to recommend that organizations endeavor to establish caring and trusting relationships between staff volunteers and youths. On the surface there are few staff who would argue against this goal. There usually is an explicit, if not implicit, understanding that trust must be present before relationships can be established. However, to achieve this goal is never easy, nor should it be taken for granted if, in fact, it is achieved.

Organizational staffing patterns must facilitate staff developing an in-depth understanding of the youths in their programs. High staff-to-youth ratios are a major impediment to facilitating development of caring and trusting relationships between staff and youths. One-to-one relationships and involvement of families and appropriate caretakers require staff to invest a considerable amount of time into structuring activities that facilitate staff/youth exchanges, creating a caring and family atmosphere, recognizing individual accomplishments of all participants, ensuring confidentiality, fostering positive interactions between youths and staff, and maintaining an open line of communication within the organization. Clearly, there are no shortcuts to developing an atmosphere that values caring and trust between program staff and youths. This is a labor intensive aspect of organizational development that is necessary in order for any type of programming to take hold and make a lasting impact on youths.

Maintenance of High Expectations

Youth organizations must seek to develop high expectations for young participants because of the importance of this message to all those involved with youths and youths themselves. This can be accomplished in a variety of ways: create a wide range of opportunities for youths, integrate cognitive enhancement activities into programs, create a respectful structure, guidelines, and rules, provide opportunities for participants to enhance their capacities to reason, solve problems, and empathize, provide life skills training, and focus on strengths and resiliencies.

Establishment of high expectations, as a result, must permeate all levels of the organization starting with the leadership (management and board of directors) down to support staff and volunteers. These expectations, in turn, will also filter into the community by having youths share with their significant adults, siblings, and peers the importance of believing in oneself and having others believe as well. This experience may be new for many youths who have historically suffered from adults and peers having low-expectations of their abilities and their dreams.

Offer of Engaging Individual and Group Activities

Youths are engaged when they are provided with an opportunity to participate in meaningful and fun activities. Achieving a balance between individual and group activities within programs serves to engage youths in a variety of modes that provide both individual time and time with peers (Gambone and Arbreton 1997). Activities should also instill curiosity and encourage youths to learn from a broad range of experiences. Creative energies are necessary to engender activities that are fun and educational, and that can possibly make important contributions to the community.

Activities such as field trips to institutions that youths would normally not consider attending, incorporate fun, provide developmentally appropriate activities, and foster creativity. As a consequence, engagement is too an important a factor to be allowed to chance. Thus, engagement must be systematically thought out, planned, and implemented.

Youth organizations, however, should strive for a good mix between individual and group activities. The former provide staff with an excellent opportunity to better become knowledgeable about participants in a way that group activities cannot. However, peer-relations are an essential aspect of youths' lives. Thus, group activities allow youths to develop confidence in working with others. Skills related to teamwork and communication, for example, will prove very useful as youths enter adulthood and are thrust into situations where they must work as a member of a team.

Opportunities for Continuing Participation

Organizations seeking to serve youths are often faced with challenges that other organizations, such as those targeting adults and seniors, do not face. Youth-serving organizations must seek to establish consistency within programs, create opportunities for youths to continue to grow within the organization, support youths in their transition to adulthood, create closure, and retain youths within programs until appropriate termination (Gambone and Arbreton 1997).

None of these goals is easy to accomplish. Consistency within programs serves to help youths develop a greater appreciation of order and structure in their experience. This consistency, in turn, will hopefully transfer over into other sectors of their lives, such as school. For example, many after-school programs specifically set aside time for youths to do homework. In many situations, tutors and staff play key roles in helping youths with their homework and special school projects. The routine established within programs serves to provide order and assists youths with prioritizing their time and activities.

Programs must also take into consideration the developmental growth that occurs among youths. As they grow and age, they must continually be challenged and grow socially, physically, and cognitively. Thus, program activities across the lifespan can help ensure that youths do not "outgrow" the organization. Counselors-in-training is one way of keeping youths actively involved with an organization after they may no longer qualify for participation based upon age.

Helping youths make an uneventful transition to adulthood will no doubt represent a significant challenge for organizations. Letting youths go after many years of actively being involved in their lives, and in many situations, helping them through very difficult times, is a challenge for any staff. However, whether the youths leave to continue their education, join the military, or seek employment, this passage can combine both the joys associated with success and the pain of not continuing to be an active participant in a youth's life.

A Diversified Funding Base

Organizations cannot function without adequate funding, and there is no such thing as funding "without strings." Adequate funding, however, goes far beyond the amount of money, but also refers to the flexibility of funds. Reliance on categorical funding—namely, money with severe restrictions on who can benefit from it and under what circumstances—can pose severe challenges for youth-serving organizations. Categorical funding severely limits an organization's ability to take a holistic perspective toward youth. Consequently, youth organizations must strive to have no more than one-third of their funding from any one source, except grassroots fundraising.

Grassroots fundraising is very important for a variety of reasons: (1) it generates money with "no strings attached"; (2) it provides community institutions such as grocery stores, restaurants, beauty parlors, etc., with an opportunity to donate prizes to the raffles; (3) it provides youths with a chance to promote the organization and recruit potential new members to youth activities; and (4) it allows an organization to come together (board, staff, volunteers, youth, parents) in pursuit of a common goal—generation of funds. This can be an annual affair for which committees can be established composed of all the major constituent subgroups.

Youth organizations that have been successful at achieving this goal have been able to reach out to foundations, corporations, and government in a manner that does not violate the integrity of the organization or create undue paperwork. Funding, as a result, must not be strictly conceptualized as only money. Organizations must also be able to tap indigenous community resources such as volunteers, space within local institutions, donations of equipment, food, transportation, etc. (Fisher 1998).

Creative ways of obtaining funding and donations should always be continually explored by youth-serving organizations. Having youths actively involved in both the planning and implementation of fundraising efforts is highly recommended. This involvement not only results in youths feeling more integrated into a program, but it also serves as an excellent means of undertaking public relations with the community, and providing youths with important skills that can be employed in other arenas.

A Community Base Whenever Possible

The location of an organization and the physical accessibility to it play important roles in helping to determine who ultimately uses and benefits from its activities (Delgado 1999b). There is an increased amount of literature focused on the value of having an organization that is located within the community it seeks to serve. Although it may be physically impossible for a youth organization to literally move from one geographical location to another in order to be physically based in the community, it may be possible to develop community-based outposts, outstation staff, or programming in community host organizations, as a means of increasing accessibility. Being community-based sends an important message to a community. Namely, "you are important enough for us to be here!"

Flexibility in program design and staff deployment are essential in conceptualizing community-based services. Further, this flexibility is also necessary in situations where an organization is based within a community. Being geographically based within a community does not guarantee access to all its sectors. Youth organizations, as a result, may wish to develop outposts in various sectors of a community in an effort to outreach to specific groups such as newcomers. It is not unusual to have program staff and conduct programming in apartments in local housing developments, in addition to the usual programming that takes place back at the organization's homebase.

However, there are many other benefits to both community and organization by having a base within the community. Staff are constantly in touch with the reality of working in the community; other agencies may follow suit and relocate into the community; residents may experience increased confidence about the future of the community; the organization will increase opportunities to collaborate with other formal or informal organizations also situated in the community; and increased geographical accessibility will allow other youths to participate.

Engagement in Community Capacity Enhancement

The concept of community capacity enhancement (Delgado, in press) has slowly gained currency within the field of social work and other helping professions. Community capacity enhancement does not occur automatically when programs focus only on enhancing youths' capacities. True, youths and their families and communities do benefit. However, community capacity enhancement is a purposeful effort at combining youths and community development in an effort to combine these two areas of focus. Historically, interventions have generally focused on one group such as individuals, families, or communities. An effort to bring these groups together within an intervention, in this case community capacity enhancement, will result in maximizing existing resources.

Youth-serving organizations can employ a variety of methods to benefit communities such as hiring local residents as staff, contracting with community institutions for the purchase of food, equipment, and other program-related expenses whenever possible, sponsoring community workshops, and assisting residents through brokering with other agencies for needed services. Youth-serving organizations should endeavor to maximize their resources whenever possible. Thus, although primarily targeting youths and their families, other sectors of the community must ultimately benefit too.

THE ROLE OF GOVERNMENT—NATIONAL, STATE, AND LOCAL

It would be irresponsible for me to write a book about new arenas and urban youth and not address the role of government in fostering youth development work. There is a prevailing belief that youths must be controlled and punished rather than given an opportunity and a voice in creating systems that are responsive to them (Hahn 1998b). Clearly, government, as well articulated by numerous national organizations, must play an active role in better enhancing youths' assets.

The National Collaboration for Youth (1998) has identified various areas for government to play a supportive role in enhancing youth development work. The following seven recommendations will result in a major step forward in getting youth development work on a national agenda: (1) tap national voluntary youth development organizations in the creation of new approaches toward reaching youths through an asset perspective; (2) create funding mechanisms that support youth development work that do not fragment youths and their struggles as currently is the case through categorical funding programs; (3) encourage and support technology transfer and replication of successful programs; (4) support capacity building and staff development of youth development organizations; (5) raise national awareness of youth development as a field of practice; (6) support information networks to facilitate the exchange of information on youth programming; and (7) support collaborative partnerships between formal and informal sectors within a community.

Efforts to carry out these recommendations at various levels of government will serve to enlist further support from other sectors such as businesses, schools, law enforcement departments, to name just three. It will take a coordinated effort on the part of all parties (after all, communities consist of all of many parties) in order for youths to receive a true chance to maximize their potential in the twenty-first century. Government can play a role of catalyst in bringing national attention to this form of practice. This attention can also result in other professions playing greater attention to youth development work as represented through the examples given in this book.

CASE STUDIES OF NEW ARENAS

The translation of theory and concepts into everyday type of practice is often best accomplished through the systematic use of case studies. Of course, there is no substitute for actual practice. However, in the absence of practice opportunities, case studies can provide practitioners with the next-best alternative, namely being being provided with a ringside seat to an actual situation. Further, case studies allow the practitioner to examine in great detail techniques, approaches, and considerations, without having to fear failing. Case studies have particular appeal for social workers because of the concurrent nature of our training (field and classroom instruction occurring at the same time and hopefully complementing each other). The careful selection of cases, in turn, can serve as a valuable educational lesson for both student and experienced practitioner.

The nine case studies presented provide the reader with a variety of settings, types of youth activities, budgets, and geographical sections of the country. The cases represent Washington, D.C. and five states (California, Georgia, Illinois, Minnesota, Missouri, New York, Texas) and nine cities (Atlanta, Chicago, Dallas, Hollywood, Jonesboro, Kansas City, New York, San Francisco, and Washington, D.C.). Unfortunately, I cannot provide greater geographical variety because of time demands and financial considerations. Nevertheless, the cases provide an in-depth appreciation of the process of developing programming targeting urban youth, the multifaceted goals often associated with youth development work, and rewards and challenges inherent in work of this type. These cases highlight many of the exemplary organizational qualities addressed earlier.

It is hoped that by reading the cases you will be able to have sufficient information to allow informed judgments concerning the activities that are most appropriate, and feasible, for your setting and location. In addition, you will be able to pick and choose between different types of activities to create an program or project that best matches your own goals, values, and circumstances. You will also be able to see how many of the principles described in chapter 5 have been manifested in the field of practice. The budgets for these programs range from zero to over $1 million, and provide a wide variety of funding amounts and configurations.

Unlike the other case illustrations used in earlier chapters, where limited information was provided, each case study used here will provide sufficient information to develop a better understanding of how practice is operationalized involving new arenas. The framework developed by Burt, Resnick, and Novick (1998) in their study of youth service organizations lends itself, with some modifications and additions, to presenting the case studies. According to the authors, youth organizations can be viewed from eight perspectives in order to develop an appreciation of labor: (1) mission, goals, and objectives; (2) current clientele; (3) service configuration; (4) type and makeup of the service integration network; (5) funding sources; and (6) evaluation activities. Resnick, Burt, and

Novick (1998) also add a brief overview of the program and an update to their framework.

This chapter borrows from their framework and includes other aspects they did not address or, if covered, did not stress. As a result, each case study consists of the following three major sections: (1) Context Setting (brief overview of the community, key institutions, and identification of factors leading to development of the project; budget and source of founding); (2) Project Specific Information (description of the process used in creating the project and the various components and aspects of the project, along with an overview of the program's staffing pattern with particular attention to the characteristics of staff—ethnic/racial, experiences, education); and (3) Lessons Learned (factors facilitating and hindering encountered in developing and implementing the project and recommendations and implications for community social work practice and education, including efforts at evaluation). These three dimensions will not only serve to ground the reader in the context of the case, but will also describe activities in sufficient detail to draw a set of lessons and implications for urban-based community social work practice.

You will no doubt discern in reading these cases that no two programs are alike, even when using the same youth development activity. This is not purposeful, and reflects the nature of the field as noted by the President's Committee on the Arts and Humanities (1996:8): "No two programs are alike. Each program reflects its creator's mission and its community's specific circumstances. The individuality of each program is testimony to this field's ingenuity."

1. Atlanta: Moving in the Spirit

The case illustration of "Moving in the Spirit" (MITS) in Atlanta is an excellent example of a project originating from faith-based organizations, utilizing dance as both a method for engaging youth, but also as a means of delivering social services in a manner that is nonstigmatizing. Youths engaging in dance can find a new perspective on their lives, as well as finding a vehicle for expressing their emotions. Structured dancing taps into the innate wishes of youths, and facilitates the development of trust between participants, and between participants and their teachers. Dance not only requires hard work and commitment, but also brings them into contact with other cultures. Dance, as a result, is not restricted to youths from middle- and upper-classes. It is a medium that is not bound by socioeconomic class.

Context Setting

Faith-based organizations have a commitment to go beyond "saving souls" and address the physical, social, and psychological needs of community residents. The role of the African-American church is well recognized nationally because of its contributions to seeking social and economic justice for its community. Community-based houses of worship are in a unique position to reach out to youth, families, and communities. Atlanta, being the birthplace of Martin Luther King Jr. serves as a context from which MITS participants derive a great deal of inspiration for their work.

Moving In the Spirit was founded in 1986. Upon graduating from college and working in a local housing development in Atlanta, Ms. Dana Marschalk, cofounder and executive director, realized the role dance could play in the lives of inner-city youngsters. Dance incorporates all of the key elements that will allow participants to succeed in life, even when not pursuing a career in dance. MITS's budget is approximately $115,000, and receives support from such local foundations and corporations as Coca-Cola, ATT&T Corporation, MasterCard, Atlanta Foundation, The Community Foundation for Greater Atlanta, and city and state government.

Project Specific Information

Moving in the Spirit's mission incorporates a variety of spiritual and social goals for youths (MITS 1998:1): "Moving in the Spirit teaches the values of respect, discipline, commitment, and responsibility through the art of dance. The organization uses dance as a fun and creative tool to encourage self-expression, give voice to issues pertinent to today's society and develop workplace values and life skills." MITS's mission, as a result, is to engage and instill in youths values and habits that will serve them well in other aspects of the life; dance, as a medium, serves to both enrich and empower youths. In addition, youths interested in theater production and stage management are given training and opportunities to develop these abilities. MITS, in essence, seeks to teach youths workplace values and life skills through the discipline and production of dance. Every dance piece incorporates important social messages from sexual education to spiritual themes such as mercy and forgiveness (Smith 1997). These messages are not only incorporated by the dancers, but they are also shared with audiences. The Martin Luther King Jr.'s dedication to achieving social and economic justice not only serves as an inspiration to the dancers, but often serves as a basis for the creation of a dance piece.

MITS consists of multiple activities addressing youths' needs across the lifespan (Lakes 1996:84):

> Moving in the Spirit offers four programs and services for critical education: Stepping Stones, The Apprentice Corporation, The Performance Company, and The Resource Network. Stepping Stones is an entry-level program using dance as a means to reinforce school curriculum. More than three hundred children, ranging in age from primary grades to high school, participate in the program on a weekly after-school classes . . . Each dance teacher in this program is required to keep a notebook in order to track the progress of their kids, monitor the incentive system for point accrual, record a daily journal entry of reflection upon their students and classes, update or revise their lesson plans, and maintain a file of parental permission/release forms.

MITS serves as an alternative in both education and performance and utilizes various programs to fulfill its mission and objectives. All MITS students have access to counselors through The Resource Network. The Resource Network, in turn, serves as a coordinating mechanism for integrating external resources into the programs to help young participants. Services such as counseling, mentor programs, and group workshops are made available through this network. Workshops serve to help participants better address substance abuse, pregnancy, and AIDS. Staff, too, participate in workshops that increase their competence on such topics as violence prevention and child psychology.

The Apprentice Corporation focuses on adolescents ages 12 to 19 and membership is determined through merit (audition). The group consists of twelve dancers who perform in Atlanta and throughout the United States. Their dances are based upon themes related to social and economic justice, in similar fashion to the messages exposed by Martin Luther King Jr. In addition to the dancing, participants are required to take classes that stress problem-solving approaches and techniques as well as creativity, to help them face the challenges of life beyond dancing.

The Performance Company is composed of a collaborative group of Atlanta-based choreographers and dancers. The Company purposefully uses dance as a medium for educating audiences about important social, cultural, and personal issues. The Performance Company presents annual performances at The Beam (MITS' theater), and in other settings. Company members, in turn, can work toward membership in the national dance tour. Many of the members of the Performance Company have worked their way through all the other programs to reach this stage. These dancers, as a result, are in positions to serve as role models for other dances in MITS and in the community at-large.

The Stepping Stones program is offered in seven community sites throughout Atlanta, as a means of facilitating participation. As already noted, it targets youngsters ages 2–13, who attend weekly classes where they learn fundamental dance techniques and means of creative self-expression. The program stresses literacy skills by having participants read, write, draw, and "create movement" from major subjects in their lives—school, family, and community. Stepping Stone players in all seven sites come together, after a year-long period, and provide a final performance in May titled "Literacy in Motion." This performance serves as a graduation from the program and provides with an opportunity to give back to their communities.

Stepping Stone dancers (approximately 15 members) interested in continuing their dance instruction can join the Junior Company. This program targets youths ages 8–12, and provides intensive instruction in a variety of dance forms—ballet, modern, jazz, and ethnic forms. This program employs a unique approach by requiring dancers to develop individual goals and objectives. Parents also play an active role in this program. The Stepping Stone dancers give performances throughout Atlanta (schools, neighborhood events, community celebrations, amusement parks, youth and senior centers).

Not every youngster has the interest or ability to engage in dance. Dance performances, after all, require the support of countless numbers of individuals besides the dancers. The work that goes on behind the scenes is just as important as the dance performance. Kinetechs is a program that provides an alternative for youths who are interested in theater from behind the scenes. Kinetechs is a technical training program that provides instruction for youths in production and stage management. Participants attend classes after school and on weekends during which they receive instruction in lighting, sound operation and design, stage management, set design, and video documentation. Youths have the opportunity to be mentored by professionals and undertake field trips to local theaters. For those with the abilities and interest of continuing this path, they can apply their skills as staff for performances at The Beam (MITS theater), and other venues.

Finally, MITS' OPTIONS Program (Orienting Peers Toward Individual Options and Self-Worth), facilitated by the Resource Network director, is a peer education program that addresses many of the social issues confronting participants in their daily lives. This program consists of a dance therapist and two peer educators. OPTIONS-sponsored workshops utilize interactional techniques in covering topics such as self-esteem, peer pressure, pregnancy prevention, decision making, and goal-stating.

Moving in the Spirit has developed a unique approach to paying youths with "MITS money" (PCAH 1996:116): "Youth earn 'MITS money' based on the number of points earned in the incentive system, and the money goes into make-believe checkbooks. The young dancers are able to use their money in Moving in the Spirit Christmas store, which is supplied with donations from individuals and local businesses."

Lessons Learned

The evaluation of MITS has generally focused on gathering data from participants, site directors, and teachers. In addition to gathering information on attendance, and other participatory factors, evaluation studies have also focused on the impact of the program on participants' other lives. For example, studies have found that 90 percent of the youths in the programs have completed high school and continued their education in college or technical training schools of various kinds. The commitment that is required of dance also serves to help them in other aspects of their non-dance lives.

Recruitment of youths into MITS programs has advantages and disadvantages. Dance is an attractive after-school activity and there are very few such programs for inner-city youths in Atlanta. Consequently, MITS does not face competition from other programs in this area. However, recruitment of males gets increasingly more difficult the older the youths get. Youths in the Stepping Stone Program are almost equally balanced between males and females. As the youths get older, however, females outnumber males by a considerable ratio. Older male dancers, in addition, are not only harder to recruit but also harder to maintain in the program.

Dance is an excellent activity for helping youths channel their energies into constructive activities. Structured dance, in turn, also provides youths with a way of expressing their emotions in an atmosphere that is receptive to this sharing. However, it is necessary for staff to be well prepared to handle the outflow of emotions. Many youths have experienced and witness much in their lives and have not been able to speak with others about this. Trust, as a result, is necessary to achieve this sharing. Staff must then be prepared to provide support, guidance, and if necessary, make referrals to appropriate sources, some of whom are social workers.

Dance companies, like their arts counterparts, are always struggling to obtain the necessary funding for their performances. MITS, unfortunately, is no different. Fundraising has historically been a challenge for MITS, and for that matter, most of the other cases in this chapter. MITS, although always managing to get the necessary funding to run its programs, is always challenged to do so. In essence, having a proven track record and evaluation results does not necessarily translate into a steady and predictable source of funding. "Soft" money is just that—soft.

2. Chicago: Gallery 37 (murals)

The case study selected complements the work of TeenStreet, reported earlier (chapter 5), and provides a perspective that involves local government. Gallery 37 targets urban youths from low-income households and communities and utilizes the arts as the primary vehicles for reaching and working with youths. Gallery 37, however, was selected for an in-depth examination because of the amount of documentation the organization does, ease of accessibility for me, the wide range of art activities it sponsors, and its influence on other youth organizations, national and international (Australia and England). Gallery 37's budget of over $1 million is funded from a wide range of sources, most notably government, foundations, and corporations.

Gallery 37 seeks to address art education and youth employment by providing youths an opportunity to learn and practice essential work skills that will stay with them for life. Its mission states (Gallery 37, 1997:1): "to provide meaningful employment and training in the arts to Chicago's youth, without regard to gender, race, or family income level; to create a mentoring program between youths and established artists; to increase public awareness of the importance of the arts and arts education; and to foster cultural awareness."

Context Setting

Gallery 37, a program of Chicago's Department of Cultural Affairs, was established in 1991, and had an operating budget of approximately $1 million, obtained from a variety of sources, and initially served 220 youths. Gallery 37 derived its name from a downtown vacant lot (Block 37) that was converted to a gallery for Chicago's youth. Its strategic location in downtown Chicago provides Gallery 37 with an excellent opportunity to bring the arts created by youths to the general public. The general public not only has an opportunity to see the finished product produced by Chicago's youths, but can also purchase it.

Project Specific Information

Gallery 37 was established with the goal of using the arts as a forum for engaging adolescents in creating critical job skills and creative thinking (Gallery 37:2):

> Working as apprentice artists under the tutelage of experienced professional artists, Gallery 37 youths create works of art in a variety of media. They also develop cognitive skills vital to the workplace, such as problem-solving, reasoning, decision-making, scheduling, punctuality, as well as interpersonal skills, including oral communication and teamwork.

Apprentices at Gallery 37 also gain work experience in the arts-related career fields. Like the professional workplace, Gallery 37 programs focus on performance and product by providing youths with an opportunity to explore their artistic talents, and in some cases, pursue a career involving the arts. Not every young person has the talent or the drive to pursue a career in the arts. However, every participant can still benefit from exploring the arts as an activity that is fun, educational, and can generate an income.

Gallery 37 has established the arts as a credible vehicle for jobs training, a significant achievement in the current climate of decreased funding and attention to the arts. The program has succeeded in challenging the ways people think about intensive the arts—pushing them to see that serious, intensive arts programs can be legitimate training grounds for the workplace, and has a marked impact on urban economic and social issues. As a result, the arts can be an effective vehicle for transforming lives and addressing many of the issues confronting Chicago's youths in the process.

Gallery 37 targets both male and female youths, ages 14–21. Although its headquarters is located downtown, Chicago's neighborhoods and parks are an integral part of Gallery 37 because of its decentralized approach to programming. Arts programming is multifaceted (literary, performing arts, media, and visual) and multisite based. Programming occurs throughout the year. During the academic year it offers programs within the city's public schools. In the summer, it offers programs in parks, schools, neighborhood centers, and downtown.

The program is located in twenty-seven Chicago neighborhoods and thirty high schools. The summer programs cover an eight-week period and consist of an apprenticeship program of twenty hours per week during which participants receive minimum wages. This program actively involves twenty other organizations in coordinating the apprenticeship. Gallery 37 also has a neighborhood-based program in fourteen Chicago Park District sites, twenty-seven neighborhood locations, of which ten are neighborhood centers.

Gallery 37, by utilizing a neighborhood base, provides youths with an opportunity to develop and exhibit their artistic talents within their respective communities. This after-school program involves approximately 400 youths who work twenty hours per week. The high school program involves thirty high schools and 1,000 students per year. This program takes place after school and requires youths to work ten hours per week during the school year, or twenty hours per week during a six-week summer period.

Gallery 37 also sells artwork created by the apprentices. Their downtown location has a specific goal of making artwork available to the public for purchase. The selling of artwork created by youths provides an important and yet often missing perspective on art—namely, that youths can make a living from this profession (Anderson 1997; Beeler 1997). The money earned through art sales is also very important to the families of the artist because many of them are low-income households. But just as importantly for the youths, it provides them with "evidence" that their talents are sufficiently well recognized that "perfect strangers" are willing to use currency to purchase the products of their artistic talents. This exchange is very often unheard off in the communities in which they reside.

Gallery 37 could not reach as many youths and provide as great a range of experiences without an active collaboration effort with numerous organizations, public as well as private. It has collaborative relationships with such organizations as Crate and Barrel, Marshall Field's Department Stores, Target, The Renaissance Chicago Hotel, Chicago Police Department, Department of Schools, in addition to many community-based organizations throughout Chicago.

Lessons Learned

Unfortunately, Gallery 37 does not employ social workers, although it staff are not adverse to working with social workers and often refer youths to agencies where social workers are employed. These organizations also serve to refer youngsters to the program and are beneficiaries of some of the artwork that is created by participants. This partnership helps participants develop a deeper understanding of the potential value of their work in the open market. Artistic value should never be solely judged by the amount of money it brings. However, urban youths from low-income backgrounds rarely have had the opportunity to witness the sale of art, particularly their own. Gallery 37 has consciously used the arts as a mechanism for helping Chicago's youths find outlets for their creative talents and in the process, acquire the necessary skills to seek employment in the arts field. The arts can play a significant role in job training and have an economic impact on the community as well as address social issues in the process of doing so.

In addition to demographic information on the participants, evaluation of programs generally consists of qualitative responses to six major areas. Data are gathered from site leaders and participants are asked a series of questions to determine the impact of the experience on their lives. Site leaders are asked to (1) Describe your project; (2) Did it deviate in any way from the proposed curriculum? If so, how? (3) Describe in detail the final artwork products created in the project (site leaders are also asked to provide both visual and nonvisual artwork—writing pieces, plays, or videos); (4) Describe the impact and affect the program had on apprentice artists, including any anecdotes and personal experiences the organization and teaching staff had with apprentice artists; (5) Did the program meet the proposed goals for benefiting the community, and in what way? How can these goals be improved upon for the next year? (6) Describe any significant growth seen in the apprentice artists in the following areas—artistic, vocational, and social. And, for demography, the number of participants, age, gender, and ethnic breakdown of participants. It is critical for program success to listen to youth—evaluation provides them with a "voice" in program structure and process.

Youths must be provided with viable options within an urban environment. Urban youths have talents and the need to belong to a group or organization. Providing a positive alternative to "street life" and gangs is not difficult if the right activity and adult guidance is available. Gallery 37 recognizes the importance of providing youths with a creative outlet. Not every youth wants to get involved with the arts, however, not every youth wants to get involved with basketball or other sports.

Gallery 37, by making participation accessible through various partnerships and collaboration at the community level, has provided viable alternatives to youths throughout Chicago. Accessibility, as a result, is much more than geographical in nature. Youths must feel that they are safe physically and psychologically in order to grow as artists and human beings. Partnerships with community-based organizations, including schools, is essential in any effort to outreach across a large geographical area, where public transportation may be very limited.

Getting youths to believe in their artistic talents is a major challenge because so few have had the encouragement to do so in their lives. The ability to take a risk and show their artwork to other youths, as well as "outsiders," is not an easy goal to achieve. However, once they take the risk, and accept constructive criticism, growth occurs. Youths must also be able to express their artistic ideas in a variety of formats, including writing. The release of artistic energies, however, can also result in youths sharing painful experiences in their lives. Thus, staff must be well prepared to address these issues either directly or through referral. Finally, the ability to work as a team is a skill that will have tremendous benefits in other aspects of youths lives. Teamwork requires youths to develop or enhance communication skills, as well as work-related skills. Some of the projects involving murals can be very dangerous if safety rules are not followed.

Gallery 37 believes that programming of this type is possible in any community in the United States. All communities have adolescents, artists, and funding to support an arts program—this is not unique to Chicago. The arts can be a very effective means of bringing together youths from very different ethnic, racial, and economic backgrounds.

3. Dallas: Junior Players (Theater)

The importance of theater goes beyond entertainment, as noted earlier. When theater is used as a youth development activity, it not only provides "voices" for youths who have historically not been heard by adults, it also provides them with structure, communication skills, an opportunity to belong to a "positive" group of peers, and self-confidence. The case study of the Junior Players reflects the work of an organization that has devoted almost half a century to youth theater, and highlights how multifaceted programming is essential in outreaching to low-income youths (Bradley 1995; Imherr 1998; Jackson 1998; Sime 1998).

Context Setting

The Junior Players' organization is the oldest nonprofit theater organization in Dallas devoted exclusively to youth. Its mission is (Junior Players' Proposal 1999:1): "to encourage intellectual growth, mental well-being and the development of life skills in the youth of Dallas through mentoring, creative expression, and participation in dramatic and arts activities." The

organization, like others in this chapter, is primarily a "one-person" operation (Ms. Kirsten Brandt, executive director), and has a budget of approximately $185,000. Most of the funds are generated from foundations and
corporations. Youth participants are not charged a fee.

Program-Specific Information

Throughout the year, Junior Players operates several programs involving
youths of various ages. Its Discover Theater summer camps and Discover
Ourselves after-school program seek to increase self-esteem and communication skills of youths by using the performing arts to improve literacy levels. Approximately 30 camps, each with a limit of 25 participants ages 6 to
12, are offered during the summer and involve between 600 to 800 youths
every year. The program utilizes adults as role models and mentors for
youth. Participants learn concentration and communication skills, working as a team, improvisation techniques, and theater games, and observe
other actors during field visits. The program covers a two-week period (10
two-hour sessions), and culminates with a Festival of Plays that is presented
to the public.

The Discover Shakespeare! program, in turn, targets adolescents, and is
a collaborative effort involving the Shakespeare Festival staff. This program
requires youths to audition and approximately 20 are selected. A total of
six free performances are presented to an audience of approximately 5,000.

The Junior Players' Theatro del Barrio (Theater of the Community) and
Peace Power programs specifically focus on "high-risk" adolescents. These
two programs help participants to share their life experiences through production of plays and also seek to help youths resolve their conflicts in non-
violent ways. The Theatro del Barrio program, in collaboration with the
Park and Recreation Department, Camp Fire Boys and Girls, YMCA, and
Buckner's Star Program, involves youths in creating a production, and
exhibiting original art work murals. The Peace Power Program is an after-
school program targeting middle schools. The program combines conflict
resolution training and drama, as a means of preventing violence among
youths.

Last, Junior Players Discover Arts After-School Workshops are offered
throughout the academic year and involve programs in drama, African
dance and drumming, and visual arts. Youths also undertake field visits to
professional children's theater productions. In 1998, a total of 35 free after-
school workshops were offered involving over 800 youth ages 6 to 12. This
program is a collaborative effort with area schools, recreation centers, and

youth agencies. Another dimension involves a collaborative effort with Project Bridge (Building Resources in Developing General Education), which places artists in long-term residences in public housing and low-income neighborhoods. This collaborative effort is sponsored, in part, by the Texas Commission on the Arts.

Lessons Learned

Evaluation usually consists of tracking attendance and participation, and, when feasible, tracking student achievement level. Participants are also required to fill out a self-evaluation of how the program has changed them. Degree of parental involvement in the programs is also a measure used in determining success. These measures and approaches, although not comprehensive, provide a picture that is useful for the purposes of programming. There is an understanding that a more systematic evaluation needs to be developed, hopefully with assistance from a local school of social work.

The Junior Players recognize the importance of involving artists who not only have artistic talent, but also have an ability to work with youth. This necessitates having patience and "flexibility" in implementing activities. Flexibility is essential because Junior Players places a tremendous amount of emphasis on the "process" of participation rather than the output. In this case, a performance.

Consistent attendance in workshops may not be possible for some youth. Consequently, it becomes important that they derive benefits from the activities taking place on the days they can attend. These activities may involve concentration exercises, team building, and games. This is not to say that a final performance is not important—it certainly is. However, the process is equally important, if not more so.

Youths who successfully complete their commitment to the program and perform in a play at its end are awarded a certificate of accomplishment. In addition, they get to actually see their names on a program. For many, this may be the first time they get public recognition that is positive.

Getting parental involvement is one of the challenges faced by many organizations, and Junior Players is no exception. There is an understanding that getting parents involved in their children's activities reinforces the lessons learned. However, the program has found that many parents feel that once their child is involved in an activity, they do not have to participate themselves. Junior Players is currently exploring establishing collaborative partnerships with local organizations as a means of increasing parental involvement. The Junior Players could not succeed in achieving its goals without an active collaborative campaign. Collaboration is an important strategy used by the organization to maximize its current resources, and reach out to youths in a wide geographical area. Partnerships with local schools, youth agencies, and recreation centers, form the nucleus of most of the community partnerships.

Finally, it is essential for organizations wishing to use theater as a youth development activity, to provide staff with necessary training and support. Youths involved in theater, for example, are encouraged to explore their emotions and to be creative. This is a wonderful experience for many youths who have traditionally not been able to do so. However, the opening up of these emotions can result in participants having to face very painful experiences and circumstances. Training of artists by social workers and other human service professionals usually entails developing skills in handling anger, trauma, sexual activity, and making referrals.

4. Hollywood: Write Now! (Writing)

Writing, as a youth development activity, can take many different forms. The act of writing can be a vehicle for helping youths express their feelings about life in the inner city or as a means of exploring their ethnic and racial identity, as addressed in chapter 7. It can also serve as a vehicle for creative outlets, as addressed in this section. Artistic expression, after all, is a means of building self-confidence and self-esteem. Thus, the act of writing serves as an excellent vehicle in a variety of arenas. The program Write Now! was selected for inclusion in this chapter because of the multifaceted nature of its activities, and because it reflects the potential of the artistic community, in this case writers in Hollywood, California, for reaching out to and engaging urban youths of color. Write Now!, in addition, is a program that has been active involving social workers as mentor trainers, and shows how they can play a role.

Context Setting

Write Now! was established as a nonprofit organization in 1995, by Jill Gurr, executive director and a writer with over twenty years of experience in film and television projects, and Leslie Stevens, a professor at the American Film Institute. Ms. Gurr's success in conducting youth-focused workshops in residential institutions, combined with her extensive experience in writing for television and film, led to her desire to create a nonprofit organization that was specifically targeting youths in institutional settings. Her contacts in the entertainment industry facilitated expanding the workshops and mounting a program.

The program is essentially a one-person operation consisting of the executive director. She does not collect a salary and there is no budget other than the time provided by the mentors and whatever funds Ms. Gurr contributes from her own personal savings. Consequently, although the organization has been in existence for several years, it has basically been run on a part-time basis, depending upon the time availability of the executive director. Ms. Gurr has a undergraduate degree in film-making. However, she also took courses in social work during her undergraduate education and volunteered in community projects during that time. Thus, she brings a combination of the arts and social services to her position.

Project Specific Information

Write Now! is a fine example of a program that taps the therapeutic dimensions of writing. This organization is based in Hollywood, and is a unique mentoring program that targets at-risk and high-risk youths (ages 8 to 18) who are in court-ordered residential institutions. These youths have histories of abuse, neglect, abandonment, and/or delinquency, and currently reside in court-ordered institutions run by the state of California. Write Now! focuses on teaching basic techniques of motion picture and television screen writing by pairing youths with professional screenwriters and actors. Its mission is "to reach as many of these 'forgotten' children around the world as possible and provide them with the attention, care, guidance and positive examples of personal responsibility that help them reclaim their lives." Write Now! primarily uses one-to-one mentoring as a means of enabling inner-city youths to build their self-esteem by "developing their unique stories into motion picture and television screenplays and creative writing, such as poetry, short stories, theatrical plays, etc." It offers workshops on screen writing, creative writing, in addition to the cyber-mentoring internet program.

The one-to-one mentoring program pairs the youths in a facility with mentors. All youths in the facility are welcomed to participate in the program and are asked to submit a short story idea. Each one who does so is paired with a mentor from the film and television community. Mentors undergo a screening process and must participate in a training program run by social workers and probation officers in the participating institution. Policies differ from facility to facility, some require facility personnel such as social workers and counselors to undertake the training or do an evaluation of the young participants before they can enroll in the program. Mentors are also provided with opportunities to meet with other, more experienced, writers to share and learn from their mentoring experiences.

Once a student completes a writing assignment, such as a screenplay, he or she may be asked to arrange for a readthrough at the participating institution. A readthrough usually consists of the mentors and the mentees sitting around a table and acting out the script, in similar fashion to the process used in the film industry itself. This activity can be very dramatic for a youth to see his/her work "played" out before a group.

Write Now! offers a variety of workshops that focus on developing the writing skills of male and female youths in the program. These workshops stress various aspects of writing for the entertainment industry. A youth in the Screenwriting Workshops can elect to participate in a group project (all participants contribute to one screenplay) or undertake his/her own individual script and share it with the group. The Creative Writing Workshops provide youths with an opportunity to create short stories, poetry, or write lyrics for songs. A newsletter titled "Psyche and Eros" is a quarterly publication written by participants and provides an opportunity for youths to contribute articles.

Theater Arts Workshops focus on youths creating and performing in plays at their host institutions. These performances allow participants to perform before all residents, as well as before invited family and friends. Act Now, a subsidiary group of Write Now! offers acting workshops where youths pair up with professional actors and learn to express their emotions through use of drama, comedy, and a variety of improvisational techniques. This workshop also serves to provide participants with skills for auditioning and developing a better understanding of the process necessary to result in a successful career in acting.

The Cyber-Mentoring Program is also unique and uses e-mail as a vehicle for linking youths with mentors from throughout the world. Write Now!, in addition to these programs, also sponsors a series of international projects that seek to broaden youths' perceptions of their world. The International Teens Sharing Unique Projects (I.T.S.U.P.) program establishes partnerships with "sister" organizations throughout the world and assists in helping to find mentors for youth. There is also an exchange component that brings groups of youths from other countries here, and sends groups of youths from this country to other countries. The sharing of different cultures and traditions between groups, particularly artistic interests and talents serves to broaden understanding, change stereotypes, and ultimately impact movie and television programs.

Write Now! not only serves to make youths critical consumers of media, but also has an impact on the mentors (Write Now! 1998:3): Through Write Now!, they learn to become discriminating about the movies and television programs that they watch and the music that they listen to. And since the mentors who volunteer in our program are the screenwriters and actors who create our entertainment, these movers-and-shakers in the film and television industries are being exposed to a world they've never known. Their deep connections with the youths will obviously influence their personal lives and their writing styles in a way that wasn't possible before. Mentors are recruited through a variety of means such as word-of-mouth and personal contacts of the executive director. However, announcements published in the Writers Guild have been the most successful.

Write Now!, like countless other organizations using new arenas as vehicles for engaging urban youth, has a number of highly innovative projects on the "planning board." It hopes to expand to include other types of artistic projects, including painting, drawing, ceramics, dance, and video production. It hopes to establish an animation studio set in a natural environment. An internship program is also planned to facilitate youths' entry into industry film-making jobs such as sound, cinematography, set design, grip and electric know-how, still photography, and production.

Lessons Learned

Write Now! is an excellent example of how local circumstances dictate how new arenas get conceptualized, planned, and implemented. Being based in Hollywood, one of the leading areas in the world for production of film and television shows, served as a ready-made source for mentors. Writing, in this case, is focused on the entertainment industry. Writing in other situations make take on different qualities altogether, as the case in Youth Communication (New York City), described in chapter 4. Youth Communication teaches writing to youths to use in journalism. Free Street's (Chicago) focus on theater used writing in the production of plays and a means of helping youths express the traumas and frustrations in their lives.

The lack of sustainable funding has severely limited Write Now! from undertaking a formal evaluation of the program, although the executive director can list many accomplishments for both young participants and the mentors. Although being based in Hollywood is a natural helping force in making Write Now! feasible, it also has limitations, particularly for a startup organization. Hollywood, according to Ms. Gurr, is a place where high-visibility is valued. Consequently, obtaining funds within this area is made much easier when an organization has an office, staff, and can generate extensive publicity. Write Now! is now in the process of developing a strategic plan for obtaining foundation and corporation funding. In addition, it is currently negotiating with a private benefactor for a large sum of money to help Write Now! reach an international audience.

5. Jonesboro, Georgia (Soccer in the Streets)

The sport of soccer has historically enjoyed a tremendous following throughout all parts of the world—with the possible exception of the United States. The holding of the 1994 World Cup in the United States, and the events leading up to the competition, served as a major impetus for getting youths to seriously consider soccer as a sport. Soccer, as a result, is widely accepted as the fastest growing sport in the United States. The case study of Soccer in the Streets (SITS) was selected because it specifically targets a sport that is relatively new in many cities, and represents an effort to use a sporting activity across the United States rather than in one geographical location. Its potential is only now being fully realized, particularly for involving youths from different ethnic and racial backgrounds and where English is not the primary language spoken in the home.

Content Setting

As already noted, Soccer in the Streets (SITS) is a national program that, although originally based in Jonesboro, uses soccer as the principal activity to attract all low-income urban youth. The program was established in 1989 by Carolyn McKenzie and has involved over 60,000 youths from more than 55 U.S. since its inception. SITS is widely considered to be the first national youth soccer organization targeting youths of color (Schutz 1997; *USA Today* 1993). Playing soccer is a mechanism for engaging youths and providing them with important skills, attitudes, and lessons that will serve them well in other aspects of their lives. It has purposefully concentrated on low-income urban youths of color because of the limited opportunities they have to seek alternatives to violence and other risk-taking behavior.

Project Specific Information

SITS specifically targets youths living in public housing developments and Section Eight housing for participation in the program. SITS seeks for participants to "gain meaningful, athletic, and educational experiences . . . [while] enhancing the confidence and self worth of children while promoting active and constructive lifestyles. Additional, there is always the opportunity for gifted players to reach the highest levels of soccer proficiency and advance to state select teams, Olympic development teams, or national team opportunities" (SITS 1998:1). According to McKenzie (Lowes 1994a:15): "Soccer was originally created for low-income people, but then it was deculturalized and suburbanized in this country . . . When I found out it was created for us in the beginning, I took it very personally, and said, 'This is one thing that will not be taken from us.' "

In 1998 SITS has a relative small operating budget, receiving funding from a variety of sources, most notably corporations, foundations, and local governments. SITS, however, like other organizations highlighted here, makes extensive use of volunteers and in-kind contributions. It is currently developing a long-range plan to increase its current budget to $5 million, allowing the organization to develop the infrastructure necessary to be national in scope. The hiring of new staff will allow the expansion of the organization to increase by twenty chapters per year over a five-year period to 100 chapters in 2005. This will allow the organization to serve five million youngsters in cities through the United States.

Soccer is a sport that can be played by many different youths. It can be played by both girls and boys and does not require that players be of a particular height, as in basketball, or weight, as in football. Thus, soccer provides a viable alternative to these two popular forms of play within urban areas. Success, like in all team-related sports, requires discipline, excellent communication between players, teamwork, and an ability for youths to follow directives (Joyner 1997; Shelman 1998). Success in the arena of soccer can easily translate into success in other arenas.

SITS has six primary goals that address the needs of youths with varying athletic abilities and aspirations: (1) teach urban youths of color how to play soccer; (2) provide a safe place for them to play; (3) provide participants with educational skills (tutoring, mentorships, field trips, cultural activities); (4) keep youths off drugs (Learning Is Fun and Exciting—L.I.F.E.); (5) teach youths about the important factors of life; and (6) obtain scholarships to high schools, colleges and universities for participants with the natural talents to continue playing (Giddens 1989; McKenzie 1998; Navarro 1996; Young 1996).

SITS has a specific set of principles that it uses to guide its work with youth (Giddens 1989:E-10):

We would like to use this [soccer] as a means to build character . . . And we want to implement certain principles. Everyone is a winner. It's not the number of points you score, but it's the amount of time you spend participating that makes you a winner. Hopefully, that will spill over into their classroom performance. The kids will spend time learning soccer terminology and the history of the sport. But more importantly we will use the sport as a means to teach responsibility, self-image building and positive thinking."

These principles, in turn, seek to prepare youths to succeed in aspects of their lives that are not necessarily sports focused.

Soccer in the Streets consists of multiple programs designed to take into account various periods of time and abilities of the players. These programs in turn systematically build up each other (*Atlanta Daily World*, 1994, 1996; Lowes 1994b). Soccer 101 is a five-session program for beginners that seeks to develop skills and competition. This program focuses on the development of basic skills and culminates in a graduation ceremony. Youths also participate in an antidrug curriculum. Successful graduates are given a certificate, uniforms, and balls if they had perfect attendance. This program is carried out at the local community level where participants live. SITS also sponsors two one-day minicamps for graduates of Soccer 101. One camp serves as a way to prepare youths for SITS recreational league play, and the other is carried out away from the neighborhood, preferably at a local college campus and a professional soccer environment.

Soccer 102 involves intramural and recreational league play with teams competing for the Soccer in the Streets Cup. Teams consisting of three, four, and five members compete against other teams of the same size. The small size of the teams, instead of the usual eleven, serves to increase the likelihood that each member gets ample opportunities to touch the ball, thereby increasing their skills. Soccer in the Streets Cup, in turn, is an annual tournament that is held in the cities that had Soccer 102 programs and involves teams of differing ages competing (ages 6–8, 9–11, 12–14, and 15–17). The Soccer in the Streets National Cup is an annual event that is held in Atlanta during August and involves teams (four, five, and seven members) from the SITS cities competing against each other.

Soccer 103 is restricted to players who have the potential to compete at a collegiate or international level and are given the opportunity to do so through competition against other teams in the United States (Gray 1996).

SITS could not have achieved its success without active collaboration between local private and public organizations and businesses helping to facilitate the implementation of the program. It is not unusual to find the Boys and Girls Clubs, houses of worship, housing authorities, and businesses, for example, sponsoring local chapters of SITS (Joyner 1997). These collaborative partnerships not only reduce the expenditure of funds, but also serve to anchor local SITS initiatives within the community.

Lessons Learned

SITS was generally a one-person operation for almost ten years. Although soccer is a growing sport throughout the United States, its popularity is only now being realized within communities of color in urban areas. The challenge of raising funds, paucity of playing fields, along with limited availability of coaches with the necessary preparation to work with children from the inner city, have proved a challenge. SITS has had minimal difficulty in finding sponsoring organizations or getting youngsters to enroll. However, difficulty in obtaining the necessary funds, including support from major national organizations such as the United States Soccer Federation, have limited expansion in the past.

The national scope of SITS has influenced how it has evaluated its programs at the local level. Evaluation efforts have focused on such process objectives as the number of participants who enroll and complete the program (60 percent), the number of local collaborative partnerships that have been established, the number of volunteers (ratio of 10 youths to 1 volunteer), the extent of parental involvement (20 youths to 2 parents), skill development (pre- and post-assessment), and the number of scholarships earned by participants—all serve to assess the effectiveness of the program.

Provision of transportation and funding (participation is free for youth) has met with considerable success in getting urban youths to participate. Soccer is an activity that can be an alternative to football and basketball for those who do not have the physical attributes to succeed in those sports. Coaching urban youths in soccer requires that specialized training be provided to coaches in working with participants. Urban youths can present numerous issues and needs that most coaches used to coaching in the suburbs are not accustomed to addressing. A holistic view of youth requires that every effort be made to not only provide a positive activity that can serve as an alternative to gangs, drugs, etc., but also to provide tutoring, mentoring, and other services.

6. Kansas City, Missouri: City Government (Midnight Basketball)

There is widespread acknowledgment that sports can be a successful activity for engaging urban youth. Historically, sports were generally an activity that had worth because it kept youths off the streets and out of trouble. However, sports activities have recently been recast into achieving greater goals for young participants. They not only provide a viable alternative to "hanging out" but can also serve as a motivator for youths to receive a wide variety of educational and social services—services that, incidentally, they would be reluctant to receive if they were not a condition of participating.

The origins of midnight basketball can be traced to the efforts of one person (G. Van Standifer), an African-American man who founded a league in Glenarden, Maryland, in June 1986. The primary targets of the program were young, unemployed, African-American men who had a great deal of time on their hands and needed constructive alternatives to prevent them from engaging in risk-taking behavior. The program was specifically set up to function during time periods when there was a high rate of crime perpetrated within the community.

Kansas City's night basketball program was selected as a case study because of the nature of the activity and the abundance of information on the program, including use of evaluation measures (Wilkins 1996). Further, this program also incorporates many of the principles addressed in chapter 3 and is a good example of other midnight basketball programs across the United States.

Context Setting

The Mayor's Night Hoops program originally started in the early 1990s at the urging of the mayor of Kansas City, who as a result of attending the 1991 Mayors Urban Summit, was inspired by the stories of success with midnight basketball programs in other cities. Kansas City was in desperate need of activities that attracted a particular age-group of young men. This program, as a result, initially focused on youths ages 14–25 and sought to increase recreational and employment opportunities for them. Offering the activity at night during a period of high rate of crime brought a different dimension to the usual basketball program that most cities and organizations had offered as part of their sporting initiatives. Participation in the program is free-of-charge to Kansas City residents. The budget for this program went from $100,000 in 1993 to over $200,000 in 1999 and is derived from both city government sources as well as grassroots fundraising efforts.

Project Specific Information

The Mayor's Night Hoops program focused on addressing five goals: creation of a recreational program that (1) would utilize basketball as the primary activity for attracting youths to participate and achieve educational and entrepreneurial goals—in short, it was much more than just a "recreational program"; (2) would attract support from both the private and public sectors as a means of getting them involved with this population group; (3) would serve as a vehicle for establishing collaboration between the City's Parks and Recreation Program and other entities that normally would not work together; (4) would establish an extensive network of support services to serve as a means of meeting the multifaceted needs of program participants; and (5) would also serve as a mechanism for providing in-service training on officiating and other activities related to basketball—this training, in turn, would provide participants with experience and prepare them for seeking employment in this area.

The collaborative relationships between different public and private organizations played a very influential role in the creation and success of the program: the Kansas City School District, Kansas City Police Department, the Greater Kansas City Community Foundation and Affiliated Trusts, Amateur Athletic Union, Urban League, Dubuque Foods, Price Chopper, KPRS radio station, Wilson Chapman Advertising, Wings and Things, among others.

The Night Hoops Program consisted of three interrelated dimensions: (1) basketball competition; (2) educational instruction; and (3) social support. The basketball competition ran throughout the summer months (June through mid-August) from 10 P.M. to 1 A.M., and initially involved 16 male teams (200 participants). However, the program expanded over the next several years to involve 480 participants on 48 teams, six of which were female. In 1994 the program was expanded to serve youths ages 10–14 on Wednesday through Fridays (7 P.M. to 9 P.M.), and Saturday mornings. There were no restrictions as to who could participate in the program as long as attendance and behavior expectations were met.

The educational dimension of the program focused on providing participants with an opportunity to learn new employment skills such as officiating at basketball games, learning about jobs, and interviewing, communication, and entrepreneurial skills. This employment perspective was supplemented with workshops on HIVAIDS, drugs, and conflict resolution. Social supports, in turn, stressed personal development, motivational training, and other activities that served to increase self-worth and tap individual assets.

The marketing of the program has involved a variety of activities and collaborations including use of local media, particularly local radio stations that youths listen to, postings in key public areas of the community, and word of mouth. The use of a promotional video developed by program staff has also been very influential in getting participants. However, the long and successful history of the program is probably its best source of publicity.

The program has recently started a business component that was pilot-tested at one site but will be expanded to a total of six sites in 1999. Program participants sell T-shirts, and food (hot dogs, candy, etc.) at the basketball games. Profits, in turn, are reinvested into the business. The "life-skills" learned in operating a business will help participants in other facets of their lives.

One of the more positive developments has been the creation of the Mayor's Urban Symposium and Tournament (MUST) in 1995, and held annually in Kansas City. A total of 12 men's and 4 women's teams from throughout the country participate in this tournament. In addition to the competition, a seminar is held for the participants. This seminar focuses on "life after basketball" and seeks to help participants examine career alternatives.

Lessons Learned

The evaluation of the program has focused on the participants, participating organizations, and level of criminal activity in the geographical areas of program sites. Process-related data were gathered on the total number of participants, and attendance at games and workshops. Out-related data were gathered on outcomes of the educational component and the success of job placements and referrals. Data were also gathered on the extent of interest in participation on the part of businesses. Crime-related data gathered between 1992 and 1993, for example, showed a decline of 25 percent in juvenile apprehensions by the police department. Within this category, violent crimes and property-related offenses witnessed the most dramatic declines (Wilkins 1996).

Any activity that is "played out" at night will have some inherent challenges for practitioners and the organizations sponsoring it. Midnight basketball is no exception. One of the biggest challenges was convincing the community at large that this program was much more than just a basketball program. The expenditure of public funds for the program caused concern on the part of the community as to why must tax dollars be spent on a game. However, through an active effort at educating the public on the multifaceted nature of the program, this criticism did not last. One of the benefits of this educational campaign has been the increased number of sponsorships that have resulted, thereby minimizing reliance on public funds.

There is little question that having the support of the highest elected public figure in Kansas City (the mayor) has not played an influential role in helping this program expand over the years. The Parks and Recreation Department's support was also instrumental. Nevertheless, the creation and support of this program required the support of key stakeholders and the community. The importance of seeking nonpublic funds for this program must be stressed if sustainability is a future goal. Evaluation, as a result, is critical in helping to silence critics and improving the quality of the program.

7. New York City: Henry Street Settlement House (arts)

Settlement houses have long had a prominent place in the profession's history and are considered by many practitioners and scholars to have served a vital role in helping shape community-based services. Settlement houses, as a result of being based in urban communities, played influential roles in helping newcomers to this country make the transition to an urbanized and industrialized society. Many staff not only worked in these communities but also lived there as well. This helped them to better understand and connect with the consumer of services.

The President's Committee on the Arts and Humanities survey of programs specifically cited Henry Street Settlement House and Hull House as important sources of inspiration for present-day arts and humanities programs across the United States (PCAH 1996:21):

> Many of the programs were started in the last half of the 1980s, but their antecedents trace their origins to the settlement house movement and community music schools. Henry Street Settlement and the Third Street Music School Settlement, both in New York City, are now over 100 years old. These organizations offered programs in the arts and culture as part of a constellation of services designed to address the needs of poor European immigrants. The same can be said of Hull House in Chicago, started in 1898 by social work pioneer Jane Addams.

The case example of Henry Street Settlement House (HSSH) was selected for four primary reasons: (1) its historical role in the history of the social work profession; (2) the role of social workers in youth programming involving the arts and sports; (3) the multifaceted approach it has taken to programs involving new arenas; and (4) the extent to its programming has actively engaged youths from various ethnic and racial backgrounds. This case study, however, will focus on the arts programs.

Context Setting

Henry Street Settlement House is located on the Lower East Side of Manhattan and has an illustrious history within the field of social work. As a settlement house, it played a pivotal role in helping thousands of immigrants to New York City during the late nineteenth century and well into the twentieth century. Its mission of helping America's newcomers continues to this day and will undoubtedly do so into the twenty-first century. HSSH's commitment to children can be traced back to the opening of its doors in 1893. In 1902 it opened one of New York City's earliest playgrounds in order to provide children with an alternative to unsafe streets for play. In 1915 it established the Neighborhood Playhouse (Henry Street's Art Center), in 1927 it opened the Henry Street Music School, and in 1975 the Arts for Living Center, now called the Abrons Art Center, was established (PCAH 1996).

The Abrons Art Center has an annual budget of approximately $800,000, derived from fees charged participants (sliding scale), foundations, corporations, and government, including the National Endowment for the Arts. Both male and female participants are served through its various programs, some of which are based in local public elementary and junior high schools. In essence, programming takes place at the center and other community-based sites, increasing accessibility for youth.

Project Specific Information

Henry Street Settlement House operates a number of youth-focused programs. A series of projects regarding the arts operate out of the Abrons Arts Center. Another set of projects operate out of the Youth Services Department. The Abrons Arts Center is currently in the midst of undertaking an extensive membership drive (2,000 by 2000!) in an effort to expand the use of its services. The campaign's goal is to increase membership and broaden the use of the Center. The Abrons Art Center offers a wide variety of programs emphasizing the visual and performing arts (dance, drama, music, and visual arts). It offers programs for both youths and adults, as well as performances for the community at large.

• The dance program "develops an awareness of space, creativity, rhythm, energy and coordination through modern, jazz, tap, ethnic and ballet for beginning, intermediate and advanced students." Students, after consultation from the dance director, are placed in dance classes based on their talents, rather than age-determined.

• The music program traces its origins back to 1925 and offers participants instruction in voice and over twenty-five instruments. It also provides students an opportunity for performing experiences with professional musicians in Henry Street events.

• The drama program provides instruction in: (1) creative dramatics (ages 5–9); (2) acting (ages 8–13); and (3) musical theater (ages 8–13)—acting, singing, and dancing. Adolescents (ages 13–19 have access to instruction in: (1) acting (introduction and advanced); (2) music and movement for theater; (3) Chinese Theater Workshop (explore contemporary and traditional Chinese Theater taught in Cantonese, Mandarin, and English); (4) play writing (through the Urban Youth Theater); and (5) introduction to theater design and production (design and production of set, lights, and sound through internships in professional theaters). The Abrons Arts Center has three indoor theaters that allow youths to perform, as well allow visiting companies and professional artists to perform.

• The visual arts program provides instruction for children as young as 2 years old to adolescents as old as 15: (1) ceramics; (2) experimental art; (3) parent/toddler art; (4) mixed media; (5) cartooning; and (6) the Saturday Visual Arts Academy. The Academy is a program for adolescents in grades 6 to 9, and seeks to develop their skills in drawing and painting in order for them to prepare a portfolio for entrance to specialized art high schools. In addition, youths visit museums, galleries, and artists' studios. The Abrons Arts Center also offers youths ages 6 to 12 a summer art camp.

The Abrons Arts Center has an Arts in Education program that is a partnership between the Center and several local public schools. As noted by the Henry Street's director of Visual Arts and Arts in education (NHS 1998:3): "It used to be that arts activities were isolated, separate from the life of the classroom. We are trying here to make the arts an integral part of basic education." This project, like the others sponsored by the Center, entails a collaborative partnership involving professionals, in this case architects. An architect visits classes every week and teaches students about architectural history and design techniques. However, students, earlier in the course of study, undertake designs of sections of their school such as the library or other designs such as "the ultimate lounge chair" in an effort to foster their creativity. Their experiences in studying and designing architecture involves them in learning math, writing, social studies, and communication skills. Attendance in these grades is over 95 percent, far above the city average.

The Urban Youth Theater (UYT) is a company composed of adolescents, male and females, ages 13 to 17. Auditions determine who will be a part of the company. Participants enroll in Master Classes through the Production Lab Workshops, which meet weekly. The goal (NHS 1996:3): "to expose youth to all parts of theater; they do not have to master each one, but we want to help them find their place. We want them to see that there is a need for their ideas on stage, and that they can make the theater in their own image."

The Urban Youth Theater brings together all of the key elements of the Abrons Arts Center (NHS 1996:4):

Helping to create America's new voice in theater—this is the mission of Urban Youth Theater. And this voice, as it's expressed in plays written by youth, is loud as it struggles with the rules and expectations of parents, and it is joyous as it remembers childhood romps. And this voice is quiet as it reveals the pain of growing up in a home where alcohol flows freely, and it is giddy as it delights in a crush on the boy next door. It is a chorus, really, made up of 30 young actors—from all boroughs of the City— who form the core of the Arts Center's newest drama project, the Urban Youth Theater.

UYT does not set as a goal to make youths professionals in theater, although many have been very successful in winning competitive scholarships to continue their studies in theater. In 1996 five male members were invited to join the Alvin Ailey Dance Theater and a female member joined the Ballet Hispanico Company (NHS 1996:4): "UYT is not trying to make everyone professional. Instead, we want kids to be open to art, and to see how theater teaches you that there are lots of ways of thinking, and lots of ways of being in this world." Thus, continuing in the arts is an option for those with the talents and the goal of doing so. Most, however, do not continue but are able to transfer the lessons learned into other areas of their lives.

HSSH's youth services programs are multifaceted in nature. The Urban Force Program's goals, for example, seeks to help youths develop greater environmental awareness, skills, and to positively change their physical environments (HSSH 1999:1): "Involve youth in active and engaging experiences that enhance their awareness of their personal potential and the environment, and; Respond to locally-identified issues and engage local community groups in program planning and implementation."

Urban Force consists of four programs (Tree Maintenance, Furniture Recycling, Recycle-A-Bicycle, and Artscape). Artscape will be the object of this case study because of its focus on the arts. The goals of Artscape are (HSSH 1999:4): "Youth learn art skills and develop a responsibility to the immediate environment and community by working with artists. Through a variety of projects such as graffiti removal, maintaining walkways and bikeways, and murals, streetscape beautification is also achieved."

The Artscape Program is multifaceted and targets 12 youths ages 14 to 17. This program's artistic aspect uses various art mediums such as mural painting, canvas art, and sculpturing. Youths are involved in a variety of activities that facilitate their expressions of emotions and creativity. Workshops focus on having them develop their artistic talents, learn math, chemistry, and other academic subjects and apply them to art projects such as mural painting. One project involved painting murals on a series of security gates within a vacant commercial complex as a way of making the premises more attractive to potential renters. Another project involved painting a large-size mural in a municipal parking lot. This use of art is very successful in achieving this development goal, in addition to beautifying the environment.

Youths also get tutoring and guidance concerning higher education as part of the program. The guidance counselor is a social worker with a community organizing background. Graduates of the program, for example, often go on to obtain a college level education and through Henry Street's employment programs are hired during the summer. Providing jobs for graduates also serves to provide youths with role models they can relate to.

This program, like the others noted in this section, takes a holistic view of youths and seeks to address their social and educational needs. Youths see a career counselor as part of their involvement. Those who need help with nonprogram-related issues see social workers in the settlement house or, where there are severe emotional needs, at a mental health clinic.

Lessons Learned

The lessons learned by HSSH must, of course, be placed within a historical context. Youth development activities have been a part of HSSH since its very origin and, as shown by the arts programs, continue to be a major part of its mission. The youth development field, too, has evolved over history and the Abrons Arts Center is an example of how the arts have continued to play a prominent role in Henry Street, just as they did in the beginning of the settlement house programs.

The programs are subject to varying formal evaluation procedures. The Artscape program, for example, involves the following aspects. Program participants undergo an intake and assessment of their strengths and needs. This assessment serves to better inform staff in the development of individual goals. There is a pre- and post-educational assessment that involves staff having access to academic records. Youths are required to show staff their report cards every quarter. Periodic follow-ups with graduates is also undertaken. Parents provide program staff with permission to access school records.

The arts programs initiated at Henry Street all take a holistic perspective toward young participants and actively seek to involve parents and schools. In addition, there is an effort to help youths develop a more balanced view toward activities. Every effort is made to help youths try new activities. Partnerships and collaborations are essential when taking a holistic view of youths. These collaborations also serve to maximize available resources in service to youths. Collaborations not involve other agencies, in this case other settlement houses, but also reach out to the artistic community.

Youths are expected to play leadership roles within the programs. However, in order to do so they must play a meaningful role in decision making within the programs. This requires that the organization makes an investment in their development of skills related to decision making. Preparation for undertaking advocacy and organizing roles is part of their experience at Henry Street. Although a difficult challenge, it is one that is essential for youths to develop their potentials. They will respond to these efforts when they realize that adults do care and are willing to work with them in the process.

8. San Francisco: Make*A*Circus

This case study does not "fit" nicely into the domains outlines in this book—namely, the arts, music, humanities, and sports.

Make*A*Circus, as it will be noted, is neither "fish nor fowl." However, the case of Make*A*Circus incorporates much of what this book is all about—reaching urban youths in a manner that increases their self-esteem, empowers them, and provides them with an avenue to make a contribution to their community. Their participation in circus-related activities provides them with a "once in a lifetime" opportunity to experience what life in a circus would be like. I know of only one other youth organization focused on using a circus theme, and it is based in Brooklyn (Miller 1999). However, Make*A*Circus's focus on developing youth self-esteem and problem-solving make it a natural choice. Make*A*Circus's uniqueness typifies a high degree of creativity, something that *New Arenas* wishes to encourage among social workers and other helping professionals, and thus it warrants inclusion.

Context Setting

Make*A*Circus was the idea of Peter Frankham, who transplanted his "The Circus with a Purpose" from London to San Francisco in 1974. His early experiences led to the establishment of a nonprofit organization stressing activities related to circus life. The organization has an operating budget of approximately $500,000. Most of its funds (55 percent) are derived from grants, with the remaining income coming from government. Recreational, park, and social service-type institutions contract out with Make*A*Circus to put on performances. Participants do not pay fees to attend the circus performances or workshops.

Program-Specific Information

Make*A*Circus's mission statement reflects the role of the performing arts in achieving social goals: "Make*A*Circus directly links the arts, children's empowerment and self-esteem. Through the magical world of the performing arts, we bring enrichment into the lives of children from all cultures and backgrounds by allowing them to participate in circus theater. Each of our programs reflects our commitment to families and children." it offers a variety of training and performing programs that take place within the Bay Area but also throughout the state of California. Some of these programs are offered through schools and community centers.

Circus Days performances consist of three separate yet interrelated acts that seek to entertain but also enhance youths' skills in the process. The first act (See The Show) consists of a professional show featuring professional circus artists. The second (Learn The Moves), in turn, involves offering the audience an opportunity to participate in a workshop of its choosing. Participants are grouped according to age and interest. The workshops cover such topics as acrobatics, clowning, juggling, tumbling and stilt-walking. The third act (Join the Circus) participants can display their newly acquired talents before the audience.

The Clown Therapy workshops specifically focus on participants who are physically and mentally challenged. Make*A*Circus hires and trains clowns to undertake workshops in facilities. These workshops are provided within centers that serve individuals with special needs, and last anywhere from eight to ten weeks. The goals of the workshops are to enhance existing and rehabilitative programming. Where possible, the workshops also involve a performance showcasing the workshop participants' clowning skills before an audience of family, friends, and other invited guests. Participants find an avenue for reactive expression in clowning. It provides them with a "license" to make fun of authority, and the roles of clowns are sufficiently flexible to accommodate most behaviors.

The Teen Apprentice program provides training and employment to at-risk youth. This program specifically targets youths, male and female, ages 14 to 19, who have indicated an interest in the performing arts, and usually involves forty or more participants. Two training cycles are offered, one in the fall (10 weeks long), and the other in the spring (15 weeks long). The program is offered through after-school workshops during which participants get training in circus skills, and are able to practice these new skills through summer work in Make*A*Circus performances. Approximately 8 teens are hired for these positions. These workshops provide participants with skills related to acrobatics, clowning, face painting, juggling, mime, and stilt walking. However, the workshops also stress development of self-esteem, confidence, leadership, self-discipline, cooperation, social skills, team building, and interview skills. These workshops and work experience provide an important foundation for youths who are interested in seeking a career in the circus. However, most youths acquire interviewing skills and self-confidence for seeking employment.

Make*A*Circus makes an active effort to provide performances in Bay Area elementary schools, and actively seeks to complement curriculum goals of the schools through provision of supporting materials such as curriculum guides, which are made available to teachers prior to performances as a means of maximizing curriculum goals. Performances actively incorporate social messages such as antismoking themes (Harib 1998:E1): "Antismoking is the theme of this year's Make*A*Circus, conveyed through a show called 'Lungman & Windpipe's Excellent Adventure.' Some of the performers start out smoking giant fake cigarettes and acting hipper than thou; by the end of three hours the evil smoke demons Tar and Nicotine have been defeated through a series of battles with the two super heroes of the title—and the antics of several hundred children showing off their impromptu circus skills."

Lessons Learned

There are tremendous advantages to using circus-related activities for reaching urban youth. The uniqueness of this theme separates Make*A*Circus from other youth-focused organizations, making marketing that much easier. The concept of a circus as a vehicle for reaching youths benefits from a general feeling that a circus will be fun. However, the very advantage is also a disadvantage—namely, youths can relate to sporting activities, the arts, etc., but what can a circus-related activity have to offer them?

Also, the concept of a circus as a youth-development organization is so unusual that many funders have a hard time thinking of its potential beyond a narrow area. Thus, it faces the challenge of not being taken very seriously by funders. After all, how "can we quantify laughter." The uniqueness of Make*A*Circus is also a barrier in the area of "what is it." It is not an arts organization, although it views its work as performing arts; it is not a social service organization, in an conventional way, although it provides services than can be considered "social." Although contact with social workers is minimal, Make*A*Circus does come into contact with them when visiting facilities or schools. Social workers, as a result, are in a position to facilitate entry into social service facilities for this organization. They are also in a position to make referrals and provide employment opportunities for graduates of the Teen Apprentice Program. Consequently, there is a role for social workers, although not one that is central in character.

Evaluation of Make*A*Circus involves participants, teachers, and staff. Funding sources, however, do not see the value of children or adolescents participating in a circus performance for a day. The Teen Apprentice Program fits more like the conventional training program most organizations offer. However, Make*A*Circus is much more than that program. Participation in Make*A*Circus can range from an afternoon to several months. Finally, safety concerns and high cost of equipment purchase and maintenance will severely limit use of most circus activities.

It is not possible to truly appreciate the impact of Make*A*Circus by watching it on video, seeing photographs, or reading about it. One must experience the joy, thrill, and fear associated with performing before an audience. It is the difference between "actual reality" and "virtual reality." Participation takes on added meaning in a circus, and Make*A*Circus provides youths who have experienced difficulties in life with an opportunity to develop self-confidence, and to do so in a manner that is fun in nature.

9. Washington, D.C.: Video/Action Fund (Humanities)

The use of video as a means of capturing a community's history has provided many organizations, particularly those targeting youth, with a mechanism that brings together many aspects associated with youth development. The skills necessary to create a video with significance cover a wide range from the technical, research, production, and writing, to actual showing and distribution of the video. Today's youths have grown up in an era where videos are an integral part of their lives. Being able to produce a video, then, is not alien to them, and provides an organization with a great opportunity to enhance their skills and accomplish a community service in the process.

The Anacostia history project, which was featured in a documentary entitled "Who's Gonna Sing Our Song?" (South East Washington, D.C.) is an excellent example of the integration of various media within a humanities context. A well-accomplished video focused on answering important questions pertaining to identity is best done using a mixture of media and activities. A community, as the case here, can best be defined from multiple perspectives, allowing a variety of interpretations to unfold. The concept of empowerment is evident throughout this project and is not restricted to the participants, with the community also benefiting from a conscious effort to enhance its capacity.

Video/Action Fund, a not-for-profit production company that produces videos on a wide range of subjects and age groups, is not a "conventional" youth-serving organization. This case, nevertheless, reflects how an organization without a specific youth-focus can contribute to youth development and, in doing so, achieve an acclaim that can be shared by other aspects of the organization. Although the budget for the video can be considered on the "high-end" for most organizations, the project is sufficiently flexible as it allows organizations to adopt or drop various dimensions to accommodate a more "modest" budget.

Context Setting

Video/Action Fund was established in 1990 and, as it embarked on the "Who's Gonna Sing Our Song" Anacostia history project, the organization's operating budget was approximately $200,000. Video/Action Fund raised $125,000 over a three-year period from a variety of local foundations and government sources, $15,000 being the largest amount from any one source. Being in the nation's capital did not play an influential role in helping Video/Action Fund have access to major funding sources and key public and private sectors. Nevertheless, Washington, D.C., typifies the struggles of other similar communities across the United States.

The project's inception can be traced to Video/Action Fund's founder volunteering at a local junior high school to tutor youths involved with "I have a Dream Foundation." She managed to enlist the support of two colleagues to act as tutors at this school. The youths, however, were much more interested in activities other than those typically associated with tutoring. The youths in this program had a room set aside for them and had the benefit of a full-time, outside-of-school person to help them. It so happened that this person had a keen interest in Anacostia, with her family being one of the original families in this community. A combination of the right people and timing played key roles in bringing the project to fruition.

The title of the video raises the question concerning who will speak about the community from a positive viewpoint rather than one that is negative and emphasizing gangs, killings, and drugs—in essence, who will sing their praises? "Who's Gonna Sing Our Song?" utilizes many of the principles common to most social workers such as empowerment, participation, community ownership, etc. This project was created by Video/Action Fund in 1991 as the Anacostia History Project with the following goal: "It was our hope that if the young people knew their own story, they would have their sense that their community mattered, and that they could draw on the strength of the past as they looked toward building a brighter future" (Video/Action Fund 1991:3).

Project-Specific Information

The project involved 60 adolescents, males and females (group called the Johnson Dreamers) over a three-year period as they progressed from junior high school to high school. They actively participated in the production of a video documenting their journey of exploration and affirmation of their

African-American identity. This journey involved the use of poetry, songs, photographs, essays, performances, and a video. Whose Gonna Sing Our Song? Project involved youths in seeking answers to such basic questions as "Who am I?" "Where did I come from?" "Where did my neighborhood come from?" "Is this place special?" Local artists and other community resources were used to help participants find the answers.

The project stresses the importance of youths having a awareness of the history of their community from a positive perspective. Unfortunately, that was very difficult for them to achieve without a special effort do so (Video/Action Fund 1991:2):

> Unfortunately, today, many of Anacostia's young people are unaware of their own important history. As is the case in so many urban areas in America, many young people in Anacostia are caught up instead in the day to day struggles of life in the inner city—violence, drugs, poverty. Anacostia's rich past is being obscured by its troubled present. As a result, many of Anacostia's youths have no idea of their community's story— and what's more, many seem to be resigned to the fact that things have always been bad there and cannot be improved.

The project was conceptualized as consisting of three distinct yet inter-related components, spanning a three-year period (following students from junior high to high school): (1) participants needed to use their own stories to discover their community's history—involvement of family, particularly elders, was instrumental in achieving the goals set out in this component; (2) participants were required to use a multimedia approach to document-ing that story and their current success—use of still and video cameras, audio recorders, music, and written materials (history was considered mul-tilayered, thus requiring a multimethod approach to recording and telling it); and (3) participants were required to "tell" their stories to the public as a means of sharing their experience with other community residents. These three components served to bring aspects of the history of Anacostia to life for the participants and the community they lived in.

Any effort to reproduce this type of project and experience should use a variety of approaches in addition to showing the video produced with the Johnson Dreamers and sharing the book written by this group: (1) conduct a series of workshops on journal writing (participants examine their own personal stories), oral histories (students interview long-time residents), and poetry/arts (participants explore how the arts can be used to communicate community history); and (2) coordinate a series of extracurricular activities that reinforce the classroom work. The latter may mean involving local school papers, displaying student work in prominent school locations, incorporating presentations during events involving adults and other youths, distributing audio clips from oral histories to local radio stations, offering to have students be interviewed on their experience, and inviting local community leaders and elders to be interviewed by students.

The workshops focus on three subject areas (Video/Action Fund 1991): (1) journal writing, with a goal to have participants examine their own personal history; (2) oral history, with a goal to have participants learn about their community's history from the perspective of those who have lived in and built the community; and (3) poetry/arts, with a goal to have participants explore how the arts can communicate history. Each of these workshops provides sufficient flexibility in allowing participants to choose their preferred approach to meeting the goals. Journal writing, for example, can use traditional written journals, video, audio recorder, photo album/scrapbook journals, card-stock paper, newspapers, etc. Materials, as a result, will vary depending upon the type of journal the students wish to create.

Lessons Learned

The potential of video to reach a wide group of people cannot be underestimated. This medium has potential to impact on communities where there is a high rate of illiteracy as well as those with high rates of literacy. Further, the product, in this case a video, can be easily shared by all those who are residents of the community and serves as a vehicle for increasing awareness of community history, a means of increasing ethnic/racial pride, and as a tool for mobilizing a community to action. "Who's Gonna Sing Our Song?" started as a history project and evolved "into a dynamic series of guest artists and workshops on oral history, video, photography and computers. The Dreamers worked side by side with local musicians, performance and media artists and storytellers whose lives are art and true success stories."

Implementing a longitudinal project spanning a period of several years offers tremendous advantages and disadvantages. It allows youths to grow with the project and is much more realistic than a project that covers a narrow time period. Further, it provides practitioners with sufficient time to make necessary adjustments—planning, after all, must be dynamic in nature. Nevertheless, there are disadvantages associated with longitudinal projects. The development of a video, for example, often is considered the "final product" everyone is working toward. If it takes an excessively long time from the participants' perspective, there is a possibility of having them lose interest in the project.

Careful consideration should be placed on the age group a project targets, particularly if it is longitudinal and will have participants entering adolescence at the end of the project. Starting with young participants, those in sixth grade for example, is an advantage over waiting until they are in the eighth or ninth grade. Starting in the sixth grade allows youths to concentrate on mastering certain competencies without factors associated with puberty influencing decisions and actions. Adolescent years take a considerable amount of energy from youths and are focused on dressing a certain way, worrying about how sexually appealing they are, etc.

However, it is advisable not to start too young because possession of critical thinking abilities is important in a project of this type. Finally, it is advisable that staff never lose sight of how youths are feeling and experiencing life. It is necessary to know what young participants are getting out of the project, and how it impacts their lives, without prying. In essence, process and outcome must always be considered by staff. Too much emphasis on one will cause problems concerning the other.

A well-executed video can have a tremendous impact on an organization, as the case with Video/Action Fund. The success of "Who's Gonna Sing Our Song?" played an instrumental role in helping the organization achieve legitimacy from the community and funders, making initiation of future projects that much easier to achieve. The production of a video, too, can serve as an archive that can be placed in local libraries, houses of worship, schools, and other key community institutions. Making copies is inexpensive and can be an excellent way to reach community members who cannot read, increasing its application for a wide range of audiences.

Exemplary organizations for youths are not born but are made through hard work, careful thought, a willingness to have adults share power with youths, and an unwillingness to just "settle" with results. Thus, organizations must be prepared to be dynamic, flexible, and able to admit mistakes when they are made. Organizational abilities, like the competencies raised in chapter 9, require the acquisition of new knowledge and competencies that reinforce the competencies required from staff, in order to carry out a mission devoted to youth development and incorporation of assets throughout the organization.

The organizational domains outlined in this chapter are sufficiently flexible in nature to allow one to consider local circumstances. Nevertheless, these domains are not just based upon my experience in conducting this type of practice. These domains have also been identified by numerous organizations working in the field of youth development and cannot be easily dismissed. In all likelihood, no organization can safely say that it has mastered all of these domains. In many ways, it reminds me about cultural competence—a journey that will never result in reaching a destination. In short, total achievement of the goal is impossible because of the dynamic nature of the field. There will also be new activities, developments, paradigms, etc., to consider in any effort to achieve the goal.

The nine case studies here highlight the exciting potential of new arenas for practice with urban youth in the United States, and illustrate how exemplary organizational qualities get operationalized on a day-to-day basis. The cases bring to life the multifaceted aspects of programming and the many considerations inherent in this type of intervention. Although most of the cases did not involve social workers playing a leadlng role in developing activities, or playing any type of role, that does not mean social workers are not capable of making important contributions to the field of youth development, as noted in several of the cases.

There is much in our education that makes this form of work natural for the profession. Our background in community-based services, combined with an understanding of human behavior and the social environment, culture, and familiarity with the consequences of oppression on undervalued groups, provides an important context from which to practice community social work. The important role of settlement houses, for example, in pioneering the use of the arts, music, humanities, and sports, stands as testament to the "natural" fit of these activities with community social work practice.

The cases also illustrate the challenges that organizations and practitioners face in working with youths, and the difficulties of operationalizing key principles such as empowerment, capacity enhancement, and participation. These principles are, and will no doubt continue to be essential elements in any form of community social work practice. Nevertheless, these challenges are just that, challenges, and not insurmountable barriers. As a result, challenges can be successfully addressed in the course of practice if anticipated and addressed in a systematic fashion. Youth development work will continue to increase in importance well into the twenty-first century. Organizations and practitioners electing this area for practice and service will undoubtedly increase numerically as more and more schools and social work programs offer youth development work as a field of practice.

Child welfare has had a strong presence in many programs across the country. However, with some exceptions, this field of practice has generally focused on child abuse and neglect and juvenile delinquency—important areas, but not encompassing youth development. As the profession of social work embraces a strengths/assets perspective, youth development work based upon this orientation will offer greater options for social work students and practitioners. Embrace of an assets paradigm may very well serve as a key motivator for practitioners to reach out to new approaches to better serve undervalued groups such as those most commonly found in the nation's cities.

Youth development work is not restricted to any one region of the country—urban, suburban or rural, nor to any one professional discipline. This perspective toward youth, as a result, facilitates social work developing new forms of partnerships that are interdisciplinary in nature, further grounding the profession in exciting new developments during the twenty-first century. These new partnerships, however, should not be restricted to the "professionally" trained. The profession must also be positive, and excited, about developing partnerships with community leaders, nontraditional settings, and other sources of indigenous support. Assets, after all, come in many different "sizes" and "types."

The broadening of collaborative options, as a result, provides sufficient flexibility within communities to take into account local circumstances and resources. The examples of collaboration presented here stress relationships that are unique as well as universal in nature. These case examples stressed the need for youth organizations to transcend the usual types of partnerships to embrace relationships that rarely, if ever, existed within the community. These new forms of relationship, however, challenged organizations to develop new language, and create projects that could not exist without collaboration.

New arenas provide social workers, youths, and communities with an opportunity to join forces in the twenty-first century. New arenas can meet pressing current needs and serve to better prepare urban youths for future roles as leaders of communities, organizations, and government. The effective leaders of the twenty-first century in the United States must be able to reach across ethnic and racial groups and create coalitions and partnerships that address undervalued groups within urban areas. Social work can play a role in helping to achieve this goal.

I find it fitting to end this chapter quoting from a message that the Johnson Dreamers ("Who's Gonna Sing Our Song?") wanted to convey through their video project (Video/Action Fund 1991:2):

> We would like to thank you for reading our book. We hope that you enjoy our book and the video. It's all about survival. We want you to know that even though there are many bad things going on in Washington, D.C., there are a lot of positive things that can come out of our young black youth. The video and the book should show youth that we can come together and do something positive without violence being involved. We also hope that you will do a project like ours so people will know that our youth are not out for a joke, but trying to be something in the world. We are the future.

PART III

—

IMPLICATIONS FOR SOCIAL WORK PRACTICE

Part 3 focuses specifically on translating the material covered in parts 1 and 2 into community social work practice with urban youth. Chapter 9 discusses a series of competencies and a framework that can be used in conceptualizing practice in new arenas. Chapter 10 identifies a series of "tensions," or challenges, that social workers will encounter in carrying practice in new arenas. Finally, chapter 11 provides me with an opportunity of making some parting comments.

CHAPTER 9

—

COMPETENCIES AND FRAMEWORK FOR COMMUNITY SOCIAL WORK PRACTICE

Frameworks for practice play an influential role in helping social workers develop systematic approaches to addressing the goals of intervention. A framework, simply stated, is an outline, or guide, that helps practitioners organize their thoughts and influences the steps they take in formulating, implementing, and evaluating an intervention. At its simplest level, a framework will consist of at least four distinct stages or phases: (1) assessment; (2) planning; (3) implementation; and (4) evaluation. This basic outline applies to both micro- and macro-focused methods. However, practitioners and academics will no doubt have different versions of this basic outline, depending upon their perspectives. Consequently, it would not be unusual to come across frameworks that can consist of anywhere from four to ten stages, and identical stages being called by different terms. These differences, as a result, serve to confuse practitioners, not to mention communities who come into contact with many different types of professionals, all of whom may be using different frameworks and terminology.

SOCIAL WORK AND YOUTH DEVELOPMENT COMPETENCIES

There are many, many, lessons that can be applied to the profession of social work and the various methods used by practitioners. By no means are these lessons restricted to one method , setting, or field of practice. This chapter, as a result, summarizes the key themes, issues, and recommendations addressed throughoutthe book, and places them within a context that raises important challenges for the social work profession as we approach the twenty-first century (Bisno and Cox 1997; Midgley and Livermore 1997). The context specifically focuses on urban areas of the country, and targets undervalued youths, particularly those who are low-income and youths of color.

The competencies addressed here, however, are not unique to youth development work and new arenas. As a matter of fact, the competencies identified can be associated with other forms of youth-related services. However, they take on added significance and are operationalized in a particular way as a result of youth development and new arenas. In essence, when social workers contextualize the competencies, they automatically seek to bring them to life in a manner that stresses the group they target.

The next decade will present our country and the profession with a series of challenges that must be successfully navigated if the profession is to maintain its relevance for undervalued population groups in urban areas.

The future of the profession is directly tied to its abilities and willingness to serve undervalued groups in urban areas. The continued marginalization of groups, many of which reside in urban areas, will continue to grow in representation based upon projected demographic trends. The segregation of these groups, combined with an punitive approach to their existence, will make service delivery challenging. Nevertheless, the history of the profession can be traced to work with undervalued urban-based groups, such as the ones addressed in this book. Consequently, this provides the profession with an opportunity to reengage in practice that, unfortunately, is seemingly more and more foreign to most social workers and the communities they supposedly seek to serve.

I am under no illusion that the arenas of practice outlined here are a panacea for all of the "ills" associated with urban life for youths. However, these arenas can play an influential role in bringing together the necessary elements, community and external, that will result in a more comprehensive approach toward urban youth (Breitbart 1998:324):

> Neighborhood cultural and environmental projects . . . cannot eradicate or fill the gaps left by missing social and economic resources or a political environment that seeks to condemn young people for hardships beyond their control. They can, however, play a critical role by increasing the safe spaces within which urban youth can explore the sources of local problems, and envision, and sometimes create, alternatives.

Clearly, policy and programming targeted cities in the United States cannot be successful without also targeting youth. The future of this country is directly tied to the future of its cities; the future of cities, in turn, is directly tied to the future of their youth. Thus, prosperity in the twenty-first century will necessitate this country maximizing its "natural" resources—in this case, its children.

Effective organizations are those that are well grounded in the operative reality of urban youths and make a concerted effort to be an active part of their entire lives, and not just one narrow dimension, and to be a part of their family's lives as well. This ambitious goal translates into an acute understanding of the daily challenges youths face in circumventing the trials and tribulations associated with urban life and providing viable alternatives (McLaughlin 1993:36): "The institutions from which inner-city youth derive support and hope are institutions that are enmeshed in the lived reality—not imagined conditions or construed circumstances—of urban youth." The same statement can easily be applied to professions! Once a profession starts to theorize about conditions and issues without being firmly anchored in witnessing how people and communities have fared, it becomes a profession without "soul," purpose, relevance, or direction.

Social work had its origins in settlement houses in urban communities across the United States. The original social workers who staffed these organizations not only worked in but also lived in the community; their contact (formal and informal) with the community became an integral part of their lives. The settlement houses, as a result, were much more than social agencies in the present-day manner; these organizations encompassed a multitude of purposes and were often thought of as being part of the community, as opposed to being in the community.

Social workers are widely acknowledged to be the originators of organized art, music, and sports as activities for preventing the onset of behavior that could result in problems. These arenas were conceived because they did not stigmatize, allowed for engagement regardless of literacy competencies, and integrated the areas of education, recreation, and therapy into activities, and did so without "professionalizing" social workers in the process—namely, professionals know what is best and they must lead individuals and communities if positive change is to occur.

Although it may seem to be unreasonable to expect social workers to live in the communities they serve, it is not unreasonable. In fact, it would be unprofessional for practitioners not to be personally cognizant of the issues, needs, hopes, and desires of the youths they serve. The community context, as a result, increases in importance when planning and staffing community-based programs involving the arts, music, humanities, and sports.

Practice within this context requires specialized skills and knowledge areas that must be taught in social work education programs and practices in human service/recreational-focused agencies. I do not suggest that education must transform social workers without meaningful artistic, musical, and athletic abilities, into high performing artists and athletes. However, just as importantly, practice takes place within the community, with community being the point of reference to all the activities that are planned.

PREMISES UNDERLYING COMPETENCIES IN NEW ARENAS

Social work competencies in new arenas have as a foundation two basic premises related to youth development work. These premises, in turn, capture the richness in diversity of roles, goals, and activities that must be mastered in order for the profession of social work to make a lasting and important contribution to this field of practice. Youth development work, according to the American Youth Policy Forum, must have as a foundation two basic premises (1995:1):

(1) Youth development is an ongoing process in which young people are engaged and invested. Throughout this process, young people seek ways to meet their basic physical and social needs and to build the competencies and connections they need for survival and success. All youth are engaged in the process of development; (2) Youth development is marked by the acquisition of a broad range of competencies and the demonstration of a full complement of connections to self, others, and the large community. Confidence, compassion, commitment and character are terms commonly used to express the attitudes and behaviors that determine whether and how learned competencies will be used.

These two premises, as a result, help guide the discussion on what kinds of competencies social workers and other helping professionals must either possess or strive to possess in order to bring to fruition this vision of community work. The move to develop youth competencies is very much in line with the trust toward greater accountability in service delivery. In addition, a clear understanding of "what it takes" to make a contribution in this field of practice lends itself to creation of field placement experiences that provide students with opportunities to better prepare themselves for this type of practice in the twenty-first century.

COMPETENCIES FOR PRACTICE IN NEW ARENAS

The translation of theory into practice is never an easy process. It takes on an even greater challenge when the application of theory is done concurrently with the initiation of practice, as is the case in social work. The identification of practice possibilities within the new arenas covered in this book are even more challenging for both the experienced practitioner and the social work student. The use of competencies, however, serves to facilitate the entire learning process and evaluation of interventions. Competencies, however, are not limited to staff, but can also be applicable to youth participants (Fruchter and Cahill 1995).

The acquisition of competencies for work with urban youth, and more specifically from a youth development perspective, takes on added significance in social work. There is much about social work education at the graduate level that lends itself to use of competencies. Professional social work education stresses concurrent field and classroom instruction, lending itself very well for the development of competencies. The use of competencies facilitates evaluating student performance in field practice. Competencies, in turn, must be able to be operationalized within a community context, an arena not foreign to the profession of social work. Further, use of competencies facilitates both process and outcome evaluation, as well as serving to translate a vision and theory into reality.

As observed by the National Collaboration for Youth (1997:2), the field of youth work/development has wide variability in terms of vision, roles, and competencies:

> the portrait of credentialing activities that emerged as information for this report was collected is consistent with the observations of others. Youth work education, training and credentialing efforts are fragmented, lacking a coherent vision and widely varying in their utilization. There is great variation in the quality of content, expertise, and instrumental approaches among staff development efforts. It is becoming more apparent by the field as a whole that all these initiatives could benefit from exploring commonalities and establishing mutual goals.

A number of researchers and national organizations have examined what core competencies are necessary for practice with youth (Center for Youth Development and Policy Research 1995; Child Youth Agency Partnership 1995; Koralek, Newman, and Colker 1995; National Collaboration for Youth 1997; Networks for Youth Development 1998a, b, c; President's Committee 1996; Taylor, Bradley, and Warren 1996; Washington State Child Care Coordinating Committee 1995). These researchers and organizations have taken a very holistic view of youth and the youth development field and have developed a set of competencies that are comprehensive in nature.

The following staff and management job descriptions integrate an assets perspective and serve to help concretize how this approach can be reflected in a "help wanted" ad (Search Institute 1998:17):

> **Youth Worker:** Needed—someone who not only builds strong relationships with youth but also takes a "community development approach" to youth development and is "on fire" with purpose and possibilities. Must be able to build bridges between youth and adults and form intergenerational teams to do community work. **Top Management:** Wanted— someone who understands systems theory, but is willing to get out of the rut of organizational "problem solving and strategic planning"—the world is too dynamic for those tools alone. A good listener who asks herself, "Who else is interested in positive youth development? Have I met with them lately?" Is willing to convene meetings across institutions and systems: nonprofit, private and public. Can lead by asking board members good questions about youth development.

The following core competencies presented into the framework outlined in this chapter are derived from a synthesis of the literature, conversations with field staff, youths, and findings from research studies conducted across the United States, and my own experiences with youth capacity enhancement practice in urban communities across the United States. These clusters of competencies are by no means exhaustive. However, the elements within each cluster represent some of the key competencies that, at a minimum, social workers must either possess or seek to acquire, in order to be successful.

A FRAMEWORK FOR COMMUNITY SOCIAL WORK PRACTICE

Social workers interested in practice involving the arts, humanities, and sports with urban youths need to use a framework that has applicability for this form of practice. There are unique aspects of practice related to new arenas that must be taken into account in the design of interventions. The framework that is being proposed for work with urban youths is one that I have developed and used in other projects specifically focused on under-valued urban communities utilizing an asset perspective (Delgado 1999a, in press). The use of this framework is particularly conducive to working with urban and undervalued groups. However, I should note that the reader may develop his/her own framework, borrowing elements from the framework presented here, and from others in the field.

Effective practice is only possible when social workers take into account context, and the contextualization of experiences is critical in any form of social work practice, regardless of method. Thus, the more applicable a framework is to a given context, in this case urban youths who are mar-ginalized because of their socioeconomic class and ethnicity/race, the more relevant, and thus effective in helping practitioners achieve their goals. On the surface this point may seem simplistic. However, my own experience has proved otherwise. It is almost as if intervention techniques and approaches are applied in practice regardless of context; as if the method is more important than the set of circumstances surrounding the need for an intervention. A "cookbook" approach toward practice with urban youths may have great appeal for some practitioners and the organizations employing them. However, a cookbook approach is undoubtedly steeped in stereotypes, misinformation, and doomed to fail in achieving any worthwhile goals.

Practitioners, as a result, must weigh very carefully their perceptions/biases of urban youths, how they systematically view urban practice, and think about how practice in new arenas will necessitate new ways of creating interventions with urban youths. This chapter provides a foundation from which practitioners can examine each of the critical stages of a framework and select methods that best meet their own individual needs and those of the organization in which they practice. Thus, I am under no illusion, nor would I welcome, that practitioners would take everything that is stated in this chapter as carved in stone and apply it to practice in their own contexts without modifying it accordingly.

Framework

Social work practitioners need tools to help them conceptualize and implement capacity enhancement activities based on the arts, humanities, and sports, to better serve youths in urban communities. The framework that follows has been successfully applied to urban-based nontraditional settings and community capacity enhancement projects such as murals, gardens, playgrounds, and sculptures. This framework consists of five distinct, yet interrelated analytical and interactional phases (Googins, Capoccia, and Kaufman 1983; Hardcastle, Wenocur, and Powers 1997). The interactional dimensions of the framework are particularly important because they emphasize the need for social workers to take into account local circumstances in applying theoretical concepts. Local circumstances and, for that matter, politics wield a tremendous amount of influence on all aspects of a framework, and the framework that is proposed in this book is sufficiently flexible to allow necessary changes to be made.

Please note that each phase of the framework places a prodigious amount of emphasis on the participation of youths and their communities, empowerment, assets, and capacity enhancement. These key aspects, as addressed earlier, must be present in all aspects of a framework in order for it to achieve the desired results. Youth development practice is no different. Thus, the principles addressed in chapter 3 must be realized in each stage of a framework. Conceptually, and value-wise, it is not possible to seek youth participation in decision making, for example, in the initial phase (identification and assessment), and not seek it during the evaluation phase. Consistency is critical!

Identification and Assessment.

Identification   The initial stage of any framework is particularly important because it sets the foundation and the direction for future stages. The initial stage in the framework used here has two distinct aspects that must be systematically carried out in youth development work, regardless of context. The first involves identifying all of the assets that can be mobilized within the community at that particular point in time—these resources can involve people (youths as well as adults), space (lots, gathering places popular with youths, building walls that lend themselves to murals, etc.). These assets, as a result, must be systematically involved in the intervention. However, prior to using them in an activity or intervention, a determination of their potential contribution and importance must be made by the practitioner.

Remember that identification, like the assessment aspect, is dynamic and the practitioner must be aware of changes within the community over time. The identification and assessment that is accomplished can best be thought of as a picture of a community at a given point in time. That picture, however, can change over time with new assets emerging and old ones disappearing. The dynamic nature of communities necessitates that every effort be made to have organizations keep abreast of changes.

Identification, the first step of this stage, as a result, can be a very straightforward activity. The process of identifying indigenous community resources is very important and plays a critical role in the identification process. Community assets, it must be noted, can be both instrumental (residents with artistic talents, space, transportation, money, donations of food, etc.), or expressive (provision of support) in nature. Thus, practitioners should not enter into the identification step with a preconceived bias of what constitutes an asset or resource. The successful launching of a program requires many different types of resources, all working in unison. Consequently, a broad vision of resources should take into account those assets that have a cultural foundation steeped in tradition, and with symbolic meaning for youths and their communities. Consequently, social workers must be culturally competent in order to successfully undertake youth development work.

Identification of assets can be accomplished in a variety of ways depending upon time constraints and resources availability. The following three approaches present the most common approaches toward assessment: (1) walking surveys in the community during which residents and key stakeholders are interviewed using a questionnaire; (2) picture-taking of community assets such as murals, parks, playgrounds, sculptures, and necessary notes taken concerning their location, significant information available from residents, etc.; and (3) key informant interviews with key residents and stakeholders concerning their perception of community assets. These approaches can accommodate a wide range in budgets and can be carried out over an extended or shortened period of time, depending upon the depth of information that is required to develop a program. In essence, not having sufficient time and funds cannot be used as excuses for not undertaking an asset assessment. There is sufficient flexibility within this stage to allow for a wide range in types of assessment!

Assessment   The assessment dimension represents the cornerstone of any effort at utilizing a youth development perspective toward intervention. Assessment has conventionally been viewed from a deficit, or needs, point of view. However, it doesn't necessarily have to be restricted to this perspective. By taking an asset approach toward youth and the community, assessment becomes the first and, as a result, the most critical stage in seeking to develop strength enhancement interventions. As already noted, the initial perspective, when taken from an asset point of view, serves to set a foundation for how a framework is operationalized throughout all of the stages.

Assessment takes on added significance in this book because there is so little information on assets within communities of color, particularly youth-related assets. Assessment, however, must be conceptualized as both assets and needs, unlike most assessments which focus on the latter. This, in turn, requires that practitioners pay careful attention to involving the community (youth as well as adults), in order to develop a more accurate picture of the community and as a means of increasing the community "ownership" of the project. Ownership is not possible without participation of the community in the decision making.

Practitioners must be creative in conceptualizing and carrying assessment studies that take into account local circumstances and result in programming based upon local knowledge. There clearly isn't one way of doing asset-determined assessment, just as there is no one way of doing needs assessments. This flexibility is both exciting and overwhelming at the same time. It is exciting because it allows the practitioner to be creative in conceptualizing and implementing this phase. The identification and assessment process is sufficiently flexible to take into account local values and needs. However, with creativity comes a concern that the process used will be subject to intense critique and possible invalidation by authorities, and that the method used may have overlooked important indigenous resources. These concerns are not unreasonable, particularly when this phase is undertaken by undervalued groups, and the phase is used as a stepping-stone for an initiative that advocates dramatic changes in service delivery.

Mapping

For the average person, the concept of a map is one that helps one locate places and roads. However, maps can also be used in a variety of other ways that can help social workers and other practitioners. The use of mapping as a tool is not entirely new to social workers. Social workers engaged in micro-practice have used maps to record client skills and abilities for a considerable period of time (Simon 1994). This form of mapping assists clinicians in developing interventions that tap client assets. However, mapping for macro-practice has only recently come of age, with the 1990s witnessing the greatest period of advancement. The infancy of this method for use in community social work practice bodes well for its future in the twenty-first century. Any method that lends itself to empowerment of undervalued communities will no doubt find a receptive audience within a profession and the communities it seeks to serve. Mapping can be as complex or simple as the practitioner and community want it to be. Consequently, it is sufficiently flexible as a tool to be modified to accomplish a wide range of goals.

The mapping of community resources is a critical step in better understanding the capacities and needs of youth. The concept of community mapping is experiencing greater popularity within youth and human service sectors, both nationally and internationally. The success of bioregional maps in Canada, for example, raises the importance of maps as tools in raising community consciousness and decision making. These bioregional maps have been used to record natural resources within a community in addition to cultural resources. Maps have historically been developed by authorities and generally have focused on roads and streets and been used for navigational purposes. However, this rather narrow view of maps does not have to be the case. Maps can fulfill many other goals and can be undertaken by "ordinary" community residents. In essence, maps can and should reflect the values of a community if they are to be relevant to its needs.

Mapping, unfortunately, has historically been used to highlight problems or deficits within communities—namely, marking where areas have excessive needs or have undergone rapid deterioration. However, mapping can just as easily be used from an asset perspective—what are the current informal resources within a community. Further, most communities have had minimal experience in helping authorities create maps that reflect their values and interests. Consequently, the concept of mapping is very alien to most undervalued groups, and this does not have to be the case. Thus, the introduction of asset mapping within an undervalued community may require that the practitioner spend additional amount of time explaining what it is and is its potential.

The literature has a number of excellent examples of youths engaging in mapping activities for the purposes of tapping indigenous assets for programming (Lewis 1998). There are a variety of ways that mapping can take place. More conventional ways of involving youth in identifying and interviewing community residents, local store owners, religious leaders, among others, in order to determine their community assets (Identification and Assessment Stage). Once these interviews are conducted, youth then take a map of the community and systematically place different colored pins on the map as a means of recording types of resources and their location within a community. Afterwards, they can analyze where these resources are located and make recommendations to organizations for where to tap existing resources and where to infuse an area with new resources.

Other efforts at mapping can involve youths taking pictures of community assets such as murals, sculptures, gardens, and community-built playgrounds, and creating a map of community "treasures" for distribution to the external community (Delgado, in press). Such efforts when combined with a well-orchestrated media campaign can prove very useful in helping a community project a positive image of itself to the outside world, and thereby break down negative stereotypes of undervalued communities.

The mapping process may entail the creation of numerous maps specifically focused on the arts, humanities, and sports, as a means of determining the best (most efficient, propitious, and feasible) form of intervention based upon a community's circumstances (assets and needs). For example, it is relatively easy to create maps of open spaces within a community that can be converted into play areas and gardens, or mapping walls that are located in prominent places within the community that can serve as a canvass for a mural. Maps of these types are not very expensive to produce or carry out, placing them within the means of communities, regardless of their income.

The process of mapping can be fun and educationally rewarding for youths. The actual activity can be constructed as a "game" that requires participants to develop ways of coding information that is important, placing the pins where the asset is located, and then discerning patterns of asset distribution within a community. Certain assets can be color-coded, such as blue for murals, red for parks or places where youth feel comfortable congregating, etc. The analytical tool of mapping can find use in other dimensions of a participant's life. However, it can play an influential role in helping to determine location, or absence, of community assets. This tool lends itself to being sufficiently flexible to account for many different types of assets, or assets that are particularly relevant to certain age groups, gender, and other dimensions.

Engagement

Goals and Activities   The concept of engagement involves two distinct perspectives. One is a goal and the other is a process. The goals of an engagement phase are quite simple—namely, how does a practitioner ensure that young participants and their significant supporters "own" the intervention. But what may appear as simple on the surface can represent a series of significant challenges, particularly when the practitioner does not have a clear idea of the extent that he/she "really" wants to input. A lack of clarity concerning the degree of input/decision making wanted can create confusion and anger on the part of participants.

Engagement, as a result, is not restricted to only one stage in a framework. It also represents a process that starts during the initial stage of the framework (identification and assessment), intensifies during the engagement stage, and ends with the final stage (evaluation). Clearly, it is of paramount importance for youths to have significant input into decisions impacting on them. Input into major decisions is not without corresponding responsibility, however. The process of engaging youths, communities, and funders, requires special attention to numerous factors, all of which will be essential in obtaining the necessary commitments to facilitate ownership of activities. The engagement of key stakeholders must be carefully conceptualized in any form of intervention. However, it takes on added importance with undervalued communities that have a history of suspicion of outsiders and a history of negative experiences of having decisions imposed upon them—decisions, incidentally, that have not led to better lives or community improvements. Thus, sufficient time, effort, and resources must be put into the engagement stage to facilitate current and future interventions.

An additional goal of engagement is to create an environment that is receptive to input from a variety of community sources, including other youths. This goal, like any other goal, can be achieved through a variety of means, depending upon local circumstances and the participants who are involved, including the organization initiating the activities. The creation of an organizational culture that empowers not just youths but also staff will facilitate the engagement process. A focus on empowerment of youths and other consumers cannot be accomplished if staff themselves are not empowered. Staff must actively convey an organizational value on empowerment. If they are not empowered, then they cannot successfully seek to empower youths. Having an organizational goal that stresses engagement, as a result, permeates all aspects of the organization. Board membership, for example, will have residents and youth in the majority, and in leadership roles, versus being there as token members.

Process and Activities   Engagement as a process necessitates staff creating mechanisms for actively seeking youth input into programming decisions. Youths may have such formal mechanisms as suggestion boxes, periodic "discussions" concerning how a project is going, membership in advisory committees, and even membership on organizational boards with full voting rights and privileges. It is important that there be multiple avenues for input since not all youths may feel comfortable speaking before a group. Input can also be on an "informal" basis with staff being receptive and encouraging youths to share their sentiments and opinions throughout the life of a project. In short, input can be both a process and an end result as evidenced through formal evaluation procedures.

A competence in the area of engagement beyond the young participants themselves is never to be underestimated, particularly when a priority is to ground youth services within the community. Consequently, the process of engagement needs to encompass a variety of arenas. Staff, as a consequence, must be prepared to reach out to families within their own homes as well as indigenous institutions that can play an important role in helping an organization undertake youth programming. For example, staff must feel comfortable in going into houses of worship within the community and meeting with their leadership. They must also be prepared to enter establishments that cater to youth such as nightclubs, video arcades, parks, etc. In essence, competence to both enter and engage in dialogue with a variety of people and in a variety of settings is critical if an organization is to reach youths who may be marginalized, and thus in school.

An ability to communicate with various sectors of the community, including elected officials, religious leaders, elders, and other persons of authority, must be stressed in the hiring and training of youth workers. Communication, as a result, necessitates staff to be able to "shift" their approaches based upon the setting. Meeting with community leaders one hour, parents of youths in another, and "hanging out" with youths in a park in another. This ability to be flexible and adjust to the setting is necessary to facilitate engagement. Youth staff, as a result, must be able to understand and respect the culture of youths and their families, including knowledge of the community and family structures and values.

Few organizations will say that open-and-clear lines of communication are unimportant. However, achievement of this goal is often very elusive within the field of human service, regardless of field of practice. Communication is a multidimensional construct. Staff must be keenly able to both convey information in a manner that is well received by youths, as well as understand the latest expressions commonly used by them. Language skills also encompass an ability to communicate in the primary language of the participant. As a result, staff who are bilingual and bicultural are very often in great demand. In addition, communication competencies also involve abilities to develop and sustain relationships with youths that are based upon mutual trust and respect. Language skills, as a result, represent a fundamental competency in youth work with youths whose parents do not have English as their primary language.

Communication competencies, as a result, must entail abilities to effectively communicate in written form and in multiple languages, as is the case with parents who are newcomers to the United States. Staff who have particular strengths in verbal communication should develop comparable skills in writing as a means of maintaining accurate and relevant record-keeping. Record-keeping has taken on greater prominence in the field of youth work, which has witnessed an increase of emphasis on evaluation. Few programs can have the luxury of hiring staff strictly based on interpersonal skills and not worry about their record-keeping.

I have placed great emphasis on engagement as a process that permeates all stages, and as a stage onto itself. An inability to actively involve youths will seriously limit any form of intervention, regardless of one's noble intentions. The engagement stage can probably best be conceptualized as the cornerstone of any intervention effort that must rely upon participant and community acceptance and cooperation in order to ensure an implementation process with minimal roadblocks.

Interventions

The ability to plan and implement programs targeting urban youth is very critical in work with new arenas. Planning within this context covers all facets from assessment to evaluation. Although there are many who would argue that the tasks associated with planning fall within the purview of administrators and program developers, line staff must still have a degree of competence in this area of practice. Planning, after all, is both a method and an activity associated with any form of intervention, micro- or macro-related.

Skills related to assessing youth and community assets and needs, for example, can play an influential role in helping to shape programs and services. Front-line staff are often in the propitious position to have a solid grasp of emerging issues and needs, as well as assets that very often go unrecognized and untapped at the programmatic level. These competencies, in turn, must be recognized in order to help inform administrators as to how best to maximize current resources, structure time periods (days and hours), and highlight which key indicators capture current issues within the community of youth.

Computer Skills   Probably no aspect of youth development work has changed as dramatically over the past decade as computer competencies, particularly their use of the internet (Hahn 1999). The following conversation, although exaggerated, nevertheless, captures the importance of staff having "net" competencies (Gauck and Boyle 1998:8):

> A youth in your program walks in to you one afternoon and begins excitedly jabbering about how she spent four hours surfing last night. She was in a Hip Hop chat room, which was great fun until some flamer came in and started shouting at everyone. So she jumped into a search engine to find a music site that a cyberpal had e-mailed her about, and hyperlinked to a page about her favorite group. She tried to download a .pif file, but her system crashed! She doesn't know if her browser is just lame or if she needs 16 more megs of RAM. While she's at it, maybe she should upgrade with a faster video card and a two-gig hard drive. She wants to know what you think. You think, "Huh?"

Competencies related to computers and the internet are critical for staff. These competencies not only allow staff access to a wealth of information, but also help them better understand and communicate with youths. Granted, poor and working-class youths generally do not have access to computers and the internet. Staff, as a result, are in the propitious position to teach them. Youth, in turn, can then help others learn these skills, including adults (Gauck 1998).

On the surface, the design and implementation of youth programming involving the arts, humanities, and sports takes into consideration many of the same points as other activities associated with social work. Areas of consideration involve attention to the development of contingencies, actively involving the ultimate beneficiaries of the intervention in helping to design the activity, establishing clear procedures and expectations of staff, creation of record-keeping systems that facilitate monitoring and making mid-course corrections as needed, etc. However, a set of dramatic differences do exist when these activities are based upon an asset foundation and seek to enhance qualities rather than ameliorate some condition. Interventions based upon individual and community assets necessitate having practitioners create mechanisms that systematically build upon and utilize assets as central components.

The development and implementation of interventions will reflect the unusual nature of the arts, humanities, and sports. These considerations must address the structure of these activities but also take into account how the arts, humanities, and sports differ between and within. Organizations with little or no expertise in the arts, for example, may have to establish partnerships with artists and/or their organizations in order to offer an arts program. Such a collaborative arrangement may be totally new to an organization used to collaborative relationships with other human service-type organizations. In essence, special considerations must be undertaken to ensure success during this phase of the framework.

Enhancement Skills   Interventions focused on urban youths of color and using the arts, humanities, or sports must address three areas in order to achieve maximum impact and use of resources: (1) enhancement of skills (physical, social, academic, leadership); (2) enhancement of creativity; and (3) enhancement of racial/ethnic awareness and pride. It is not necessary to prioritize all three areas equally. In fact, organizations and practitioners may want to highlight just one, and there is nothing wrong with that. However, all three must be present to a certain degree in order for organizations to successfully address the challenges facing urban youths. The term enhancement is used very deliberately because it presupposes that youths have these skills to begin with, and an intervention will enhance versus develop them.

Enhancement of skills should prepare youths for undertaking activities that are fun and meaningful for the present, but also help prepare them to assume leadership roles in the future. Providing opportunities for youths to develop their creative talents and problem-solving skills provides a foundation for future undertakings. Preparation of youths to speak before public groups, for example, is developing an important leadership skill. Leadership of groups is another. The future, after all, belongs to today's youth. Acquisition of leadership skills, in turn, will not only serve their communities well, but also the nation.

Enhancement of creativity is an essential goal for youth programs. An ability to be creative and having the self-confidence to take chances results in growth. New arenas, such as the arts, require the artist to push limits and seek new interpretations and understandings. This, however, is not possible if youths are afraid of venturing out of the world they know and feel comfortable with. Creativity, unfortunately, is not a skill that is often valued in education, particularly at the elementary and high school levels. Thus, there are few places youths can acquire the skills and confidence to make the contributions they are quite capable of making.

Enhancement of racial/ethnic awareness and pride fulfills many different important goals. It not only helps youths function in a multicultural world when they know more about groups that are different from themselves, but also develops skills that facilitate functioning within mixed racial and ethnic groups. This ability to function within diverse groups will serve youths very well as they prepare to enter the world of work. Ethnic and racial pride, in turn, is essential if youths are to have the confidence to venture out into a new and challenging world, one that will require them to have a solid grasp of themselves and a willingness to make the external world develop a more realistic view of communities of color, a view that is not dominated by deficits and stereotypes.

Funding   Interventions must actively seek to utilize external funding as a means of further enhancing community capacity (Delgado, in press; Lakes 1996; Lerner 1995). As a result, efforts to "recirculate" funding by buying locally is one way of accomplishing this goal. Hiring and training local residents is another.

The effort to keep as much funding within the community as possible further serves to "anchor" the program within the community, and for residents to benefit from youth activities even though they may not be participating directly in them. Such an effort is not unusual or difficult to accomplish since there are countless numbers of instances were a product or service can be purchased within the community. Catering events, for example, may involve local restaurants or grocery stores. Purchase of airplane tickets can also be purchased through local travel agents. I have gone so far as to purchase gasoline using local gas stations.

Transformation of Environment   Interventions that also serve to dramatically change the unpleasant aspects of the environment are also important. Activities that physically result in a transformation of an area that would normally be a "blight" on the community have multiple benefits—young participants, their families, and community all benefit. For example, the transformation of a wall from one that is covered with graffiti to one with a mural not only beautifies an area but also serves as a message board to the outside world concerning themes of importance to a community. The transformation of an abandoned lot, from one that is a repository of broken glass, trash, cars into a park where concerts and exhibitions can be held, can be an impressive contribution by youths to their community.

Bringing together youths, professional artists and performers, athletes, and other personnel with a community capacity enhancement agenda (hopefully some of whom are social workers), can serve as a powerful formula for creating partnerships that enhance the capacities of all parties to successfully work together to bring about social change. Consequently, collaborative partnerships should be an integral part of any form of intervention involving new arenas (Lakes 1996). The nature and extent of collaboration, of course, will be determined by local circumstances. However, the principles associated with collaborative partnerships must always be present!

It is important to stress that youth development goals are not achievable without meaningful participation on the part of the most important stakeholder—the youths themselves (Lakes 1996:133): "seeking answers to our more vicious social problems is possible when citizens of all ages come together in a common struggle—a grassroots, voluntary activism that recognizes the educational process within political empowerment. Young people are integral to learning communities where pedagogy informs development." A strengths perspective toward youth, as a result, can only have a true and lasting impact if youths are integral parts of the decision making, implementation, and evaluation process. In essence, interventions must be youth-centered and determined.

Activities Programming   Staff competencies in the area of programming and group work are critical components of their daily work routines. Social groupwork, as noted in earlier chapters, has its origins in communities and youth-related activities such as sports, etc. This legacy, unfortunately, has been lost and it is not uncommon to find social workers with minimal or no competencies in working with groups. These activities invariability take place within a group modality, requiring youth staff to be able to compose and facilitate groups. Groups also provide participants with an opportunity to strengthen their relationship skills with peers.

The ability to effectively respond to youths' needs necessitates possessing competencies in both motivating youths and planning daily activities. Motivational work is very important in helping urban youths to surmount the numerous obstacles they encounter in school and community. Motivational messages, therefore, have greater impact when the person making the speech, so to speak, has shared many of the experiences youths are facing, and has successfully met the challenge.

An ability to plan daily activities and motivate youths to actively participate is very much a part of youth work. Youths, like adults, are not always willing to carry out their daily activities. Staff, as a result, must be competent in selecting appropriate activities for the goals of the program as well as taking into consideration the "state of mind" of participants on that particular day. In essence, successful programming of activities must systematically weigh goals versus circumstances. Failure to achieve this balance through flexibility may seriously undermine the ultimate goals of any program.

Advocacy/Networking   The disadvantaged position many urban youths of color face in our society very often requires staff to use advocacy techniques to ensure that youths' rights are not violated. Advocacy competencies, in these instances, require staff to play pivotal roles in obtaining necessary resources for youths and also bringing about system changes. Youths who are consistently being monitored by school authorities and law enforcement systems will often turn to staff to advocate for them. Staff, in turn, must be comfortable with this role. It is not unusual, after all, for advocacy work to entail pushing others into carrying out their responsibilities. Such pushing, however, may not make many friends for a youth worker, and the staff member must be prepared for the consequences of being a successful advocate. Advocacy is not just a technical process—there is also an emotional component that must be recognized and addressed in training and supervision.

Networking competencies, on the other hand, require staff to have an in-depth knowledge of external systems, as well as in-depth knowledge and skills related to finding appropriate schooling experiences for youths, and helping them make informed career choices. Referral and follow-up are not unusual activities for youth staff. Staff may also be called upon to help significant adults in a participant's life, and must be prepared to assist as much as possible in this area.

Achievement of youth development goals, like those associated with cultural competence, can best be conceptualized as a journey without a final destination. In short, there is always room for improvement and change in interventions stressing strengths and new arenas.

Counseling/Referral   Anyone who has worked with urban youths in a sustained manner will attest to the tremendous amount of issues they confront on almost a daily basis. These issues fall into expressive (counseling and advice), instrumental (advocacy, tutoring, etc.), and informational (referral) areas. Thus, any provider wishing to make a significant impact on youths must assume a variety of roles that very often are not part of a standard job description. A good coach, for example, cannot simply view his/her role as teaching fundamentals and serving as a catalyst. A good coach is also a counseling, tutor, advocate, etc. Possession of an ability to utilize a wide range of intervention strategies enhances the value of staff to an organization.

Staff flexibility in designing intervention activities can never be minimized. Thus, youth staff must possess multiple competencies and an ability to fulfill multiple roles within an organization. Interventions must take into account the operative reality of the youth it seeks to assist. This "relevance," in turn, is greatly increased when youths play an influential role in the decision-making process through such mechanisms as advisory committees, suggestion periods, etc.

Flexibility in role acquisition serves to allow staff and organizations to be more responsive to participant and community issues and needs. Instead of youth "fitting" into interventions, interventions must "fit" youth interests and needs. It represents the difference between planning for and planning with constituents. Staff that are "specialists" in the most narrow definition of the term make responsive programming difficult, if not impossible, to achieve when addressing urban youths. An ability to be creative in designing interventions allows both staff and youths to take calculated risks in devising ways of meeting goals. The use of creativity, however, is generally in short supply as a result of schooling that rarely places a value on it. Consequently, any effort at sparking creative urges should always be encouraged and supported. Sometimes creative ideas when implemented do not achieve the goals that they originally set out to meet. However, the encouragement of creative solutions and ideas must not be put down because it didn't result in success.

The necessary staff and organizational competencies to effectively carry out interventions will surely test any staff or organization. These competencies, however, are not beyond the reach of those wishing to better serve urban youth. No organization or staff member possesses all of the requisite competencies. Thus, acquisition of these abilities will require active and sustained efforts through provision of workshops, consultation, and attendance at youth development conferences. Assessment of staff performance, with an emphasis on strengths and areas for improvement must play an important role in any form of evaluation.

Evaluation

Evaluation of new arena projects should not only enrich our understanding of the effectiveness of programs but must also serve as an ongoing vehicle for improving programs (Presidents Committee 1996). The goals of evaluation for the young, as a result, are no different than those for any other age group. The challenges, however, when taking a youth development approach stressing assets can be considerable. The following youth coordinator's comments on the challenges evaluators face in measuring youth development work notes the ease in which to measure something occurring versus it not occurring (Witt and Crompton 1996:30): "Part of the problem of doing a cost-benefit evaluation analysis of the program is that you cannot measure what didn't happen. We save lives, but how can you measure a shooting that didn't occur because the kid was in the program?"

There are numerous challenges and rewards associated with evaluating youth development projects. It is not viable to concentrate onlyon process or outcome evaluation. The need for the type of information provided by both is essential for programming. The projects centered on the use of arts, humanities, and sports will present practitioners with a set of challenges on how best to evaluate their impact on individuals, families, and communities. Nevertheless, these challenges must be successfully addressed if there are hopes of receiving, or continuing to receive funds, for programming. There are a number of approaches to evaluating these forms of intervention which will be described and analyzed in this section.

Evaluation is a very important phase in any form of intervention, be it deficit- or asset-driven. The process of evaluation will uncover important information about how to best structure services to maximize their benefits. The information gathered through evaluation will also serve as a basis for seeking additional funding. Thus, there is very little dispute concerning the virtue of evaluating an intervention. However, the subject of evaluation rarely elicits a welcome sign from practitioners, regardless of setting, population group targeted, or services provided. In fact, it is rare to find a staff member who has been through an evaluation process where the experience was positive and professionally enhancing. Consequently, efforts at evaluating youth development interventions will no doubt encounter similar reactions. If staff and youths are not involved in developing the evaluation, they will in all likelihood not see its relevance for their lives.

Staff Abilities to Undertake Evaluation   Staff, and not necessarily just senior management, must have evaluation competencies. All staff must have some degree of competence in helping to plan and conduct evaluations of youth programs (Leffert et al. 1996). Skills in both helping program evaluators design methodologies and instruments can prove invaluable in helping organizations develop better and more cost-effective ways of designing youth programs. Abilities to conduct interviews, focus groups, and other methods of gathering data will help ensure that the data do reflect the reality of youth in programs. Both of the dimensions of evaluation, helping to structure evaluation and helping to carry it, out will require organizations to put resources into staff development stressing these aspects of job functions.

Outcome Studies   Morrison, Alcorn, and Nelums (1997) note that programs that stress problem-oriented services are at an advantage over youth development programs when it comes to evaluating outcomes. Problem-focused services facilitate the creation of short-term outcomes and are relatively easier to measure. Youth development, however, stresses long-term enhancement of typical development, and thereby lends itself to longitudinal studies and measures. Thus, evaluation of youth development activities places them at a distinct disadvantage in "proving" their worth when compared to problem-focused activities.

The continued growth in the field of youth development has resulted in increased expectations on the part of funders for the kind of programs that demonstrate their impact on youth (Leffert et al. 1996:1):

> While many funders understand the limitations, they also want to ensure that the programs they support are making a difference in the lives of young people. There, they usually require program providers to clearly demonstrate several indicators of why their program should receive funding: their youth development goals and/or outcomes and how their program will facilitate them; evidence that their program has "what it takes" to be a good program; and—eventually, evidence of some positive impact on the lives of the young people involved.

Programs making extensive use of outcome studies usually have very well-defined objectives, process as well as output and impact, that are both realistic, based upon their budgets, and that specifically take into account local circumstances. Organizations wishing to undertake such studies must invest anywhere from 10 to 20 percent of their operating budgets (Leffert et al. 1996). Such expenditure of funds, which can very easily be "invested" into programming activities, can seem like a "princely" sum to pay in many communities that have few formal, if any, resources directed to youth development work. Lerner (1995) argues, quite convincingly, that evaluation of youth development initiatives can only be best accomplished through a collaborative partnership having youths and their families (two key stakeholders) playing active and meaningful roles. Their participation must be evident throughout all stages of the evaluation process from the design phase to the implementation and analysis phases. The concept of empowerment, as a result, will guide the evaluation effort. True empowerment, however, cannot be achieved without maximum participation of youths and families.

The results of an evaluation effort stressing participatory principles will not only result in an evaluation where the results have meaning to the most important stakeholders, but will also serve to enhance youths' capacities in the process. Any evaluation of youth development activities must also note the availability of residents and the manner in which they were identified and used in creating an intervention. Evaluation must not exclusively focus on problems and accomplishments, which is usually the case with most forms of evaluation.

A recent meta-analysis of evaluations conducting by youth organizations targeting at-risk youth noted a not-surprising result (Witt and Crompton: 1996). The most frequently cited approach to evaluation was no formal evaluation (30%). The second most frequently cited approach (20%) either used or planned to use crime statistics as indicators of program impact. The third most popular approach (19%) used surveys to obtain data from participants, parents or other significant adults, on program quality or outcomes. Testimonies or case studies followed in popularity (14%). Finally, only 4 percent utilized a pre/post study of changes— school grades, test scores, leisure-related attitudes, and behavior.

Police records, although subject to bias due to selective enforcement factors, often represent an attractive source of data for evaluation, particularly in cases where the funders have particular interest in curbing crime-related behavior committed by youths within communities. It is also not unusual to find programs relying on school attendance and performance records as a means of supplementing participate testimonials and other forms of qualitative data. These types of data are collected as a regular part of doing business by these systems and do not require extraordinary expenditure of funds in order to gather them. Consequently, their availability makes them a natural source of data to supplement other types that are more program specific.

Performance Assessment   Assessment of staff performance must play an important role in evaluation efforts. Performance assessment competencies must be viewed from two perspectives—staff skills in assessing youths and staff skills in assessing themselves. Staff ability to assess their own performances is very important. Not only does it help them organize and manage their workloads, it helps them ascertain when they need assistance from supervisors and other personnel. Their ability to assess themselves also allows them to serve as role models for youths. As in any profession, an ability to reflect on one's own practice and performance is a critical ability that ensures quality delivery of services and professional growth.

Youth work can be very demanding upon staff and their ability to identify when and how they need support plays an important role in preventing burnout and misjudgments that can ultimately result in youths not receiving the quality services they are entitled to. Staff must be capable of identifying their strengths and areas for improvement if they are to be successful in this or any other field. A willingness to be "honest" and "straightforward" concerning their attributes and needs will help supervisors and organizations develop the appropriate support mechanisms such as in-service training, supervision, consultation, and attendance at appropriate conferences.

There is little doubt that the profession can ill afford to ignore the arts, humanities, and sports as vehicles for reaching out to urban youths, particularly those of color who are widely considered marginal in a society about to approach the twenty-first century. The history of the social work profession in the settlement house movement highlights how some of the activities being proposed for the twenty-first century can be traced back to the nineteenth century. However, I am as well aware that few schools of social work have courses, or for that matter modules, specifically focused on using these approaches in the planning of community-based services. Although field placements may incorporate new arenas, in all likelihood there are few. This is probably the result of policies related to placing students in settings where they can obtain MSW supervision. Many of the settings utilizing new arenas of social work practice may not employ graduate-level social workers—thus, a vicious circle occurs.

Schools of social work are in an excellent position to provide leadership in this arena and "legitimize" this form of practice through the offering of courses, using readings, providing field placements, holding conferences, and conducting workshops on the topic. Morrison, Alcorn, and Nelums (1997:331) are cognizant of the profession's potential in the field of youth development services and issue an important challenge to the profession:

> We believe that social work education has much to offer preventive youth and family development programs. The staff of such programs must be professionally trained, and social work, because of its broad, value-based approaches, is better equipped than other professions to provide the tools and perspectives to increase staff effectiveness. New, broader theoretical paradigms and growing knowledge about effective approaches for the development of youth, their families, and communities provide unprecedented opportunities for social work to make a significant difference in the lives of youth. Social work education must listen and respond to the needs of youth and the staff that serve them.

Nevertheless, the challenge for the profession is far greater than one might imagine, even though the benefits may far outweigh the costs. Much groundwork must be accomplished before a social work program can provide a coherent and comprehensive educational program using the arts, humanities, and sports. An extensive review of the professional literature did not uncover many publications written by social workers for social workers. Consequently, a prime source of information on these forms of practice is not available.

The competencies and framework covered in this chapter provide an initial step forward in helping the profession of social work better understand the parameters of youth development work, as well as the core competencies that must be mastered by social workers interested in practice with youth. As noted in the case examples used throughout, some social work practitioners are involved in these arenas, highlighting the viability of these methods for urban practice. These individuals have ventured out into arenas that rarely think of social workers as possible staff for programs. Unfortunately, there are not enough social workers to meet the ever-increasing need in these new arenas of practice. There is, in addition, a tremendous need for evaluation studies that report on process, output, and impact objectives related to these programs as a means of documenting their success and identifying areas that need improvement. Nevertheless, there are countless numbers of studies focused on identifying youth-related problems and highlighting the need for organizations to reach them. In essence, it becomes a catch-22 situation!

All facets of the profession must come forth with a noble, and sustainable, effort at producing social work practitioners with the necessary skills to use new arenas of practice in meeting the needs of urban youth, regardless of color, and do so within a community context. However, urban youths of color are in the greatest need due to the issues of racism and classism that they face in this society as we approach the twenty-first century. If the social work profession is to wield the influence it is potentially capable of exerting, it must actively seek out new arenas that lend themselves to the strengths it brings in serving undervalued communities.

The new arenas created through the use of the arts, humanities, and sports, like others not addressed in this book and awaiting social work attention, can open up important doors for practitioners working in organizations that have historically not employed social workers such as recreationally focused agencies, houses of worship, and community development corporations, to name just three types of settings. Social workers can make important contributions through their employment in new organizations. Further, the interdisciplinary possibilities that will result from practice in new arenas will provide rewards and challenges for the profession that cannot be left solely to field of practice; social work curriculum (classroom and field placement) must integrate content related to interdisciplinary practice. Interdisciplinary based research will open up new vistas for improving the lives of urban youths, their families, and communities. Nevertheless, the future for the profession can look bright, exciting, and very rewarding should it exercise its potential to venture out into new arenas and do so with enthusiasm and skill.

Failure on the part of the profession to initiate practice in new arenas can prove very damaging to social work in the long run, and seriously undermine the profession's ability to exercise creativity, initiate bold initiatives, and limit the types of professionals we can work with on behalf of undervalued groups and communities. There is widespread recognition that youth work, particularly that related to development, will continue to increase in importance in the twenty-first century, creating unprecedented demand for qualified staff (Boyle 1998e).

Further, and probably the most damaging consequence of a failure to act, is the continued negative reputation that the profession will engender—namely, we are rigid, narrow-focused, and incapable of venturing out of an office to work. A profession more interested in status and job security than on reform and seeking of ways to better engage undervalued communities is destined to become obsolete, or at best irrelevant. This reputation is an antithesis of our reputation during the late nineteenth century. Ironically, I am not advocating highly "innovative" approaches to the profession—if these recommendations are placed within a historical context, it is more specifically the nineteenth century!

There is no question that social work practitioners need the benefits associated with the use of a framework that provides sufficient structure to influence process, but that is sufficiently flexible to take into account local issues and circumstances. The framework presented in this chapter is specifically focused on youth development work with urban youths, and provides social work practitioners with an approach through which practice can materialize, and is sufficiently flexible to take into account local circumstances.

The targeting of urban youth for the framework does not mean it does not have applicability to other contexts such as those found in suburbia or rural areas of the United States. However, the context serves to influence how the framework gets operationalized and, by having an urban context, issues that are particularly pronounced in this area will have greater prominence—oppression related to poverty and ethnic/racial backgrounds. Further, indigenous resources usually found in urban areas, too, will have greater relevance to practice for those using the framework, by specifically highlighting the need and importance of using these assets in all facets of the framework.

This framework has both analytical and interactional dimensions that facilitate its practice application within communities and allow local circumstances to dictate many facets related to implementation. However, this framework is only as good as the practitioner using it. In short, a framework is nothing more than a sophisticated outline of what needs to be done in order to bring about a desired change. Practitioners who are not culturally competent nor have an ability to work with undervalued groups will experience a very arduous time in applying the framework presented in this chapter. A tool, after all, is only as good as the skills of the practitioner using them. A practitioner who does not feel "comfortable" in undertaking certain types of work will not be successful in using the tool!

CHAPTER 10

—

SOME REFLECTIONS ON SOCIAL WORK AND YOUTH DEVELOPMENT WORK: FOURTEEN DILEMMAS

The field of social work will encounter numerous "dilemmas" as it ventures forth into the field of youth development work. The field of youth development is full of rewards and challenges that will arise as professionals seek to better reach out to and engage urban youths. The rewards of working with youth have been well articulated throughout this book. This field of practice has tremendous potential for influencing future generations well into the twenty-first century. However, there are numerous challenges that will be encountered that will require deliberate and systematic attention by providers. These challenges, in many ways, will strike at the heart of many of social work's traditional values concerning empowerment.

In this chapter I will identify fourteen dilemmas I encountered in the process of writing the book and at times I will propose solutions or recommendations. These areas of "tension" are an integral part of this field of practice. Both author and reader can argue that these areas of tension are not the only ones in the field, nor are they necessarily restricted to youth work, nor are they new. Heath and McLaughlin (1993) identified several of these themes in the early 1990s. Nevertheless, these areas of tension continue in the field. However, I believe that these foourteen themes strike at the core of the youth work field of practice, and the issues that cut across other age groups have a particular form of manifestation among youths that warrants special attention.

1. "Process" versus "Product"

I could not help but reflect on numerous practice situations when there were two possible approaches to take in making programming decisions—but involving youths in the decision-making process would result in a considerable expenditure of time and resources when it would have been so much easier to make the decision for them. On the other hand, facilitating youth ownership of the process could easily be a final goal, with the benefits of the experience, regardless of the success or failure of the project, representing "the bottom line." However, the pressures placed on program staff to "show" results, often misplaced on a "final product" that could be paraded or shown to the funder, made a decision on process versus outcome difficult to make because so much was riding on the outcome.

Practitioners must weigh the final outcome ("product"), with the importance of "process." They will undoubtedly be faced with these types of situations in their practice. However, I am biased toward valuing process much more than outcome for youths, since their experience will stay with them a lifetime and can influence future decisions concerning participation in programs. It would be wise for practitioners to conceptualize this dilemma along the lines that a "product" without meaningful process is nothing more than an artifact. The process, although labor intensive, must never be lost sight of by youth workers. A more active role on the part of staff may yield a product that has meaning for both youths and funders.

2. Assets versus "Business as Usual"

Sometimes it is so easy to take a "business as usual" approach toward services. This approach is well understood by virtually all service providers, with a distinct vocabulary that brings professionals from different disciplines together. In addition, this approach is usually what the funders want to see addressed by staff. Consequently, a "business as usual" approach is very seductive because of the comfort level many practitioners have with it. In essence, why rock the boat?

The identification of assets is a very labor intensive process because so few individuals and organizations have developed the ability to do so, nor has it been fostered by funding sources. Thus, as more individuals and organizations search for humanistic and successful ways of reaching urban youths, the greater is the need for a concerted effort involving communities, organizations, universities, and funding sources to come together through collaborative endeavors.

Identification of youth and community assets will require that practitioners set aside enough time to create an atmosphere that facilitates asset identification, namely, time to allow dialogue and use of a vocabulary that allows youths to understand the meaning of assets. Youths, like their adult counterparts, are very adept at identifying what is pathological, missing, or a failure in their lives and communities. They already possess the awareness of these aspects of their lives and have a ready vocabulary to allow them to express themselves. However, they no not necessarily have had extensive experience in identifying the positives (strengths) that they possess or that are available within the community. Nor do they possess the vocabulary to identify these assets. Consequently, I am very fond of saying that gathering information on assets requires three times as much time as gathering information on deficits.

3. Cultural Competence versus "We Are All Human Beings"

The importance of youths being able to function in a work that is increasingly becoming more diverse is critical to their growth. This growth must be thought of along a series of dimensions—an understanding of different worldviews, values, cultural traditions, languages, etc. This understanding, in turn, will hopefully translate youths into better functioning human beings who understand and accept those who are different from themselves.

I am firmly convinced that youths, in many ways, are far ahead of adults in confronting the challenges associated with living in a multicultural world. Youths have been exposed to more individuals from different cultural backgrounds than their adult counterparts, and have done so in environments such as schools that involve countless numbers of contacts. This exposure, combined with exposure to music, movies, etc., has necessitated that youths develop coping strategies for interacting with peers who do not share their same ethnic/racial backgrounds. These experiences, as a result, can prove invaluable in future undertakings within the community, such as in the world of work.

4. Monitoring versus Evaluation

Although there may not be much of a distinction in the field, there is a tremendous difference between monitoring and evaluation. The former is usually a simplistic process that focuses almost all of its attention on reporting numbers, most likely how many participants in a program or activity, with very little effort and attention being paid to quality and growth. Monitoring is relatively easy to undertake and takes very little effort that can be well directed to other aspects of programs. However, its value is very limited, and does not do much for enhancing program quality since it does not really look at quality.

Quality, in turn, places its emphasis on determining both process and outcome of an intervention—quality versus quantity. Further, it seeks to gather information on what changes must occur to make the program that much more effective and efficient. No program is perfect. The information gathered through evaluation will serve to inform future efforts. Nevertheless, program evaluation does require considerable thought and effort, which often translates into money.

An asset approach toward evaluation seeks to actively involve youths in all facets of an evaluation. Youths must play an active and meaningful role in helping to create the measures that will be used to judge their progress within a program. Who best to describe the changes in their lives other than the individuals the program targets? However, unlike the more common approaches where youths are asked to answer a series of questions pertaining to their experiences, evaluation based upon assets takes a significantly different approach.

An evaluation process that actively involves participants in all facets also enhances the capacities of participants to both undertake or respond to future evaluation efforts. Evaluation, after all, is usually a mystery to the community, with its own language and procedures. However, if youths play active roles in the evaluation, they increase their knowledge and skills in the process.

Evaluation, in turn, must be conducted in a manner that consistently takes into account local circumstances. These circumstances may involve having instruments and interviewers that reflect the cultural tradition of the groups being targeted by the program. It may also entail having interviews conducted in nontraditional settings, etc.

5. Single-Sex versus Mixed Programming

There is clearly much to be gained from undertaking programming combining males and females. If programming activities are to provide youths with experiences that will better prepare them for living in this society, then learning how to interact with the opposite sex is a worthwhile goal. This form of programming provides staff with a golden opportunity to help shape gender relations. However, having stated that, there is much to be said for single-sex programming, particularly for girls. In addition, creation of a "sense of family," which is often one of the goals of programs, necessitates having both boys and girls co-actively involved.

Sporting activities, however, tend to be an exception because of the almost universal dominance of single-sex competition. The combination of the sexes lends itself to creation of activities that help prepare youths for adult roles. In essence, girls' activities have historically focused on helping them assume future adult roles while boys' activities have generally focused on physical development.

I found, and the literature bears it out, that activities that are single-sex facilitate the emergence of issues that would otherwise not surface in a constructive manner in mixed-sex groups. Further, there seems to be more opportunities for males to find programs to meet their needs compared to those available to their female counterparts. This emphasis (resource allocation) on male-related programming systematically limits opportunities for females. When programming does target females, it invariably concentrates on teenage pregnancy and sexual behavior. This focus, unfortunately, provides a highly stereotype view of females. Programming related to leadership, for example, seems to be almost thought of as being within a male purview. Consequently, staff must endeavor not only to reach more females but also to expand the options of programs available to them.

6. Inclusive versus Exclusive Diversity

I was struck by the multiple ways diversity can be conceptualized by agencies, communities, and youths. The subject of gay, lesbian, transsexual, and transgender, for example, is rarely addressed in the conceptualization of diversity within youth programs. In fact, it is not unusual to have these youngsters separate and apart from more "mainstream" programs as a way of keeping them safe and having services specifically target their unique needs. This effort to separate, however, does not address the intolerance youths may have toward those who are "different" from themselves.

Youth programming must have a broad definition of diversity that goes far beyond ethnicity, race, socioeconomic class, and gender. This definition must also address affectional preferences, disabilities, religious beliefs, etc. In essence, programs must never shy away from addressing population groups other than those that are visibly represented within their programs. Communities, after all, consist of all of these groups. Staff are in a unique position to make a lasting and quite important impact on youths when addressing issues of diversity that go beyond a narrow focus.

7. Parental Involvement versus No Involvement

Although the more successful programs in the youth field have made a deliberate attempt to involve parents in a variety of ways and forums, parental involvement can be a problem. On one level young participants' parents and significant adults play very influential roles in shaping their perceptions of life and other adults. These individuals may often represent the only form of support system in their lives. Consequently, involving them seems logical and advantageous. The more active the support system, the higher the likelihood that young participants can have people who will advocate for them, provide moral support, and serve as role models of positive adults.

Nevertheless, there very often is ambivalence concerning involving parents and other significant adults in youth development work. Staff, and sometimes rightly so, have heard horror stories about abuse and neglect being perpetrated by adults in a participant's life, the same individuals that the youths are trying to escape by joining a program. Consequently, involving these adults may not be the wisest decision on the part of program staff. Thus it is very important that staff to be able to differentiate between parents/adults who are positive and stabilizing forces in a participant's life from those who are not. It is recommended that youth programs make a deliberate effort to involve adults under the right circumstances. In short, any decision that does not take into account circumstances is a poor decision.

8. Youth Input versus Decision Making

There are very few practitioners, regardless of professional discipline, who would argue against having youths play a role in influencing decisions impacting on their lives. Social workers, for example, have no doubt spent countless hours reading and listening to lectures on the importance of empowerment in the field of practice. Nevertheless, there is a dramatic difference between seeking youth "input" into the final decision and having youth "make" the final decision. This distinction is much more than a matter of semantics because it focuses at the very core of empowerment.

It is easy for practitioners working with adults to grasp the importance of a client's or a community's exercising self-determination. However, youths, since they are under legal age for making their own choices, cannot do the same. Thus we are caught in a dilemma of careful crafting situations so that their input is taken seriously rather than that their input is the final decision. It is important that practitioners never try to give the impression that youths actually have the final decision when in fact they do not. Youths are very perceptive about these games. In fact, youths would be greatly appreciative if practitioners have a clear sense of how much power youths have rather than give the illusion that they have a degree of power that they really do not.. This honesty, particularly from an adult, is a refreshing experience for them.

9. "Magic Bullet" versus Long-Term Commitment

There are many practitioners, policy makers, organizations, and communities that are searching for a "magic bullet" that can be used to address the needs of youth. Unfortunately, I must agree with many of those in the field that there is no such creature, so to speak. The answers are complex and require long-term commitments in order to have a chance at achieving the ultimate goal—namely, creating an environment that values youths and provides the opportunities for them to maximize their potential.

The complexity of society, and an understanding that youths cannot easily be compartmentalized according to their needs and issues, dictates a holistic approach that requires major commitment of resources and political will in order for youth to thrive. The holistic health movement can serve as an role model for the profession. The inclusion of a spirituality dimension is also needed to meet physical, social, psychological, and spiritual aspects of youth.

A "magic bullet" has much appeal to some practitioners and policy makers. This simplistic view of life interferes with the development of a comprehensive approach that is long-term as opposed to short-term. Practitioners working with youths realize the incredible set of pressures that they face on a daily basis and how these forces impede youth from seeking positive alternatives. Unresponsive school systems, lack of employment that pays a livable wage and has a future, and the constant threat of violence, physical and psychological, that claims countless numbers of urban youth on an hourly basis.

10. "The Lone Ranger" versus "It Takes a Village"

There isn't much debate about the importance of a concerted effort involving other organizations, formal and informal, in working together on behalf of youth. The professional literature highlights this as an important theme in better coordinating services and maximizing available resources. However, the reality of achieving collaborative partnerships is never easy, requiring numerous meetings and constant monitoring to ensure that all parties are doing what they promised to do. We live in a society that has historically championed competition. Competition, for many of us in the human service field, has been so deeply ingrained that we do not question the value of it.

We spend anywhere from sixteen to twenty-one years competing in school. After we complete our formal education we are thrust into the field and told to work cooperatively across departments and organizations. However, we have very little experience in doing so, and we do not have the skills or the trust to accomplish this goal. Further, we are then told that we should work collaboratively with the youths we seek to serve—partners, if you wish. Not an easy task to say the least. It's much easier, if not less effective, to work alone. To collaborate requires a considerable amount of time and effort that must be systematically taken into account during planning and implementation of programs. Funders, as a result, must also take it into account.

11. Social Workers versus the World

If we social workers are to make significant inroads into the field of youth development, we must be prepared to work collaboratively with other professionals, and not necessarily psychologists, psychiatrists, and other mental health professionals. We must be prepared to work alongside recreation personnel, coaches, artists, musicians, clergy, and just "ordinary" people who have taken it upon themselves to make a difference in a youngster's life. These partnerships, however, will necessitate that we learn new languages, techniques, approaches, and feel "comfortable" in settings that historically have not been seen as home to social workers.

It will take a tremendous amount of patience on all sides before social work can have a significant presence and contribution to the field of youth work. It will mean that communities will once again be home to us, just as they were over a hundred years ago during the birth of our profession. Further, it will necessitate that social work education be prepared to provide the necessary training for youth work, and share a leadership role in promoting this form of practice.

As a result, child welfare, as a field of practice, must be redefined to include working with youths. It can no longer be restricted to school social work, juvenile delinquency, and child abuse and neglect. These are very important areas of practice for social work. However, they are not the only areas involving youth. This broadening of child welfare will also serve to bring in other fields of practice involving youth.

12. An Asset versus a Deficit Paradigm

It may seem obvious from this book that the future of social work involvement in youth development must embrace an asset paradigm. I have not attempted to hide this bias. An asset paradigm is not restricted to any one age-group, setting, community, or method. It has appeal and relevance for all forms of practice. Obviously, local circumstances and situations will influence how it gets operationalized. However, it is never a question as to whether a youth or community have strengths. The question is what they are and how can we tap them in designing interventions? This fundamental difference between these two questions makes an incredible degree of difference in the nature of programming.

However, I realize that a deficit paradigm has tremendous resiliency, pardon the pun. It is a very seductive paradigm through its elevation of us as professionals because of its reliance on diagnosis and treatment. This elevation, unfortunately, provides us with a false sense of importance, a sense of importance that separates us from consumers and their reality. Although a strengths perspective, in various forms, has been an integral part of the profession since the inception of social work, pathology has and continues to reign supreme. Much work lies ahead in undertaking research using an asset paradigm, and introducing it into all facets of our social work curriculum and fields of practice. Funders have played an important role in fostering reliance on a deficit perspective by their stressing classification systems that place youths and other undervalued groups into categories in order for services to qualify for reimbursement. Consequently, I am under no illusion concerning the uphill battle that lies ahead as we venture forth in promoting a strengths perspective for urban youth.

13. Asset-Based Practice with All Youths versus Some Age-Groups

One of my colleagues (Irene Fassler) has raised this subdilemma in her writings and presentations. Namely, at what point do we practitioners start thinking of youths as having assets. Conventional wisdom states that it usually occurs during preadolescence—for some reason, younger children do not have assets?

I believe that youths of all ages have assets that can be tapped in developing programs and activities. These assets, however, must be placed within a developmental stage perspective.

The process of determining what strengths can be tapped at what developmental stage will prove challenging, but also rewarding. This information will help us develop mechanisms for tapping and enhancing these strengths throughout the life-cycle. The concept of empowerment, as a result, doesn't necessarily "kick-in" at a particular age. Empowerment practice, at least as I conceptualize it, must find its way into practice with all age-groups for it to have true meaning. Youths will no doubt benefit, and indirectly everyone, when they have experience in practicing methods that help actualize their abilities. The earlier their experience begins, the greater their potential as they grow up.

14. Specialist versus Generalist

Social work education has struggled over how to structure curriculum to best prepare social workers for practice. The struggles have taken many shapes and foci. However, the struggle of specialist versus generalist has been significant. The pressure to specialize is very often driven by outside forces that have historically placed greater value on the specialist. However, in the area of youth development in new arenas, the need is for the generalist—namely, staff who not only have a willingness to assume multiple roles, but do so because of the value of this orientation.

The needs youth present necessitate that staff be flexible in how they conceptualize their role. A generalist approach provides youth-serving organizations with the greatest flexibility in designing and delivering programs. This flexibility, in turn, is built into the job descriptions, hiring process, evaluations, etc., as a means of better serving youth. In short, staff are expected to fulfill multiple roles, and the necessary support (supervision and training) are provided to ensure that this occurs.

This chapter has served me as a vehicle to highlight key issues and areas of tension in the field of working with youth. By no means are the issues listed the "only ones" in the field. Nevertheless, these issues proved particularly problematic and must be seriously addressed by the profession. The field of youth development, like any other, is not immune from tensions.

Some would argue that a field without tensions is a field in decline. That is certainly not the case with youth development. Debate and dialogue will cause the field to grow in a manner that is more inclusive and result in greater creative energies being directed to better serve the needs of youth.

I hope that in raising these issues and suggesting possible solutions the reader is better alerted to them as they manifest themselves in practice, and as a result, is better able to respond to them in a positive and systematic manner. The dilemmas outlined here touch upon major issues and considerations in our society, further complicating finding "solutions" to them. Issues related to diversity, gender, competition versus cooperation, and the role of youth our world have implications far beyond youth development and services.

CHAPTER 11

EPILOGUE

I could not simply end my book with chapter 10. These ten chapters did not provide me with a chance to raise some final points that needed to be highlighted, or that were not addressed in earlier chapters. The idea of a book is usually confined to a "prospectus" that states its goals, highlights the significance of its content, and lays out a brief outline of all of the chapters and how they interrelate to each other in achieving the overall goal for the book. At no time is there a section that allows an author to comment on how the journey of writing a book (which usually entails several years), will evolve and his hopes and fears in undertaking such a venture. Consequently, it isn't until a book is completed that an author has a full appreciation of how the experience manifested itself and how the journey involved many "twists" and "turns." Countless decisions must be made as content matter is transmitted to paper. This chapter, as a consequence, is intended to provide a sense of the excitement of the journey.

I could not help but be impressed by the energy and enthusiasm displayed by youths and staff who work in this field. Youth development displays tremendous potential for growth in the twenty-first century and this potential, when combined with the energy usually associated with youth, converts into a sense of importance and excitement. This is not to say that I have not come across excitement and energy in other fields. However, it did not match that found in youth development practice. The enthusiasm of staff, in turn, reminded me of the staff involved in the Great Society Programs of the 1960s and early 1970s. Staff not only possessed a desire to tackle very difficult challenges but have done so in a manner that taps their creativity and a willingness to "do whatever is necessary" to accomplish their goals.

This energy is a welcomed experience when placed within the context that human services have been under siege from a variety of sources, and have seriously undermined our mission to address the needs of undervalued population groups in a way that is affirming of cultural background, empowering, and nonstigmatizing. The profession's venture into the youth field from an asset perspective will no doubt help us recapture the sense of accomplishment and joy that our work once symbolized many years ago. Consequently, practitioners should be warned that they must be prepared to "catch" this fever and be prepared to enter an exciting period of professional growth as a result—a period which, incidentally, will result in their coming into contact with other professionals they normally would not work with, and in engaging youths and their communities in a manner they are not accustomed to.

However, with excitement comes anxiety and uncertainty. The rapidly changing composition of communities combined with dramatic changes in the economy, politically, and socially, are bound to create a tremendous amount of ambiguity in practice. Any effort at "searching the soul" will result in tremendous uncertainty and debate between different schools of thought about how the profession should go in the twenty-first century. There will be those who would argue that the youth development field should be left to educators and recreation specialists. Others will argue that the youth population of this country, particularly youths who are marginalized, cannot be ignored by a profession that historically worked with youths in urban areas in the nineteenth century. Clearly, this debate and dialogue is essential for the profession before we can make any significant strides in this field. A lack of dialogue and debate, however, will result in a status quo for the profession, something that I believe is unproductive and quite harmful for social work in the long run.

The potential of youth development to be converged with community development is very exciting because it not only represents an investment in the present, but also in the future of youth, their families, and communities. The twenty-first century will no doubt witness important developments in the area of community capacity enhancement. Bringing youth development within this practice framework will serve to increase the likelihood that youths will play important roles in the creation of initiatives that address community capacity enhancement. In short, youth development and community development are so interrelated that it would be artificial to separate the two. Social work, as a result, can make an important contribution to bringing these two arenas together in a coherent and conceptually sound manner.

On a less uplifting note, I could not help but seriously wonder about the tremendous strides that social work education must make in order to play a significant role in the field of youth development. Conversations with colleagues across the United States, combined with reviews of countless school brochures, left me with the impression that there is only a minimal amount of attention being paid to this form of practice in schools and departments of social work. Thus, a considerable amount of energy and resources will need to be invested into making the profession more responsive to youth development. This, unfortunately, will take a number of years to at least set the foundation for this form of practice, let alone make significant progress and contributions to the field. As a result, I am not under an illusion that the journey to achieving the above goal is short and free of numerous "land mines." Nevertheless, the longest journey does start with the first step! No journey worth taking is ever easy. Growth, which is a goal most social workers and other helping professions seek, can be both pleasing and painful at the same time.

I have had numerous students who came out of an arts and humanities background. Many had undergraduate degrees or extensive work experience in these areas. The opportunity to combine video, for example, and youth groups, opens up countless possibilities for social work intervention. Thus, the "stretch" between applying the concepts addressed in this book to "real life" situations is not out of the question. As already noted, not every social worker will have this background, or have an interest in youth development. However, for those who either have such a background or interest, the potential for contributions is great.

Social work can, and must, play an active and influential role in helping America realize this dream for all youths, regardless of ethnic/racial background and economic circumstances. In so doing, social work will carve out a niche in the twenty-first century that it had historically occupied at the turn of the twentieth century—a niche that I believe will serve to reconnect us with undervalued groups such as low-income youths of color residing in urban areas. Then, and only then, can the profession place the requisite emphasis on the "social" aspects of its work! A youth development perspective fits well within a community capacity enhancement approach. However, as noted by Poole (1998:165): "Nevertheless, to prepare students for effective practice within the community capacity-building paradigm, adjustments must be made in how we transmit theoretical knowledge and applied research." Social work educators, through their teaching and practice, must develop ways of conveying new approaches for practice in the twenty-first century.

It is only fitting to end this book with a quote from the Carnegie Corporation of New York, one of the nations most influential foundations in the area of youth development (1992:77):

In a youth-centered America, every community would have a network of affordable, accessible, safe and challenging opportunities that appeal to the diverse interests of youth. Youth development services would provide meaningful opportunities for young people to pursue individual interests as well as contribute to their communities. They would be organized through responsive program, organizational and community structures. They would be rooted in a solid foundation of research- and practice-based knowledge of the needs of children and adolescents and supported by a dependable and diverse financial base. Finally, they would be grounded on suggestions from youth themselves."

REFERENCES

Abrahamson, M. 1996. *Urban Enclaves: Identity and Place in America.* New York: St. Martin's Press.

Abramovitz, M. 1998. Social work and social reform: An arena of struggle. *Social Work* 43: 512–526.

Academy for Educational Development. 1997. *Girls Programming in New York City.* New York: AED

Acosta, A. and V. Hamel. 1995. *CSAP Implementation Guide: Hispanic/Latino Natural Support Systems.* SAMHSA. Rockville, Md.: Center for Substance Abuse Prevention.

Aguliar, M. A. 1996. Promoting the educational achievement of Mexican-American young women. *Social Work in Education* 18: 145–156.

Alder, P. A. and P. Alder. 1998. *Peer Power: Preadolescent Culture and Identity.* New Brunswick, N.J.: Rutgers University Press.

Alexander, B. 1997. Juvenile arson on steady rise as prevention programs die. *Youth Today* 6(1): 53–55.

Alexander, B. 1998a. White House plugs in to youth workers for school violence remedies. *Youth Today* 7: 8–10.

Alexander, B. 1998b. Museums fling open doors to youth programs. *Youth Today* 7: 16–18.

Alexander, B. 1999. U.S. juvenile justice gets busted. *Youth Today* 8: 56, 29.

Alexander, J. 1995. Introduction. In L. Costello, ed., *Part of the Solution: Creative Alternatives for Youth,* p. ii. Washington, D.C.: National Assembly of State Arts Agencies.

Allen, L., J. Denner, H. Yoshikawa, E. Seidman, and J. L. Aber. 1996. Acculturation and depression among Latina urban girls. In B. J. R. Leadbeater and N. Way, eds., *Urban Girls: Resisting Stereotypes, Creating Identities,* pp. 337–352. New York: New York University Press.

American School Health Association. 1995. *STD Fact Sheet.* Research Triangle Park, N.C.: ASHA.

American Youth Policy Forum. 1997. *Some Things Do Make a Difference for Youth: A Compendium of Evaluations of Youth Programs and Practices.* Washington, D.C.: AYPF.

Anderson, J. 1997. Kids get their 15 minutes of fame. *Chicago Tribune,* November 5, p. 3.

Apfel, N. and V. Seitz. 1996. African-American adolescent mothers, their families, and their daughters: A longitudinal perspective over twelve years. In B. J. R. Leadbeater and N. Way, eds., *Urban Girls: Resisting Stereotypes, Creating Identities,* pp. 149–170. New York: New York University Press.

• Archibold, R. C. 1998a. In the schools, a week to open eyes and ears to the thrill of the arts. *New York Times,* May 20, p. A22.

• Archibold, R. C. 1998b, An arts revival grows in New York schools. *New York Times,* May 23, pp. A1, A14.

Archibold, R. C. 1999. To improve learning and attendance, schools are drumming up interest in after-school programs. *New York Times,* March 24, p. A25.

Aronowitz, S. and W. DiFazio. 1994. *The Jobless Future.* Minneapolis: University of Minnesota Press.

Aspen Institute. 1997. *Voices from the Field: Roundtable on Comprehensive Community Initiatives for Children and Families.* Washington, D.C.: Aspen Institute.

Atlanta Daily World. 1994. "Soccer in the Streets" kids sit with Clinton during world cup. July 17, p. 2.

Atlanta Daily World. 1996. "Soccer in the Streets" becomes national affiliate of the United States Soccer Federation. December 28, p. 4.

Auer, T. 1995. Denver's neighborhood cultures—Colorado. In L. Costello, ed., *Part of the Solution: Creative Alternatives for Youth,* pp. 48–53. Washington, D.C.: National Assembly for State Art Agencies.

Austin, J. and M. N. Willard. 1998. Introduction: Angles of history, demons of culture. In J. Austin and M. N. Willard, eds., *Generations of Youth: Youth Cultures and History in Twentieth-Century America,* pp. 1–20. New York: New York University Press.

• Baca, J. F. 1990. Preface. In E. S. Cockcroft and H. Barnet-Sanchez, eds., *Signs from the Heart: California Chicano Murals,* pp. 1–3. Albuquerque: University of New Mexico Press.

Badshah, A. A. 1996. *Our Urban Future: New Paradigms for Equity and Sustainability.* New York: Oxford University Press.

Ball, A. and S. B. Heath. 1993. Dances with identity: Finding an ethnic self in the arts. In S. B. Heath and M. W. McLaughlin, eds., *Identity and Inner-City Youth: Beyond Ethnicity and Gender*, pp. 69–96. New York: Teachers College Press.

Barker, C. 1995. Creative entrepreneurs: The Ya/Yas of New Orleans. In L. Costello, ed., *Part of the Solution: Creative Alternatives for Youth*, pp. 34–41. Washington, D.C.: National Assembly of State Arts Agencies.

Barton, W. H., M. Watkins, and R. Jarjoura. 1997. Youths and communities: Toward comprehensive strategies for youth development. *Social Work* 42: 483–493.

Beeler, A. 1997. Schools' urban canvas: Chicago is summer patron to young artists. *Boston Sunday Globe*, August 24, p. 16.

Belluck, P. 1998. Fighting youth crime, some states blend adult and juvenile justice. *New York Times*, February 11, pp. A1, A26.

Bemby, R. and A. Tufono. 1996. The real deal: The evolution of Seattle, Washington's, at-risk youth program. In P. A. Witt and J. L. Crompton, eds.. *Recreation Programs that Work for At-Risk Youth*, pp. 81–94. College Park, Pa.: Venture.

Benavidez, M. and K. Vozoff. 1995. Soothing the arching heart of young Los Angeles California. In L. Costello, ed.,. *Part of the Solution: Creative Alternatives for Youth*, pp.28–33. Washington, D.C.: National Assembly of State Art Agencies.

Benson, P. L. 1996a. Beyond the "village" rhetoric: What makes a healthy community for children and adolescents. *Assets* Magazine 1: 3–4.

Benson, P. L. 1996b. Random acts of asset-building. *Wingspread* 18: 7–9.

Bernardi-Reis, N. 1996. Taking it from the streets. *Performing*, May 23, pp. 13–14.

Bernstein, S. 1964. *Youth on the Streets: Work with Alienated Youth Groups*. New York: Association Press.

Berryman, J. W. 1978. The rise of organized sports for preadolescent boys. In R. A. Magill, M. J. Ash, and F. L. Smoll, eds., *Children in Sport: A Contemporary Anthology*, pp. 115–121. Campaign, Ill.: Human Kinetics.

Betson, D. M. and R. T. Michael. 1998. Why so many children are poor. *The Future of Children* 7: 25–39.

Bisno, H. and F. Cox 1997. Social work education: Catching up with the present and the future. *Journal of Social Work Education* 33: 373–387.

Blakely, E. J. and M. G. Snyder. 1997. *Fortress America: Gated Communities in the United States*. Washington, D.C.: Brookings Institution Press/Lincoln Institute of Land Policy.

Blum, R. W. 1995. Enhancing resilience: Toward a new model of adolescent health. In S. Halpern et al., eds., *Contract with America's Youth: Toward a Youth Development Agenda*, pp. 10–11. Washington, D.C.: American Youth Policy Forum.

Bok, M. and J. Morales. 1997. The impact and implications of HIV on children and adolescents: Social justice and social change. *Journal of HIV/AIDS Prevention and Education for Adolescents and Children* 1: 9–34.

Bowles, E. 1995. *Community Development and the Arts*. Pittsburgh: Manchester Craftsmen's Guild.

Boyer, E. J. 1996. Marshaling hearts: Youth; Privately sponsored LAPD karate program gives children discipline, self-esteem, alternative to gangs. *Los Angeles Times*, August 23, p. B-1.

Boyle, P. 1998a. Write stuff, wrong place: Graffiti wars. *Youth Today* 7: 56, 48–49.

Boyle, P. 1998b. In the apple, community service earns youth development dollars. *Youth Today* 7: 48–49.

Boyle, P. 1998c. How democratic are youth organizations? *Youth Today* 7: 14.

Boyle, P. 1998d. Coalition helps to make programs real. *Youth Today* 7: 25.

Boyle, P. 1998e. "More youth workers" pitch soars from cop's lips to Clinton's list. Now what? *Youth Today* 7: 18–19.

Boyle, P. and J. Wolfson. 1998. Youth agencies clamor to stay after school. *Youth Today* 7(1): 22, 24, 26, 28.

Boynton, C. W. 1998. Academy offers Latinos beacon of hope. *Boston Globe*, March 7, pp. B1, B11.

Braddock, J. H., II, M. P. Dawkins, and G. Wilson. 1995. Intercultural contact and race relations among American youth. In W. D. Hawley, D. Willis, and A. W. Jackson, eds., *Toward a Common Destiny: Improving Race and Ethnic Relations in America*, pp. 237–256. San Francisco: Jossey-Bass.

Bradley, D. 1995. Theater reaches out to teens under siege. *Dallas Morning News*, June 21, pp. 1C, 11C.

Breggin, P. R. and G. R. Breggin. 1998. *The War Against Children of Color*. Monroe, Maine: Common Courage Press.

Breitbart, M. M. 1995. Banners for the street: Reclaiming space and designing change with urban youth. *Journal of Planning Education and Research* 15: 35–49.

Breitbart, M. M. 1998. "Dana's mystical tunnel": Young people's design for survival and change in the city. In T. Skelton and G. Valentine, eds., *Cool Places: Geographies of Youth Cultures*, pp. 305–327. London: Routledge.

Bronner, E. 1999. For the homeless, rebirth through Socrates. *New York Times,* March 8, pp. 1, 22.

Brooke, J. 1998. Indians proudly revive a tradition of running. *New York Times,* August 2, p. 20.

Brookins, G. K., A. C. Peterson, and L. M. Brooks. 1997. Youth and families in the inner-city: Influencing positive outcomes. In H. J. Warberg, O. Reyes, and R. P. Weissberg, eds., *Children and Youth: Interdisciplinary Perspectives,* pp. 45–66. Thousand Oaks, Calif.: Sage.

Brooks, D. D., R. Althouse, and D. Tucker. 1996. African-American male head coaches: In the "red zone," but can they score. *Journal of African American Men* 2: 93–112.

Brooks-Gunn, J. and G. J. Duncan. 1998. The effects of poverty on children. *The Future of Children* 7: 55–71.

Brown, C. G. 1995. Devising a national youth development strategy. In S. Halpern et al., eds., *Contract with America's Youth: Toward a Youth Development Agenda,* pp. 14–16. Washington, D.C.: American Youth Policy Forum.

Brown, D. 1998. State grapples with kids charged with murder. *New Brunswick Telegraph Journal,* August 18, p. A8.

Brown, D. 1997. *Thorsons Principles of Art Therapies.* London: Thorsons.

Brown, D. W. 1995. *When Strangers Cooperate: Using Social Conventions to Govern Ourselves.* New York: Free Press.

Burt, M. R., G. Resnick, and E. R. Novick. 1998. *Building Supportive Communities for At-Risk Adolescents: It Takes More Than Services.* Washington, D.C.: American Psychological Association.

Butterfield, F. 1994. Teen-age homicide rate has soared. *New York Times,* October 14, p. A22.

Butterfield, F. 1998a. Guns blamed for rise in homicides by youths in 80s. *New York Times,* December 10, p. A25.

Butterfield, F. 1998b. Decline of violent crimes is linked to crack market. *New York Times,* December 28, A16.

Cabral, E. 1994. Taking a closer look at the news: A new report examines media coverage of minorities. *Ford Foundation Report,* 25, 26–29.

Caffey, A. 1998. Young actors have a stage to call home: Opening of JP arts center is a boost for arts groups. *Boston Globe,* March 1, City Weekly Section, pp. 1, 8.

Cahan, S. and Z. Kocur. 1996. Introduction. In S. Cahan and Z. Kocur, eds., *Contemporary Art and Multicultural Education,* pp. xix–xxix. New York: Routledge.

Calamese, B. 1999. Mural project draws teen artists. *Boston Sunday Globe*, February 21, City 3.

Canada, G. 1998. *Reaching Up for Manhood: Transforming the Lives of Boys in America*. New York: Beacon Press.

Carley, G. 1997. The getting better phenomenon: Videotape applications of previously at-risk high school student narratives. *Social Work in Education* 19: 115–120.

Carnegie Corporation of New York, *see* CCNY.

Carnegie Council on Adolescent Development, *see* CCAD.

CCAD (Carnegie Council on Adolescent Development). 1989. *Turning Points: Preparing American Youth for the 21st Century*. Washington, D.C.: CCNY.

CCAD. 1992. *A Matter of Time: Risk and Opportunity in Nonschool Hours*. Washington, D.C.: CCNY.

CCAD. 1993. *Promoting Adolescent Health: Symposium on Research Opportunities in Adolescence*. Washington, D.C.: CCNY.

CCAD. 1994. *Consultation on Afterschool Programs*. Washington, D.C.: Carnegie Corporation of New York.

CCAD. 1995. *Great Transitions: Preparing Adolescents for a New Century*. Washington, D.C.: CCNY.

CCNY (Carnegie Corporation of New York). 1994a. Saving youth from violence. *Carnegie Quarterly* 39: 1–5.

CCNY. 1994b. Charting new paths to safety. *Carnegie Quarterly* 39: 6–15.

CCNY. 1994c. *Starting Points: Meeting the Needs of Our Youngest Children*. New York: CCNY.

CCNY. 1996. *Years of Promise: A Comprehensive Learning Strategy for America's Children*. New York: CCNY.

Center for Youth Development and Policy Research. 1995. *Core Competencies of Youth Workers*. Washington, D.C.: Academy for Educational Development.

Chaiken, M. R. 1998. *Kids, Cops, and Communities*. Washington, D.C.: U.S. Dept. of Justice, Office of Juvenile Justice Programs.

Chantelat, P. and M. Fodimbi. 1994. Young people, forms of sport sociability and citizenship: Analysis of an "inner-city" in the agglomeration of Lyon. Paper presented at the Annual Meeting of the International Sociological Association.

Chavis, D. M. and A. Wandersman. 1990. Sense of community in the urban environment: A catalyst for participation and community development. *American Journal of Community Psychology* 18: 55–80.

Chavis, M. E. 1997. *Altars in the Street: A Neighborhood Fights to Survive.* New York: Bell Tower.

Children's Defense Fund. 1994. *The State of America's Children: Yearbook 1994.* Washington, D.C.: Children's Defense Fund.

Children's Defense Fund. 1998. *The State of America's Children: Yearbook 1998.* Washington, D.C.: Children's Defense Fund.

Child Welfare League of America, *see* CWLA.

Child Youth Agency Partnership. 1995. *Core Competencies for Youth Workers: Self Assessment.* Chicago: Author.

Choi, A. 1998. Rash of youth suicides fails to interest U.S. Senate. *Youth Today* 7: 52–53.

Christenson, P. G. and D. F. Roberts. 1990. *Popular Music in Early Adolescence.* Washington, D.C.: CCAD.

Cimons, M. 1995. Sure, the action and yelling are part of the draw. But when it comes to martial arts, instilling discipline and teaching kids to walk away from fights are the re . . . ; Kick backs. *Los Angeles Times*, September 26, p. 12.

Cisneros, H. G. 1996a. The university and the urban challenge. *Cityscape: A Journal of Policy Development and Research*, December, pp. 1–14.

Cisneros, H. G. 1996b. Regionalism: The new geography of opportunity. *Cityscape: A Journal of Policy Development and Research*, December, pp. 35–53.

Cobb, N. 1998. Meet tomorrow's teens. *Boston Globe*, April 28, pp. C1, C6.

Cockcroft, E. 1984. The story of Chicano park. *Aztlan* 15: 79–103.

Coleman, J. S. and T. Hoffer. 1987. *Public and Private High Schools: The Impact of Community.* New York: Basic Books.

Coleman, S. 1994a. Project doesn't shrink from using "tough love" with inner-city kids. *Atlanta Journal and Constitution*, April 14, p. E16.

Coleman, S. 1994b. Their aim is create an "Avenue of the arts." *Boston Globe*, April 17, p. 1.

Coleman, S. 1998a. After a few lost serves, Dorchester tennis club rallies. *Boston Globe*, April 26. City, p. 14.

Coleman, S. 1998b. July 26. Diving into life lessons: In scuba class, youths learn to reach the top. *Boston Sunday Globe*, City, 9, 11.

Collingwood, T. R. 1997. *Helping At-Risk Youth Through Physical Fitness Programming.* Champaign, Ill.: Human Kinetics.

Collins, A. 1998. *Our Children at Risk: Children and Youth Issues, 1998.* Chicago: YMCA of the USA.

Collins, E. G. and P. Scott. 1978. Everyone who makes it has a mentor. *Harvard Business Review*, July/August, 89–101.

Conniff, R. 1998. The joy of women's sports. *The Nation,* August 10/17. pp. 26–30.

Corcoran, J. 1998. Consequences of adolescent pregnancy/parenting: A review of the literature. *Social Work in Health Care* 27: 49–67.

Corcoran, M. E. and G. J. Chaudry. 1998. The dynamics of childhood poverty. *The Future of Children* 7: 40–54.

' Costello, L., ed. 1995. *Part of the Solution: Creative Alternatives for Youth.* Washington, D.C.: National Assembly of State Art Agencies.

' Cotter, H. 1998. A neighborhood nurtures its vibrant cultural history: Pride of place for art and artists in the barrio. *New York Times,* March 16, pp. B1, B3.

Council on Crime in America. 1997. *Preventing Crime, Saving Children: Monitoring, Mentoring, and Ministering.* New York: Manhattan Institute.

Cowell, A. 1998. Now, teen-agers turn to crime. *New York Times Week in Review,* February 1, pp. 1, 4.

Cowger, C. D. 1992. Assessment of client strengths. In D. S. Saleebey, ed., *The Strengths Perspective in Social Work Practice,* pp. 139–147. New York: Longman.

Cox, G. and G. T. Powers. 1998. Against all odds: An ecological approach to developing resilience in elementary school children. In R. R. Greene and M. Watkins, eds., *Serving Diverse Constituencies: Applying the Ecological Perspective,* pp. 135–166. New York: Aldine De Gruyter.

Crowe, K. 1998. RI DCYF initiates a youth advisory board. *Common Ground* 15: 9.

Currie, E. 1998. Solutions for a nation where children kill. *New York Times,* April 12, section 2, p. 37.

Curry, J. 1990. Going to the hoop to redirect lives. *New York Times,* February 6, p. 39.

Curry, T. 1997. Rheedlen's rise and shine. *HOPE* 6: 88–92.

Curtis, L. A. and V. Kimble. 1995. Common sense policy for inner-city youth investment. In S. Halperin et al., eds., *Contract with America's Youth: Toward a National Youth Development Agenda,* pp. 44–45. Washington, D.C.: Center for Youth Development and Policy Research.

CWLA (Child Welfare League of America). 1998. *1998 Children's Legislative Agenda: Children'98 America's Promise.* Washington, D.C.: CWLA.

Damon, W. 1997. *The Youth Charter: How Communities Can Work Together to Raise Standards for All Our Children.* New York: Free Press.

De Anda, D. et al. 1997. A study of stressors, and coping strategies among middle school adolescents. *Social Work in Education* 19: 87–98.

Dedman, B. 1998. Where children play, grown-ups often brawl. *New York Times*, July 29, p. A10.

De Jong, P. and S. D. Miller. 1995. How to interview for client strengths. *Social Work* 40: 729–736.

De Leon, B. 1996. Career development of Hispanic adolescent girls. In B. J. R. Leadbeater and N. Way, eds.. *Urban Girls: Resisting Stereotypes, Creating Identities*, pp. 380–398. New York: New York University Press.

Delgado, M. 1979. A grass-roots model for needs assessment in Hispanic communities. *Child Welfare* 58: 571–576.

Delgado, M. 1981. Using Hispanic adolescents to assess community needs. *Social Casework: The Journal of Contemporary Social Work* 62: 607–613.

Delgado, M. 1995. Community asset assessment and substance abuse prevention: A case study involving the Puerto Rican community. *Journal of Child and Adolescent Substance Abuse* 4: 57–77.

Delgado, M. 1996. Community asset assessments by Latino youths. *Social Work in Education* 18: 169–178.

Delgado, M. 1997. Strength-based practice with Puerto Rican adolescents: Lessons from a substance abuse prevention project. *Social Work in Education* 19: 101–112.

Delgado, M. 1998. *Social Services and the Latino Community: Research and Strategies*. New York: Haworth Press.

Delgado, M. 1999a. *Social Work Practice in Non-Traditional Urban Settings.* New York: Oxford University Press.

Delgado, M. 1999b. Involvement of the Hispanic community in ATOD research. In M. R. De La Rosa, B. Segal, and R. Lopez, eds., *Conducting Drug Abuse Research with Minority Populations*, pp. 93–105. New York: Haworth Press.

Delgado, M. In press. *Community Social Work Practice: An Assets Perspective.* New York: Oxford University Press.

Delgado, M. and K. Barton. 1998. Murals in Latino communities: Social indicators of community strengths. *Social Work* 43: 346–356.

Del Pinal, J. and A. Singer. 1997. Generations of diversity: Latinos in the United States. *Population Bulletin* 52: 1–48.

De Vincent, A. 1996. Categories for the expression of new forms of youth activities in research on social integration. *International Sociological Association-Research Committee on Clinical Sociology* 45: 145.

De Vita, C. J. 1996. The United States at mid-decade. *The Population Bulletin* 50: 1–48.

Deyhle, D. 1998. From break dancing to heavy metal: Navajo youth, resistance, and identity. *Youth* 30: 3–31.

Djuranovic, D. 1995. A sporting chance: Children from war-torn and impovished countries find peace and hope on: A hockey field. *Atlanta Journal and Constitution,* July 24, p. A7.

Dryfoos, J. D. 1998. Carving up the kids. *Youth Today* 7: 62.

Dryfoos, J. G. 1990. *Adolescents at Risk: Prevalence and Prevention.* New York: Oxford University Press.

Dryfoos, J. G. 1995. Foreword. In R. M. Lerner, *America's Youth in Crisis: Challenges and Options for Programs and Policies,* pp. vii-viii. Thousand Oaks, Calif.: Sage.

Dryfoos, J. G. 1998. *A Look at Community Schools in 1998.* New York: National Center for Schools and Communities, Fordham University.

Duehr, G. 1998. Showing it like it is. *Cambridge Chronicle,* June 25, pp. L1, L6.

Dunning, J. 1997. A dance of imagination shapes a child's view of life and the world. *New York Times,* November 29. p. A23.

Dupper, D. R. and J. Poertner. 1997. Public schools and the revitalization of impoverished communities: School-linked, family resource centers. *Social Work* 42: 415–434.

DuRant, R., D. Krowchuck, and S. Kreiter. 1999. Weapon carrying on school property among middle school students. *Archives of Pediatric and Adolescent Medicine,* p. 153.

Durrence, J. 1998. YMCA, Boys and Girls Clubs, beacons among nation's outstanding after-school programs. *Youth Today* 7: 16–18.

Duster, T. 1995. Postindustrialization and youth unemployment: African Americans as harbingers. In K. McFate, R. Lawson, and William Julius Wilson, eds., *Poverty, Inequality, and the Future of Social Policy: Western States in the New World Order,* pp. 461–486. New York: Sage.

Dykeman, C., J. R. Nelson, and V. Appleton. 1996. Building strong working alliances with American Indian families. In P. L. Ewalt et al., eds., *Multicultural Issues in Social Work,* pp. 336–350. Washington, D.C.: NASW.

Early, G. 1998. Performance and reality: Race, sports and the modern world. *The Nation,* August 10/17, pp. 11–19.

Eckolm, E. 1998. Shaolin Temple journal; Where Zen and Kung Fu got off to a flying start. *New York Times,* March 28, p. 12.

Editorial. 1998. After school as after thought. *Youth Today* 7: 2.

Educational Development Center. 1994. Why student video production? *News from the Center for Children and Technology* 2: 1–6.

Educational Video Center. 1994. *Yo-TV Production Handbook: A Guide to Video by Students for Students.* New York: EVC.

Educational Video Center. 1998. *About EVC.* New York: EVC.

Egoscue, P. 1998. Children are hurting for some exercise. *New York Times,* Sunday, May 10, NESP 8.

Elliott, D. S. 1993. Keynote presentation: Health-Enhancing and Health-Compromising behaviors during adolescents. In *Promoting Adolescent Health. Symposium on Research Opportunities in Adolescence,* pp.17–22. Washington, D.C.: CCAD.

Elliott, D. S. 1994. *Youth Violence: An Overview.* Philadelphia: Center for the Study of Youth Policy, University of Pennsylvania School of Social Work.

Erkut, S., J. P. Fields, R. Sing, and F. Marx. 1996. Diversity in girls' experiences: Feeling good about who you are. In B. J. R. Leadbeater and N. Way, eds., *Urban Girls: Resisting Stereotypes, Creating Identities,* pp. 53–64. New York: New York University Press.

Ewalt, P. L., E. M. Freeman, S. A. Kirk, and D. L. Poole, eds. 1996. *Multicultural Issues in Social Work.* Washington, D.C.: NASW.

Ewalt, P. L., E. M. Freeman, A. E. Fortune, D. L. Poole, and and S. L. Witkin, eds. 1998. *Multicultural Issues in Social Work Practice and Research.* Washington, D.C., NASW.

Farrell, W. C., J. H. Johnson Jr., M. Sapp, R. M. Pumphrey, and S. Freeman. 1996. Redirecting the lives of urban black males: An assessment of Milwaukee's midnight basketball league. *Journal of Community Practice* 2: 91–107.

Fassler, I. 1998. The voices of children and youth in the democratic process. *New Designs for Youth Development* 14: 36–40.

Feagin, J. R. 1998. *The New Urban Paradigm: Critical Perspectives on the City.* Lanham, Md.: Rowman and Littlefield.

Feber, B. J. 1996. Battle on youth smoking brings hope and caution. *New York Times,* November 29, pp. A1, B18.

Feetham, S. 1997. Families and health in the urban environment: Implications for programs, research, and policy. In H. J. Warberg, O. Reyes, and R. P. Weissberg, eds., *Children and Youth: Interdisciplinary Perspectives,* pp. 321–359. Thousand Oaks, Calif.: Sage.

Felien, E. 1993. 300 residents march and remember those shot and killed in area. *Southside Pride.* Minneapolis Community Calendar, December, p. 2.

Fellin, P. 1995. *The Community and the Social Worker.* Itasca, Ill.: F. E. Peacock.

Ferguson, R. F. 1990. *The Case for Community-Based Programs that Inform and Motivate Black Male Youth.* Washington, D.C.: Urban Institute.

Finch, K. 1998. Maintaining troubled youth in the community. *Common Ground* 15: 7.

Fine, G. A. and J. Mechling. 1993. Child saving and children's cultures at century's end. In S. W. Heath and M. W. McLaughlin, eds., *Identity and Inner-City Youth: Beyond Ethnicity and Gender*, pp. 120–146. New York: Teachers College Press.

Finn, J. L. and B. Checkoway. 1998. Young people as competent community builders: A challenge to social work. *Social Work* 43: 335–345.

Fisher, D. 1998. How much funding do you really need to build assets? *Assets Magazine*, Autumn: 10–11.

Fishman, S. 1998. Their eyes are on the camera: Video project links young people to cinema verite. *Boston Sunday Globe*, July 19, 12 City.

Flanagan, W. G. 1993. *Contemporary Urban Society.* New York: Cambridge University Press.

Flora, J. A. 1990. *Strategies for Enhancing Adolescents' Health Through Music Media: A Commentary on "Popular Music in Early Adolescence" by Peter G. Christensen and Donald F. Roberts.* Washington, D.C.: CCAD.

Foley, J. and H. Pick. 1995. Healthy cities: Survival strategies for recreation and parks. *Parks and Recreation* 30: 68–72.

Ford, R. 1998. Razor's edge. *Boston Globe Magazine*, May 24, 12: 22–28.

Ford Foundation. 1998. A movie named desire: A filmmaker explores the sexuality of teenage girls. *Ford Foundation Report* 29: 28–29.

Fox, J. R. 1990. Mission impossible? Social work practice with black urban youth gangs. *Social Work* 30: 25–31.

• Francis, R. 1994. A message for youth. In S. Cahan and Z. Kocur, eds., *Contemporary Art and Multicultural Education*, p. 45. New York: Routledge.

Frank, I. C. 1996. *Building Self-Esteem in At-Risk Youths: Peer Group Programs and Individual Success Stories.* Westport, Conn.: Praeger.

⌐ Franklin, M. C. 1998. Young artists pay homage to Monet. *Boston Sunday Globe*, October 4, P5–P6.

Fraser, M. W., ed. 1997. *Risk and Resilience in Childhood.* Washington, D.C.: NASW.

Freedman, M. 1993. *The Kindness of Strangers: Adult Mentors, Urban Youth, and the New Voluntarism.* San Francisco: Jossey-Bass.

Freeman, C. 1998. Desert odyssey: An Idaho wilderness program brings troubled kids from the streets to the sticks to discover what it means to be responsible. *HOPE* 17: 54–60.

Freeman, E. M. 1990. The black family's life cycle: Operationalizing a strengths perspective. In S. Logan, E. M. Freeman, and R. G. McRoy, eds., *Social Work Practice with Black Families*, pp. 55–72. New York: Longman.

Freeman, E. M. 1994. African-American women and the concept of cultural competence. *Journal of Multicultural Social Work* 3: 61–76

Freeman, E. M. 1998. School social work at its crossroad: Multiple challenges and possibilities. *Social Work in Education* 20: 83–89.

Free Street Programs. 1998. Mission and History. Chicago: Free Street.

Freking, K. 1992. Night basketball for LR teen-agers on board's agenda. *Arkansas Democrat Gazette*, May 2, p. 2B.

Freudenberg, N. and A. Radosh. 1998. *Protecting Youth, Preventing AIDS: A Guide for Effective High School HIV Prevention Programs*. New York: Academy for Educational Development.

Fried, J. P. 1999. Testifying against gun makers, mother recalls night her son was slain. *New York Times*, January 9, p. A14.

Fruchter, N. and M. Cahill. 1995. Developing youth competencies: School reform through collaboration. In S. Halpern et al., eds., *Contract with America's Youth: Toward a Youth Development Agenda*, pp. 40–42. Washington, D.C.: American Youth Policy Forum.

Furby, L. and R. Beyth-Marom. 1990. *Risk-Taking in Adolescence: A Decision-Making Perspective*. Washington, D.C.: CCAD.

Gallery 37. 1996. *Gallery 37: 1996 Program Report*. Chicago: Gallery 37.

Gallery 37. 1997. *Gallery 37: Chicago's Job Training Program in the Arts for Urban Youth*. Chicago: Gallery 37.

Gambone, M. A. 1993. *Strengthening Programs for Youth: Promoting Adolescent Development in the JTPA System*. Philadelphia: Public/Private Ventures.

Gambone, M. A. and A. J. A. Arbreton. 1997. *Safe Havens: The Contributions of Youth Organizations to Healthy Adolescent Development*. Philadelphia: Public/Private Ventures.

Garbarino, J., N. Dubrow, K. Kostelny, and C. Pardo. 1992. Children in Danger: Coping with the Consequences of Communiity Violence. San Francisco: Jossey-Bass.

Gardner, J. 1997. Writing off the walls. *HOPE* 6:93.

Gardner, J. W. 1994. Foreword. In M. W. McLaughlin, M. A. Irby, and J. Langman, eds., *Urban Sanctuaries: Neighborhood Organizations in the Lives and Futures of Inner-City Youth*, pp. ix–xii. San Francisco: Jossey-Bass.

Garr, R. 1995. *Reinvesting in America*. Reading, Mass.: Addison Wesley.

Gates, A. 1998. 3 aliens visit earth: take us to your culture. *New York Times*, January 15, p. B5.

Gauck, J. 1998. Kids teach adults to get on-line. *Youth Today* 7: 13.

Gauck, J. and P. Boyle. 1998. Net gain: The whys and wheres of the web. *Youth Today* 7: 8–10.

Gaunt, K. D. 1998. Dancin' in the streets to a black girl's beat: Music, gender, and the "ins and outs" of a double-dutch. In J. Austin and M. N. Willard, eds., *Generations of Youth: Youth Cultures and History in Twentieth-Century America*, pp. 272–292. New York: New York University Press.

George, L. 1992. *No Crystal Star: African-Americans in the City of Angels.* New York: Anchor Books.

Giddens, M. L. 1989. McKenzie hopes youth get a kick out of "Soccer in the Streets." *Atlanta Journal and Constitution*, December 28, p. E-10.

Giddens, M. L. 1991. Soccer in streets promotes sport for inner city. *Atlanta Journal and Constitution*, November 11, E-15.

Glentzer, M. 1996. Art with a heart. *HOPE* 4: 62–69.

Goldberg, V. 1999. Outreach, the wandering museum's speciality. *New York Times*, January 10, Arts and Leisure, part 2, pp. 41, 43.

Goldman, S. 1995. Project bridge: An artist in their midst—Texas. In L. Costello, ed., *Part of the Solution: Creative Alternatives for Youth*, pp. 66–71. Washington, D.C.: National Assembly of State Art Agencies.

Goldstein, A. P. and B. Glick. 1994. *The Prosocial Gang: Implementing Aggression Replacement Training.* Thousand Oaks, Calif.: Sage.

Goodman, S. and B. Tally. 1993. Portfolio assessment: The tape's great, but what did they learn? *The Independent* (Film and Video Monthly), August/September, pp. 30–33.

Goodwillie, S. 1993. *Voices from the Future: Our Children Tell Us About Violence in America.* New York: Crown.

Googins, B., V. Capoccia, and V. A. Kaufman. 1983. The interactional dimension of planning: A framework for practice. *Social Work* 28: 273–277.

Goplerud, E. N. 1994. What works: Essential elements of effective youth development programs. In *Building Resiliency: What Works*, pp. 25–27. Washington, D.C.: National Assembly.

Gordon, G. 1998. RI focuses on positive youth development. *Common Ground* 15: 14.

Gorov, L. 1997. A tentative peace: LA injunction thwarts gang, raises legal issue. *Boston Globe*, July 11, pp. A1, A12.

Gottlieb, B. H., ed. 1988. *Marshaling Social Support: Formats, Process, and Effects.* Beverly Hills: Sage.

Graeber, L. 1998. Taking the arts to teen-agers. *New York Times*, March 13, p. B40.

Gray, M. F. 1996. Program puts soccer in the city streets. *Atlanta Journal and Constitution*, April 18, p. D1.

Greene, R. R. and G. Barnes 1998. The ecological perspective, diversity, and culturally competent social work practice. In R. R. Greene and M. Watkins, eds., *Serving Diverse Constituencies: Applying the Ecological Perspective*, pp. 63–95. New York: Aldine De Gruyter.

Greene, R. R. and L. McGuire. 1998. Ecological perspective: Meeting the challenge of practice with diverse populations. In R. R. Greene and M. Watkins, eds., *Serving Diverse Constituencies: Applying the Ecological Perspective*, pp. 1–27. New York: Aldine De Gruyter.

Griffin-Wiesner, J. and K. Hong. 1998. A closer look at the asset categories, part 2. *Assets* Magazine, Autumn: p. 5.

Gross, J. 1998. Young blacks link tobacco use to marijuana. *New York Times*, April 22, pp. A1, A28.

Guest, H. E. 1995. A national youth agenda: Returning the community interest to the community. In S. Halpern et al., eds., *Contract with America's Youth: Toward a National Youth Development Agenda*, pp. 26–27. Washington, D.C.: American Youth Policy Forum.

Guterman, N. B. and M. Cameron. 1997. Assessing the impact of community violence on children and youths. *Social Work* 42: 495–505.

Gutierrez, L. 1990. Working with women of color: An empowerment perspective. *Social Work* 35: 149–154.

Hacker, G. A., R. Collins, and M. Jacobson. 1987. *Marketing Booze to Blacks.* Washington, D.C.: Center for Science in the Public Interest.

Hagedorn, J. M. 1988. *People, Folks: Gangs, Crime, and the Underclass in a Rustbelt City.* Chicago: Lakeview Press.

Hager, S. 1984. *Hip Hop: The Illustrated History of Break Dancing, Rap Music, and Graffiti.* New York: St. Martin's Press.

Hahn, A. 1998a. High standards. *Youth Today* 7: 54.

Hahn, A. 1998b. Research challenges assumptions about youth work. *Youth Today* 8: 54.

Hahn, A. 1999. Technology gap in impoverished youth field. *Youth Today* 9: 54.

Haldane, D. 1998. Ballet aficionados toe line, study finds. *Los Angeles Times* (Orange Co. ed.), April 28, p. B-3.

Halpern, S., J. Cusack, G. Raley, R. O'Brien, and J. Wills. 1995. *Contract with America's Youth: Toward a National Youth Development Agenda.* Washington, D.C.: American Youth Policy Forum.

Hamburg, D. A. 1990. *Life Skills Training: Preventive Interventions for Young Adolescents. Report of the Life Skills Training Working Group.* Washington, D.C.: CCAD.

Hamburg, D. A. 1992. *Today's Children: Creating a Future for a Generation in Crisis.* New York: Times Books.

Hamburg, D. A., S. G. Millstein, A. M. Mortimer, E. O. Nightingale, and A. G. Peterson. 1993. Adolescent health promotion in the twenty-first century: Current frontiers and future directions. In S. G. Millstein, A. C. Peterson, and E. O. Nightingale, eds., *Promoting the Health of Adolescents: New Directions for the Twenty-First Century,* pp. 375–388. New York: Oxford University Press.

Hamilton, S. F. and M. A. Hamilton. 1994. *Opening Career Paths for Youth: What Can Be Done? Who Can Do It?* Washington, D.C.: American Youth Policy Forum.

Hansot, E. 1993. Misperceptions of gender and youth: Learning together, learning apart. In S. B. Heath and M. W. McLaughlin, eds., *Identity and Inner-City Youth: Beyond Ethnicity and Gender,* pp. 196–209. New York: Teachers College Press.

Hardcastle, D. A., S. Wenocur, and P. R. Powers. 1997. *Community Practice: Theories and Skills for Social Workers.* New York: Oxford University Press.

Harlib, L. 1998. No smoking allowed at this circus. *Marin Independent Journal,* July 6, pp. E1, E3.

Harris, F. R. and L. A. Curtis, eds. 1998. *Locked in the Poorhouse: Cities, Race, and Poverty in the United States.* Lanham, Md.: Rowman and Littlefield.

Harris, O. 1997. Race, sport, and future orientation. *Journal of African-American Men* 2: 131–150.

Haymes, S. N. 1995. *Race, Culture, and the City.* Albany: State University of New York Press.

Haynes, K. S. 1998. The one-hundred-year debate: Social reform versus individual treatment. *Social Work* 43: 501–509.

Heath, S. B. and M. W. McLaughlin, eds. 1993. *Identity and Inner-City Youth: Beyond Ethnicity and Gender.* New York: Teachers College Press.

Heide, K. M., ed. 1998. *Young Killers: The Challenge of Juvenile Homicide.* Thousand Oaks, Calif.: Sage.

Heller, B. 1996. Nike's P.L.A.Y. for the neighborhoods. *HOPE* 1: 44–51.

Hellison, D. R. and N. J. Cutforth. 1997. Extended day programs for urban children and youth: From theory to practice. In H. J. Walberg, O. Reyes, and R. P. Weissberg, eds., *Children and Youth: Interdisciplinary Perspectives,* pp. 223–252. Thousand Oaks, Calif.: Sage.

Henderson, A. and S. Champlin, eds. 1998. *Promoting Teen Health: Linking Schools, Health Organizations, and Community.* Thousand Oaks, Calif.: Sage.

Henkin, N. Z., N. Santiago, M. Sonkowsky, and S. Tunick. 1997. Intergenerational programming: A vehicle for promoting intra- and cross-cultural understanding. *Journal of Gerontological Social Work* 28: 197–209.

Henry Street Settlement House. 1999. *Urban Force*. New York: HSSH.

Herszenhorn, D. and S. Hirsh. 1996. Healing neighborhoods with comprehensive community building. *New York Times*, December 8, p. 61.

Higgins, C. 1988. *Youth Motivation: At-Risk Youth Talk to Program Planners*. Philadelphia: Public/Private Ventures.

Hillman, E., M. F. Hovell, L. Williams, R. Hofstetter, and E. Burdyshaw. 1991. Pregnancy, STDS, and AIDS prevention: Evaluation of new image teen theatre. *AIDS Education and Prevention* 3: 328–340.

Hingson, R. and J. Howland. 1993. Promoting safety in adolescents. In S. G. Millstein, A. C. Peterson, and E. O. Nightingale, eds., *Promoting the Health of Adolescents: New Directions for the Twenty-First Century*, pp. 305–327. New York: Oxford University Press.

Hollenbeck Youth Center. 1998. *Inner-City Games, Los Angeles*. Los Angeles: HYC.

Holmes, S. A. 1998. Hispanic births in U.S. reach record high. *New York Times*, February 14, p. B1.

Horatio Alger Association. 1998–1999. *The State of Our Nation's Youth*. Alexandria, Va.: HAA.

Howard, B. 1997a. Assets vs. risks: The selling of rival youth development strategies. *Youth Today* 6(1): 18–21.

Howard, B. 1997b. Study shows how to take the guess work out of youth work. *Youth Today* 6(1): 49, 50–51.

Hughes, D. M. and N. Nichols. 1995. Changing the paradigm to community youth development. In S. Halpern et al., eds., *Contract with America's Youth: Toward a Youth Development Agenda*, pp. 30–32. Washington, D.C.: American Youth Policy Forum.

Humke, R. P. 1996. Multiple strategies for reaching at-risk youth. In P. A. Witt and J. L. Crompton, eds., *Recreation Programs that Work for At-Risk Youth*, pp. 161–169. College Station, Pa.: Venture.

Huston, A. C., ed. 1992. *Children in Poverty: Child Development and Public Policy*. New York: Cambridge University Press.

Hutchinson, M. R. and D. Poole. 1998. Adolescent health and school health: It's time to meet the challenge. *Health and Social Work*, pp. 3–7.

Imherr, K. 1998. Twinkle, twinkle, little stars. *Dallas Morning News*, July 24, p. 15C.

Immen, W. 1996. Scientists, spin-doctors and cigarettes. Canadian *Globe and Mail*, August 20, p. A6.

Inciardi, J., D. Pottieger, and A. Lockwood. 1993. *Women and Crack Cocaine*. New York: MacMillan Press.

IPR Datanote. 1998. *Puerto Ricans and Other Latinos in the United States: March 1996*. New York: PRLDEF Institute for Puerto Rican Policy, 20, 1–2.

Isaacs, M. R. 1992. *The Impact of Community Violence on African-American Children and Families: Collaborative Approaches to Prevention and Intervention Workshop Summary*. Arlington, Va.: National Center for Education in Maternal and Child Health.

Jackson, M. 1998. When having fun requires some acting. *Dallas Morning News*, July 26, p. 24C.

Jacobs, S. 1999. Fighting for their lives: Boxing requires discipline and focus, giving young men an outlet like no other. *Boston Globe*, January 19, p. E-3.

James, T. 1993. The winnowing of organizations. In S. B. Heath and M. W. McLaughlin, eds., *Identity and Inner-City Youth: Beyond Ethnicity and Gender*, pp. 176–195. New York: Teachers College Press.

Jankowski, M. S. 1991. *Islands in the Street: Gangs and American Urban Society*. Berkeley: University of California Press.

Janofsky, M. 1998a. Some midsize cities miss trend as drug deals and killings soar. *New York Times*, January 15, pp. A1, A16.

Janofsky, M. 1998b. Decline in gun violence bypasses Philadelphia. *New York Times*, May 20, p. A14.

Jarret, R. L. 1995. Growing up poor: The family experiences of socially mobile youth in low-income African-American neighborhoods. *Journal of Adolescent Research* 10: 111–135.

Jason, L. A. 1997. *Community Building: Values for a Sustainable Future*. Westport, Conn.: Praeger Press.

Jimenez, R. 1997. Tobacco gear big draw to kids. *Boston Globe*, December 15, pp. C1, C4.

Johnson, D. 1998. Many schools putting an end to child's play. *New York Times*, April 7, pp. A1, A18.

Johnson, K. 1999a. For New York, 25-year losing streak. *New York Times*, January 13, pp. A1, C20–21.

Johnson, K. 1999b. Separate but unequal: 2 schools' tales. *New York Times*, January 14, pp. C-21, C-24, C-25.

Johnson, K. and J. Curry. 1999. Sending authority for athletics back to the schools. *New York Times*, January 15, pp. C21–C23.

Johnson, R. L. 1997. Health perspectives on urban children and youth. In H. J. Walberg, O. Reyes, and R. P. Weissberg, eds., *Children and Youth: Interdisciplinary Perspectives*, pp. 299–320. Thousand Oaks, Calif.: Sage.

Jones, K. M. 1994. *Say It loud!: The Story of Rap Music*. Millbrook, Conn.: Millbrook Press.

Jones, L., L. Newman, and D. Isay. 1997. *Our America: Life and Death on the South Side of Chicago*. New York: Scribner.

Jordan, D. A. 1996. Youth summits: Exploring collaboration to maximize opportunities. In P. A. Witt and J. L. Crompton, eds.. *Recreation Programs That Work for At-Risk Youth*, pp. 97–106. State College, Pa.: Venture.

Joyner, D. 1997. Soccer goals' area program is aimed at teaching self-confidence, conflict resolution. *Clayton* (Ga.) *News/Daily*, March 31, p. 14.

Junior Players' Proposal. 1999. Dallas, Texas: JPP.

Kahlenberg, R. 1998. Ringing up successes: Boxing club has rigorous regimen but produces champions. *Los Angeles Times*, April 2, p. F-47.

Kahn, R. 1998. Youths see favoritism in city's golf-study program. *Boston Globe*, July 29, p. B1, B3.

Kaplan, C. P., S. Turner, E. Norman, and K. Stillson. 1996. Promoting resilience strategies: A modified consultation model. *Social Work in Education* 18: 158–168.

Katz, C. 1998. Disintegrating developments: Global economic restructuring and the eroding of ecologies of youth. In T. Skelton and G. Valentine, eds., *Cool Places: Geographies of Youth Cultures*, pp. 130–144. London: Routledge.

Katz, J. and E. Dickey. 1995. Forward. In L. Costello, ed., *Part of the Solution: Creative Alternatives for Youth*, p. i. Washington, D.C.: National Assembly of State Arts Agencies.

Kawakami, T. 1996. July 3. Ready to rumble; Fernando Vargas' Olympic boxing training started long ago when he sought out challenges on the streets of Oxnard. *Los Angeles Times*, p. C-1.

Kay, P., A. Estepa, and A. Desetta, eds. 1998. *Things Get Hectic: Teens Write About the Violence that Surrounds Them*. New York: Touchstone Books.

Keating, W. D. 1996. Introduction. In W. D. Keating, N. Krumholz, and P. Star, eds., *Revitalizing Urban Neighborhoods*, pp. 1–6. Lawrence: University of Kansas Press.

Kellogg Foundation. 1996. *Keeping Tomorrow in Sight: Communities Building Futures by Improving the Health of Mothers and Children*. Battle Creek, Mich.: KF.

Kellogg Foundation. 1998a. *Safe Passages Through Adolescence: Communities Protecting the Health and Hopes of Youth*. Battle Creek, Mich.: KF.

Kellogg Foundation. 1998b. *Executive Summary—Safe Passages Through Adolescence: Communities Protecting the Health and Hopes of Youth*. Battle Creeck, Mich.

Kelly, B. T., D. Huizinga, T. P. Thornberry, and R. Loeber. 1997. *Epidemiology of Serious Violence.* Washington, D.C.: U.S. Dept. of Justice, Office of Juvenile Justice and Delinquency Prevention.

Kennedy, R. 1997. A girls' choir in spotlight. *New York Times*, November 24, pp. A1, A24.

• Kenyon, K. 1997. Stories from the streets. *HOPE* 7: 77–78.

Kimball-Baker, K. and E. C. Roehlkepartian. 1998. Firm footing for asset builders everywhere. *Assets* Magazine, Autumn: 12–13.

Klein, M. W. 1995. *The American Street Gang: Its Nature, Prevalence, and Control.* New York: Oxford University Press.

Komro, K. A., F, B. Hu, and B. R. Flay. 1997. A public health perspective on urban adolescents. In H. J. Walberg, O. Reyes, and R. P. Weissberg, eds., *Children and Youth: Interdisciplinary Perspectives*, pp. 253–298. Thousand Oaks, Calif.: Sage.

Koralek, D. G., R. L. Newman, and L. J. Colker. 1995. *Caring for Children in School-Age Programs*, vols. 1 and 2. Washington, D.C.: Teaching Strategies.

Kotlowitz, A. 1991. *There Are No Children Here: The Story of Two Boys Growing Up in the Other America.* New York: Anchor Books.

Kresnak, J. 1998. Murder case debacle may spur changes. *Youth Today* 7: 40–41.

Kretzmann, J. P. and J. L. McKnight. 1993. *Building Communities from the Inside Out: A Path Toward Finding and Maintaining a Community's Assets.* Evanston, Ill.: Center for Urban Affairs and Policy Research, Northwestern University.

Krimsky, S. and D. Golding, eds. 1992. *Social Theories of Risk.* Westport, Conn.: Praeger.

Krueger, M. 1998. Finding the soul of youth work. *Youth Today* 7: 51.

• Lakes, R. D. 1996. *Youth Development and Critical Education: The Promise of Democratic Action.* Albany: State University of New York Press.

Lal, S. R., D. Lal, and C. M. Achilles. 1993. *Handbook on Gangs in Schools: Strategies to Reduce Gang-Related Activities.* Thousand Oaks, Calif.: Corwin Press.

Landre, R., M. Miller, and D. Porter. 1997. *Gangs: A Handbook for Community Awareness.* New York: Facts on File.

Langley, C. P. 1996. Project Phoenix in Raleigh, North Carolina. In P. A. Witt and J. L. Crompton, eds., *Recreation Programs that Work for At-Risk Youth*, pp. 187–194. College Station, Pa.: Venture.

Langman, J. and M. W. McLaughlin. 1993. Collaborate or go it alone? Through decisions for youth policy. In S. B. Heath and M. W. McLaughlin, eds., *Identity and Inner-City Youth: Beyond Ethnicity and Gender*, pp. 147–175. New York: Teachers College Press.

Lantier, G. 1998. Youth statistics swell, but is that swell for youth programs? *Youth Today* 7: 50–51.

Lasley, J. R. 1992. Age, social context, and street gang membership: Are "youth" gangs becoming "adult" gangs. *Youth and Society* 23: 434–451.

Lawrence, D. H. 1998. Positive youth development promotes pathways of growth. *Common Ground* 15: 9.

Lawrence, E. 1995. Voices of youth: The arts and preservation in Vermont. In L. Costello, ed., *Part of the Solution: Creative Alternatives for Youth*, pp. 22–27. Washington, D.C.: National Assembly of State Arts Agencies.

Lawrinsky, R. 1997. Transforming the soul of a city. *HOPE* 10: 20–23.

Lazzari, M. M., H. R. Ford, and K. J. Haughey. 1996. Making a difference: Women of action in the community. *Social Work* 41: 197–205.

Leadbeater, B. J. R. and N. Way. 1996. Introduction. In B. J. R. Leadbeater and N. Way, eds., *Urban Girls: Resisting Stereotypes, Creating Identities*, pp. 1–12. New York: New York University Press.

Leeds, J. 1997. Downhill racers: Inner-city youths get to show their stuff and have some fun at what is believed to be the first official soapbox derby in South Central Los Angeles. *Los Angeles Times*, May 5, p. B-1.

Leffert, N., R. N. Saito, D. A. Blyth, and C. H. Kroenke. 1996. *Making the Case: Measuring the Impact of Youth Development Programs*. Minneapolis: Search Institute.

Lefkowitz, F. 1998. Getting the picture. *HOPE* 16: 66–69.

Leonard, M. 1998. Where are the kids? *Boston Globe*, April 19, pp. G1, G2.

Lerner, R. M. 1995. *America's Youth in Crisis: Challenges and Options for Programs and Policies*. Thousand Oaks, Calif.: Sage.

Lerner, R. M. 1999. Foreword. In P. C. Scales and N. Leffert. *Developmental Assets: A Synthesis of the Scientific Research on Adolescent Development*, pp. ix–xi. Minneapolis: Search Institute.

Lerner, R. M. and C. D. Ryff. 1978. Implementation of the life-span view of human development: The sample case of attachment. In P. B. Baltes, ed., *Life-Span Development and Behavior*, vol. 1, pp. 1–44. New York: Academic Press.

Leventhal, H. and P. Keeshan. 1993. Promoting healthy alternatives to substance abuse. In S. G. Millstein, A. C. Peterson, and E. O. Nightingale, eds., *Promoting the Health of Adolescents: New Directions for the Twenty-First Century*, pp. 260–284. New York: Oxford University Press.

Lewin, T. 1998. Birth rates for teen-agers declined sharply in the 90's. *New York Times*, May 1, p. A21.

Lewis, A. 1998. Youth map greater roles for themselves. *Youth Today* 7: 24–25.

Linden, J. A. V. and C. I. Fertman. 1998. *Youth Leadership: A Guide to Understanding Leadership Development in Adolescents.* San Francisco: Simon and Schuster.

Loeber, R. and D. P. Farrington. 1998. *Serious and Violent Juvenile Offenders.* Thousand Oaks, Calif.: Sage.

Logan, S. 1996. A strengths perspective on black families: Then and now. In S. L. Logan, ed., *The Black Family: Strengths, Self-Help, and Positive Change,* pp. 8–38. Boulder: Westview Press.

Lowes, M. 1994a. Bolstered by world cup, youth soccer to take to streets. *Chicago Tribune,* January 14, p. 23.

Lowes, M. 1994b. Program gives inner-city soccer kick start. *Chicago Tribune,* April 22, p. 15.

Lurie, T. 1991. Black and Hispanic art museums: A vibrant cultural resource. *Ford Foundation Letter* 22: 6–7, 13.

MacGregor, H. E. 1998. Kid gloves; While the head of La Colonia's boxing club has turned youths from the tough streets into champions, his main offering is hope. *Los Angeles Times,* September 26, p. B-2.

MacKenzie, H. 1998a. Young salts get their hands on the helm. *Boston Sunday Globe,* July 19, p. 16 City.

MacKenzie, H. 1998b. Teens take a course in rudiments of responsibility. *Boston Sunday Globe,* August 23, p. 12 City.

Magen, Z. 1998. *Exploring Adolescent Happiness: Commitment, Purpose, and Fulfillment.* Thousand Oaks, Calif.: Sage.

Magid, K. and C. A. McKelvey. 1989. *High Risk: Children Without a Conscience.* New York: Bantam Books.

Males, M. A. 1999. *Framing Youth: 10 Myths About the Next Generation.* Monroe, Maine: Common Courage Press.

Manning, J. 1999. Performers at an early stage. *New York Times,* January 1, pp. B1, B34.

Marbella, J. 1995. Dancing into the future—Maryland. In L. Costello, ed., *Part of the Solution: Creative Alternatives for Youth,* pp. 8–13. Washington, D.C.: National Assembly for State Art Agencies.

Marshall, J., Jr. and L. Wheller. 1996. *Street Soldier: One Man's Struggle to Save a Generation—One Life at a Time.* New York: Dell.

Masten, A. 1994. Resilience in individual development: Successful adaptation despite risk and adversity. In M. C. Wang and E. W. Gordon, eds., *Educational Resilience in Inner-City America: Challenges and Prospects,* pp. 3–25. Hillsdale, N.J.: Erlbaum.

Martin, D. 1998. On city's playing fields, a turf war: More sports and teams mean shortage of space in parks. *New York Times*, April 5, pp. 31, 34.

Martin, E. P. and J. M. Martin. 1995. *Social Work and the Black Experience.* Washington, D.C.: NASW Press.

Martin, J. M. and E. P. Martin. 1985. *The Helping Tradition in the Black Family and Community.* Washington, D.C.: NASW Press.

Martinez, F. B. 1992. The impact of gangs and drugs in the community. In R. C. Cervantes, ed., *Substance Abuse and Gang Violence*, pp. 60–73. Newbury Park, Calif.: Sage.

Maxwell, B. and M. Jacobson. 1989. *Marketing Disease to Hispanics: The Selling of Alcohol, Tobacco, and Junk Foods.* Washington, D.C.: Center for Science in the Public Interest.

McBride, R. 1995. A.P.P.L.E. corps: A unique partnership—Arizona. In L. Costello ed., *Part of the Solution: Creative Alternatives for Youth*, pp. 14–21. Washington, D.C.: National Assembly of State Art Agencies.

McCord, J., ed. 1997. *Violence and Childhood in the Inner-City.* New York: Cambridge University Press.

McCubbin, H. I., E. A. Thompson, and J. E. Fromer, eds. 1998. *Resiliency in Native American and Immigrant Families.* Thousand Oaks, Calif.: Sage.

McCubbin, H. I., E. A. Thompson, A. I. Thompson, and J. A. Futurell, eds. 1998. *Resiliency in African-American Families.* Thousand Oaks, Calif.: Sage.

McKay, M. M., J. Stoewe, K. McCadam, and J. Gonzales. 1998. Increasing access to child mental health services for urban children and their caregivers. *Health and Social Work* 23: 9–15.

McKenzie, C. 1998. Personal communication, November 23.

McKnight, J. L. 1995. *The Careless Society: Community and Its Counterfeits.* New York: Basic Books.

McKnight, J. L. and J. Kretzmann. 1990. *Mapping Community Capacity.* Evanston, Ill.: Center for Urban Affairs and Policy Research, Northwestern University.

McLaughlin, M. W. 1993. Embedded identities: Enabling balance in urban contexts. In S. B. Heath and M. W. McLaughlin, eds., *Identity and Inner-City Youth: Beyond Ethnicity and Gender*, pp. 69–93. New York: Teachers College Press.

McLaughlin, M. W. and S. B. Heath. 1993. Casting the self: Frames for identity and dilemmas for policy. In S. B. Heath and M. W. McLaughlin, eds., *Identity and Inner-City Youth: Beyond Ethnicity and Gender*, pp. 210–239. New York: Teachers College Press.

McLaughlin, M. W., M. A. Irby, and J. Langman. 1994. *Urban Sanctuaries: Neighborhood Organizations in the Lives and Futures of Inner-City Youth.* San Francisco: Jossey-Bass.

McLoyd, V. C. 1994. Research in the service of poor and ethnic/racial minority children: A moral imperative. *Family and Consumer Science Research Journal* 23: 55–66.

McLoyd, V. C. and D. M. H. Jozefowicz. 1996. Sizing up the future: Predictors of African-American adolescent females' expectancies about their economic fortunes and family life courses. In B. J. R. Leadbeater and N. Way, eds., *Urban Girls: Resisting Stereotypes, Creating Identities*, pp. 355–379. New York: New York University Press.

McQuaid, C. 1998. Program puts young at arts. *Boston Globe*, March 1, pp. F1, F7.

McRoy, R. G. 1990. A historical overview of black families. In S. L. Logan, E. M. Freeman, and R. G. McRoy, eds.,. *Social Work Practice with Black Families: A Culturally Specific Perspective*, pp. 3–17. New York: Longman.

McWhirter, J. J., B. T. McWhirter, A. M. McWhirter, and E. H. McWhirter. 1993. *At-Risk Youth: A Comprehensive Response.* Pacific Grove, Calif.: Brooks/Cole.

Mears, T. 1997. Miami spice. *HOPE* 7: 74–76.

Meier, B. 1998. Data on tobacco show a strategy aimed at blacks. *New York Times*, February 6, pp. A1, A16.

Melaville, A. I. and M. J. Blank. 1991. *What It Takes: Structuring Interagency Partnerships to Connect Children and Families with Comprehensive Services.* Washington, D.C.: American Youth Policy Forum.

Melnick, M. J. and D. Sabo. 1994. Sport and social mobility among African-American and Hispanic athletics. In G. Eisen and D. K. Wiggins, eds.. *Ethnicity and Sport in North American History and Culture*, pp. 221–241. Westport, Conn.: Greenwood Press.

Mendel, R. A. 1995. *Prevention or Pork? A Hard-Headed Look at Youth-Oriented Anti-Crime Programs.* Washington, D.C.: American Youth Policy Forum.

Mexic-Arte Museum. Undated. *Mission.* Austin, Texas: MAM, p. 1.

Midgley, J. and M. Livermore. 1997. The developmental perspective in social work: Educational implications for a new century. *Journal of Social Work Education* 33: 573–585.

Mieckowki, T. 1990. Crack distribution in Detroit. *Contemporary Drug Problems* 17: 9–30.

Mihoces, G. 1993. "Streets" puts soccer on cities' playlots. *USA Today* (Sports Section), July 6. p. 20.

Miller, K. 1999. The school is a circus. *Life*, March 15, pp. 80–81.

Millstein, S. G., A. C. Petersons, and E. O. Nightingale, eds. 1993. *Promoting the Health of Adolescents: New Directions for the Twenty-First Century*. New York: Oxford University Press.

Mincy, R. B., ed. 1994. *Nurturing Young Black Males: Challenges to Agencies, Programs, and Social Policy*. Washington, D.C.: Urban Institute Press.

Minkler, M. and N. Wallerstein. 1997. Improving health through community organization and community building. In E. Minkler, ed., *Community Organization and Community Building for Health*, pp. 30–52. New Brunswick: Rutgers University Press.

Mitchell, S. G. and S. L. Logan. 1996. Reconceptualizing youth violence: Implications for change. In S. L. Logan, ed.,. *The Black Family: Strengths, Self-Help, and Positive Change*, pp. 83–107. Boulder: Westview Press.

Moe, R. and C. Wilkie. 1997. *Changing Places: Rebuilding Community in the Age of Sprawl*. New York: Holt.

Moore, J. W. 1991. *Going Down to the Barrio*. Philadelphia: Temple University Press.

Moore, J. W. and J. M. Hagedorn. 1996. *Drugs, Posses, Gangs, and the Underclass in Milwaukee*. Progress report submitted to the National Institute on Drug Abuse (National Institute on Drug Abuse grant number DA07128. Rockville, Md.: NIDA.

Morrison, J. D., S. Alcorn, and M. Nelums. 1997. Empowering community-based programs for youth development: Is social work education interested? *Journal of Social Work Education* 33: 321–333.

Moving in the Spirit. 1998. *Teaching Workplace Values and Life Skills Through the Discipline of Dance*. Atlanta: Moving in the Spirit.

Moyers, B. 1995. *What Can We Do About Violence?* New York: Public Broadcasting Services.

Musick, J. 1993. *Young, Poor, and Pregnant: The Psychology of Teenage Motherhood*. New Haven: Yale University Press.

National Assembly. 1998a. *After-School Care in Brief*. Washington, D.C.: NA.

National Assembly. 1998b. *Positions for Youth: Public Policy Statements of the National Collaboration for Youth 1998*. Washington, D.C.: NA.

National Campaign to Prevent Teen Pregnancy. 1997. *Whatever Happened to Childhood? The Problem of Teen Pregnancy in the United States*. Washington, D.C.: NCPTP.

National Coalition for the Homeless. 1997. *America's Homeless Children: Will Their Future Be Different?* Washington, D.C.: NCH.

National Collaboration for Youth. 1997. *Credentialing Activities in the Youth Development Field.* Washington, D.C.: NCY.

National Commission on Resources for Youth. 1974. *New Roles for Youth—in the School and the Community.* New York: Citation Press.

National Research Council. 1993. *Losing Generations: Adolescents in High-Risk Settings.* Washington, D.C.: NRC.

Navarro, M. 1996. A new sport on the West Grove block. *Miami Herald,* July 28, p. 24.

Neale, R. 1995. Hugs and kisses, a big kid's play—Virginia. In L. Costello, ed., *Part of the Solution: Creative Alternatives for Youth,* pp. 72–79. Washington, D.C.: National Assembly of State Art Agencies.

Networks for Youth Development. 1998a. *Core Competencies for Youth Work.* New York: NYD.

Networks for Youth Development. 1998b. *A Guided Tour of Youth Development.* New York: NYD.

Networks for Youth Development. 1998c *The Handbook of Positive Youth Outcomes.* New York: NYD.

News from Henry Street. 1996. Urban youth theater: New voices and new talent. New York: NHS.

News from Henry Street. 1998. The Abrons Arts Center look towards the millennium: Expanding teaching potential through the arts. Winter, p. 3. New York: NHS.

New York Times. 1998a. Editorial: Hooked on young smokers, January 16, p. A26.

New York Times. 1998b. Girls seek equal use of all fields for softball. May 10, p. 26.

New York Times. 1998c. Teenager to face trial in killing at casino. September 8, p. A19.

New York Times. 1998d. Crime drops in '97; Murders are at 30-year low. November 23, p. A16.

Noble, G., P. Egan, and S. McDowell. 1977. Changing the self-concepts of seven-year-old deprived urban children by creative drama or video feedback. *Social Behavior and Personality* 5: 55–64.

Ochoa, V. 1990. San Diego to the Mexican border. In E. S. Cockcroft and H. Barnet-Sanchez, eds., *Signs from the Heart: California Chicano Murals,* pp. 51–53. Albuquerque: University of New Mexico Press.

O'Donnell, J., J. Ferreira, R. Hurtado, E. Ames, R. E. Floyd, and L. M. Sebren. 1997. Partners for change: Community residents and agencies. *Journal of Sociology and Social Welfare* 25: 133–151.

O'Donnell, J., E. A. Michalak, and E. B. Ames. 1999. Inner-city youths helping children: After-school programs to promote bonding and reduce risk. In Ewalt et al., *Multicultural Issues in Social Work: Practice and Research*, pp. 191–201. Washington, D.C.: NASW Press.

Office of Juvenile Justice and Delinquency Prevention. 1996. *Juvenile Offenders and Victims: 1996 Update on Violence.* Washington, D.C.: OJJDP.

Ogbu, J. U. 1997. Understanding the school performance of urban blacks: Some essential background knowledge. In H. J. Warberg, O. Reyes, and R. P. Weissberg, eds., *Children and Youth: Interdisciplinary Perspectives*, pp. 190–222. Thousand Oaks, Calif.: Sage.

Oldenburg, R. 1991. *The Great Good Place.* New York: Paragon House.

Olsen, M. R. 1983. Foreword: Social support networks from a British perspective. In J. K. Whittaker and J. Garbarino, eds., *Social Support Networks: Informal Helping in the Human Services*, pp. xi–xx. New York: Aldine.

Osofsky, J. D., S. Wewers, D. M. Hamm, and A. C. Fick. 1993. Chronic community violence: What is happening to our children? *Psychiatry* 56: 36–45.

Osterman, P. 1995. Apprenticeship programs for the American youth labor market. In S. Halpern et al., eds., *Contract with America's Youth: Toward a Youth Development Agenda*, pp. 48–59. Washington, D.C.: American Youth Policy Forum.

Ozer, E. M., C. D. Brandis, S. G. Millstein, D. K. Knopf, and C. E. Irwin. 1997. *America's Adolescents: Are They Healthy?* San Francisco: University of California, National Adolescent Health Information Center.

Padilla, F. M. 1993. *The Gang as an American Enterprise.* New Brunswick, N.J.: Rutgers University Press.

Palumbo, M. J. 1997. Art work in progress. *Boston Herald*, November 25, pp. 41–44.

Pantalone, J. 1995. Working their way into the arts—Rhode Island. In L. Costello, ed., *Part of the Solution: Creative Alternative for Youth*, pp. 54–59. Washington, D.C.: National Assembly of State Arts Agencies.

Partee, G. 1996. *Youth Work, Youth Development, and the Transition from Schooling to Employment in England.* Washington, D.C.: American Youth Policy Forum.

Pennington, H. 1995. Learning and doing: A new vision. In S. Halpern et al., eds., *Contract with America's Youth: Toward a Youth Development Agenda*, pp. 33–34. Washington, D.C.: American Youth Policy Forum.

Phinney, S. 1995. Ethnic identity and self-esteem: A review and integration. In A. M. Padilla, ed., *Hispanic Psychology: Critical Issues in Theory and Research*, pp. 57–70. Thousand Oaks, Calif.: Sage.

Pinto, B. 1998. Viewing youth as resources. *Common Ground*, 15: 6.

Pittman, K. 1998. Move over, Greenspan. *Youth Today* 7: 55.

Pittman, K. 1998b. Beyond participation. *Youth Today* 8: 55.

Pittman, K. and M. Cahill. 1991. *A New Vision: Promoting Youth Development.* Commissioned Paper No. 3. Washington, D.C.: Academy for Educational Development, Center for Youth Development and Policy Research.

Pittman, K. and W. E. Fleming. 1991. *A New Vision: Promoting Youth Development, Testimony Before the House Select Committee on Children, Youth, and Families.* Washington, D.C.: Center for Youth Development and Policy Research.

Pittman, K. and M. Wright 1991. *Bridging the Gap: A Rationale for Enhancing the Role of Community Organizations in Promoting Youth Development.* Washington, D.C.: Center for Youth Development and Policy Research at the Academy for Educational Development.

Poertner, J. and J. Ronnau. 1992. A strengths approach to children with emotional disabilities. In D. S. Saleebey, ed., *The Strengths Perspective to Social Work Practice*, pp. 111–121. New York: Longman.

Poinsett, A. 1996. *The Role of Sports in Youth Development: A Report of a Meeting Convened by the Carnegie Corporation of New York.* New York: Carnegie Corporation.

Policy Exchange, The. 1998. *The Measure of Success: What Are the Policy Implications of the New National Indicators of Child Well-Being.* Washington, D.C.: Institute for Educational Leadership.

Poole, D. L. 1997. Building community capacity to promote social and public health: Challenges for universities. *Health and Social Work* 22: 163–170.

Popple, K. 1996. Community work: British models. *Journal of Community Practice* 3: 147–180.

President's Committee on the Arts and the Humanities. 1996. *Coming Up Taller: Arts and Humanities Programs for Children and Youth at Risk.* Washington, D.C.: GPO.

Price, R. H., ed. 1990. *School and Community Support Programs that Enhance Adolescent Health and Education.* Washington, D.C.: CCAD.

Pring, J. 1997. Graffiti artists get the picture. *Boston Globe*, November 28, pp. B1, B11.

Prothrow-Stith, D. 1991. *Deadly Consequences.* New York: HarperCollins.

Purdy, M. 1995. Drug turf is safer as dealers avoid streets. *New York Times*, January 2, pp. 1, 27.

Pynoos, R. S. and K. Nader. 1988. Psychological first aid and treatment approach to children exposed to community violence: Research implications. *Journal of Traumatic Stress Studies* 1: 445–473.

Quinn, T. 1990. The door: Providing skills, hope, and a haven. *Ford Foundation Newsletter* 21: 1–7, 16–17.

Radin, C. A. 1998a. Anti-gang group faces growing problems. *Boston Globe*, May 26, pp. A1, A8.

Radin, C. A. 1998b. Harbor opening to city youths. *Boston Sunday Globe*, July 26, pp. B1, B8.

Raimar, B. 1995. Youth and modern lifestyles. In J. Fornas and B. Goran, eds., *Youth Culture in Late Modernity*, pp. 120–144. London: Sana.

Rathbone, C. 1997. *On the Outside Looking In: A Year at an Inner-City High School*. New York: Atlantic Monthly Press.

Reardon, C. 1996a. Striking a richer chord. *Ford Foundation Report* 27: 8–13.

Reardon, C. 1996b. Tapping the arts in other communities. *Ford Foundation Report* 27: 13.

Redding, S. 1997. Urban myth: The family in hard times. In H. J. Walberg, O. Reyes, and R. P. Weissberg, eds., *Children and Youth: Interdisciplinary Perspectives*, pp. 92–118. Thousand Oaks, Calif.: Sage.

Rees, S. 1998. Empowerment of youth. In L. M. Gutierrez, L. M. Parsons, and E. O. Cox, eds., *Empowerment in Social Work: A Sourcebook*, pp. 130–145. Pacific Grove, Calif.: Brooks/Cole.

Reppucci, N. D. 1987. Prevention and ecology: Teen-age pregnancy, child sexual abuse, and organized youth sports. *American Journal of Community Psychology* 15: 1–22.

Rhodes, J. E. and A. B. Davis. 1996. Supportive ties between nonparent adults and urban adolescent girls. In B. J. R. Leadbeater and N. Way, eds., *Urban Girls: Resisting Stereotypes, Creating Identities*, pp. 213–225. New York: New York University Press.

Ribadeneira, D. 1998. Church-led camp helps urban teens find their voice, change their tune. *Boston Globe*, July 30, p. B4.

Ribadeneira, T. W. 1998. Soccer field just one goal for the YMCA. *Boston Globe* (City Weekly), May 3, pp. 1, 11.

Richards, N. 1996. Schools in all states need repair, report says. *Education Week*, July 10, p. 8.

Riggins, S. H. 1992. The media imperative: Ethnic minority survival in the age of mass communication. In S. H. Riggins, ed., *Ethnic Minority Media: An International Perspective*, pp. 1–20. Newbury Park, Calif.: Sage.

Rimer, S. 1998. First steps to reclaim streets are precise, joyful, loud. *New York Times*, January 12, p. A11.

Rook, A. 1998. At-risk youth art programs come up tall. *Youth Today* 7: 14–17.

Rosenbaum, J. E., D. Stern, M. Agnes, S. F. Hamilton, S. E. Berryman, and R. Kazis. 1994. *Youth Apprenticeship in America: Guidelines for Building an Effective System.* Washington, D.C.: American Youth Policy Forum.

Rotheram-Borus, M. J., S. Dopkins, N. Sabate, and M. Lightfoot. 1996. Personal and ethnic identity, values, and self-esteem among Black and Latino adolescent girls. In B. J. R. Leadbeater and N. Way, eds., *Urban Girls: Resisting Stereotypes, Creating Identities,* pp. 35–52. New York: New York University Press.

Rothman, J. 1994. *Practice with Highly Vulnerable Clients: Case Management and Community-Based Service.* Englewood Cliffs, N.J.: Prentice Hall.

Rubin, B. ed.,. 1980. *Small Voices and Great Trumpets: Minorities and the Media.* New York: Praeger.

Sagawa, S. 1998. *Ten Years of Youth in Service to America.* Washington, D.C.: American Youth Policy Forum.

Sailes, G. A. 1996a. Editor's comments. *Journal of African American Men* 2: 2–10.

Sailes, G. A. 1996b. Betting against the odds: An overview of black sports participation. *Journal of African American Men* 2: 11–22.

Saito, R. N. and D. A. Blyth. 1995. *Understanding Mentoring Relationships.* Minneapolis: Search Institute.

Saldana, D.. 1995. Acculturative stress: Minority status and distress. In A. M. Padilla, ed., *Hispanic psychology: Critical Issues in Theory and Research,* pp. 43–54. Thousand Oaks, Calif.: Sage.

Saleebey, D. S., ed. 1992. *The Strengths Perspective in Social Work Practice.* New York, Longman.

Saleebey, D. S. 1996. The strengths perspectives in social work practice: Extensions and cautions. *Social Work* 41:296–305.

Sallis, J. F. 1993. Promoting healthful diet and physical activity. In S. G. Millstein, A. C. Peterson, and E. O. Nightingale, eds., *Promoting the Health of Adolescents: New Directions for the Twenty-First Century,* pp. 209–241. New York: Oxford University Press.

Sampson, R. J. 1997. The embeddedness of child and adolescent development: A community-level perspective on urban violence. In J. McCord, ed., *Violence and Childhood in the Inner-City,* pp. 31–77. New York: Cambridge University Press.

Sanders, S. 1998. Settlement houses survive—and thrive. *NASW News* 43: 3.

Santiago, E. 1995. A Puerto Rican stew. *New York Times Magazine,* October 1, pp. 34, 36.

Sarri, R. C. 1996. An agenda for child and youth well-being. In P. R. Raffoul and C. A. McNeece, eds., *Future Issues for Social Work Practice*, pp. 141–150. Boston: Allyn and Bacon.

Scales, P. C. and N. Leffert. 1999. *Developmental Assets: A Synthesis of the Scientific Research on Adolescent Development.* Minneapolis: Search Institute.

Schinke, S., M. Jansen, E. Kennedy, and O. Shi. 1994. Reducing risk-taking behavior among vulnerable youth: An intervention outcome study. *Family and Community Health* 16: 49–56.

Schiraldi, V. 1998. Making sense of kids who kill. *Youth Today* 7: 52.

Schoen, C., K. Davis, C. DesRoches, and A. Shekhdar. 1998. *The Health of Adolescent Boys: Commonwealth Fund Survey Findings.* New York: Commonwealth Fund.

Schorr, L. 1989. *Within Our Reach: Breaking the Cycle of Disadvantage.* New York: Anchor Books.

Schorr, L. B. 1997. *Common Purpose: Strengthening Families and Neighborhoods to Rebuild America.* New York: Anchor Books.

Schubiner, H., R. Scott, and A. Tzelepis. 1993. Exposure to violence among inner-city youth. *American Journal of Diseases of Children* 146: 214–219.

Schultz, J. 1997. Inside boxing: Boxing notebook: Atlanta boosted by new gym. *Atlanta Journal and Constitution*, September 14, p. C-10.

Schutz, A. 1997. Soccer in the Streets founder honored by sporting goods magazine. *Jonesboro* (Ga.) *Clayton News/Daily*, February 20, p. 1.

Schwartz, D. B. 1997. *Who Cares? Rediscovering Community.* Boulder: Westview Press.

Schwartz, M., ed. 1982. *TV and Teens: Experts Look at the Issues.* New York: Addison-Wesley.

Search Institute. 1996. *Healthy Communities, Healthy Youth.* Minneapolis: SI.

Search Institute. 1997. *The Asset Approach: Giving Kids What They Need to Succeed.* Minneapolis: SI.

Search Institute. 1998. *Helping Youth Thrive: How Youth Organizations Can—and Do—Build Developmental Assets.* Minneapolis: SI.

Seefeldt, V. 1993. *Overview of Sports Programs in the United States.* Washington, D.C.: CCAD.

Seefeldt, V., M. E. Ewing, and S. Walk. 1991. Overview of youth sports in the United States. Paper commissioned by the Carnegie Council on Adolescent Development. New York: CCAD.

Seidel, R. W. and N. D. Reppucci. 1993. Organized youth sports and the psychological development of nine-year-old males. *Journal of Child and Family Studies* 2: 229–248.

Seidman, E. 1991. Growing up the hard way: Pathways of urban adolescents. *American Journal of Community Psychology* 19: 173–200.

Seidman, E. and S. E. French. 1997. Normative school transitions among urban adolescents. In H. J. Warberg, O. Reyes, and R. P. Weissberg, eds., *Children and Youth: Interdisciplinary Perspectives*, pp. 166–189. Thousand Oaks, Calif.: Sage.

Sharff, J. W. 1998. *King Kong on 4th Street: Families and the Violence of Poverty on the Lower East Side*. Boulder: Westview Press.

Sheley, J. F. and J. D. Wright. 1995. *In the Line of Fire: Youth, Guns, and Violence in Urban America*. New York: Aldine De Gruyter.

Shelman, J. 1998. Suburbs' game now city kids. *Cincinnati Post*, May 6, p. 33.

Shorris, E. 1997. In the hands of the restless poor. *Harper's Magazine*, September: 50–59.

Short, J. F., Jr. 1997. *Poverty, Ethnicity, and Violent Crime*. Boulder: Westview Press.

Sickmund, M., A. L. Stahl, T. A. Finnegan, H. N. Snyder, R. S. Poole, and J. A. Butts. 1998. *Juvenile Court Statistics 1995*. Washington, D.C.: U.S. Dept. of Justice, Office of Juvenile Justice and Delinquency Prevention.

Sime, T. 1998. '60s setting tames disturbing "Shrew." *Dallas Morning News*, July 30, p. 1C.

Simeonsson, R. J., ed. 1994. *Risk, Resilience, and Prevention: Promoting the Well-Being of All Children*. Baltimore: Brookes.

Simon, B. L. 1994. *The Empowerment Tradition in American Social Work: A History*. New York: Columbia University Press.

Simon, D. and E. Burns. 1997. *The Corner: A Year in the Life of an Inner-City Neighborhood*. New York: Broadway Hardcover.

Simons, J. M., B. Finlay, and A. Yang. 1992. *The Adolescent and Young Adult Fact Book*. Washington, D.C.: Children's Defense Fund.

Simpson, B. 1997. Towards the participation of children and young people in urban planning and design. *Urban Studies* 34: 5–6.

Sipe, C. L., P. Ma, and M. A. Gambone. 1998. *Support for Youth: A Profile of Three Communities*. Philadelphia: Public/Private Ventures.

Skelton, T. and G. Valentine. 1998. *Cool Places: Geographies of Youth Cultures*. London: Routledge.

Smith, G. 1997. Heart of gold, will of steel. *HOPE* 7: 64–68.

Smith, P. 1997. Dancers present movement with message. *Arts*, June 17, p. 2.

Smith, T. J. 1997. Introduction. In: *Some Things Do make a Difference: A Compendium of Evaluations of Youth Programs and Practices*, pp. vii–xii. Washington, D.C.: American Youth Policy Forum.

Smith, T. J. and K. Jucovy. 1996. *Americorps in the Field: Implementation of the National and Community Trust Act in Nine States.* Washington, D.C.: American Youth Policy Program.

Smith, T. W. 1998. Boxing; Off the streets, into the ring is boxing program's goal. *New York Times,* May 2, p. 35.

Smokowski, P. R. 1998. Prevention and intervention strategies for promoting resilience in disadvantaged children. *Social Service Review* 72: 337–364.

Snyder, H. N. and M. Sickmund. 1995. *Juvenile Offenders and Victims: A National Report.* Washington, D.C.: Office of Juvenile Justice and Delinquency Prevention.

Soccer in the Streets. 1998. Jonesboro, Ga.: Soccer in the Streets.

Sorin, G. 1990. *The Nurturing Neighborhood: The Brownsville Boys Club and Jewish Community in Urban America 1940–1990.* New York: New York University Press.

Specht, H. and M. E. Courtney. 1994. *Unfaithful Angels.* New York: Free Press.

Stake, R. E. 1995. *The Art of Case Study Research.* Thousand Oaks, Calif.: Sage.

Stauss, J. H. 1995. Reframing and reinforcing American Indian family strengths. In C. K. Jacobson, ed., *American Families: Issues in Race and Ethnicity,* pp. 105–118. New York: Guilford Press.

Steinber, J. 1999. The coming wave is washed up. *New York Times,* January 3, section 4, p. 4.

Steinhardt, L. 1994. Creating the autonomous image through puppet theatre and art therapy. *The Arts in Psychotherapy* 21: 205–218.

Stolberg, S. G. 1998a. U.S. awakes to epidemic of sexual diseases. *New York Times,* March 9, pp. A1, A14.

Stolberg, S. G. 1998b. Rise in smoking by young blacks erodes a success story. *New York Times,* April 3, p. A20.

Stolberg, S. G. 1998c. Surgeon general warns of rise in ethnic smoking. *New York Times,* April 30, p. A16.

Stover, C. 1998. The poetry of science. *HOPE* 17: 61–63.

Stuker, J. 1995. South Carolina's abc project: Making a difference in education. In L. Costello, ed., *Part of the Solution: Creative Alternatives for Youth,* pp. 42–47. Washington, D.C.: National Assembly of State Arts Agencies.

Sullivan, A. 1996. From enter to muse: Recasting the role of women in relationships with urban adolescent girls. In B. J. R. Leadbeater and N. Way, eds., *Urban Girls: Resisting Stereotypes, Creating Identities,* pp. 226–253. New York: New York University Press.

Sum, A., N. Fogg, and N. Fogg. 1997. Confronting the demographic challenge: Future labor market prospects of out-of-school young adults. In A. Sum, S. Mangum, E. deJesus, G. Walker, D. Gruber, M. Pines, and W. Pring, eds. *A Generation of Challenge: Pathways to Success for Urban Youth*. Baltimore: Johns Hopkins University Institute for Policy Studies.

Swenson, C. R. 1995. Professional understanding of community: At a loss for words? In P. Adams and K. Nelton, eds., *Reinventing Human Services: Community and Family-Centered Practice*, pp. 223–243. New York: Aldine de Gruyter.

Swenson, C. R. 1998. Clinical social work's contribution to a social justice perspective. *Social Work* 43: 527–537.

Symons, C. W., B. Cinelli, T. C. James, and P. Groff. 1997. Bridging student risks and academic achievement through comprehensive school health programs. *Journal of Social Health* 67: 220–228.

Taylor, C. 1990. Sports and recreation: Community anchor and counterweight to conflict. *Journal of Peace Psychology* 2: 342–349.

Taylor, C. S. 1993. *Girls, Gangs, Women, and Drugs*. East Lansing: Michigan State University Press.

Telander, R. 1995. *Heaven Is a Playground*. Lincoln: University of Nebraska Press.

Tennille, G. 1994. Night court. *Arkansas Democrat Gazette*, July 10, pp. 8C, 10C.

Terry, D. 1994, September 18. Gangs: Machiavelli's descendants. *New York Times*, 26.

Texeira, E. 1989. 1989. In a late night sport, the game is fighting crime. *New York Times*, February 12, p. 51.

Texeira, E. 1994. *Building Resiliency: What Works!* Washington, D.C.: National Assembly.

Texeira, E. 1996. Young boxers given grants for equipment. *Los Angeles Times*, May 1, p. B3.

Texeira, E. 1998a. Boxing program for youths seeks volunteer trainers. *Los Angeles Times*, June 24, p. B-4.

Texeira, E. 1998b. For Cleveland women, a night basketball league of their own. *New York Times*, August 2, p. 21.

Tilghman, R. 1995. The family arts agenda: A lighthouse for rough waters— Oregon. In L. Costello, ed., *Part of the Solution: Creative Alternatives for Youth*, pp. 60–65. Washington, D.C.: National Assembly of State Arts Agencies.

Tobar, H. 1996. A fighting chance; De La Hoya refurbishing gym to help youngsters, neighborhoods. *Los Angeles Times*, October 12, p. B-1.

Toland, P. H. and D. Gorman-Smith. 1997. Families and the development of urban children. In H. J. Walberg, O. Reyes, and R. P. Weissberg, eds., *Children and Youth: Interdisciplinary Perspectives*, pp. 67–91. Thousand Oaks, Calif.: Sage.

Torregrosa, L. L. 1998. Latino culture whirls onto center stage: Even as they capture the spotlight, performers question their identity. *New York Times*, March 26, pp. B1, B6.

Traver, N. 1998. Teachers balk at extended day. *Youth Today* 7: 26.

Trust for the Public Land. 1994. *Healing America's Cities: Why We Must Invest in Urban Parks*. San Francisco.

Tucker, M. 1999. Museums experiment with new exhibition strategies. *New York Times*, January 10, Arts and Leisure, part 2, pp. 40, 46.

Tyler, K. 1996. Collaboration: One community's story. *Assets* Magazine 1: 8–10.

Unger, D. G. and A. Wandersman. 1995. The importance of neighbors: The social, cognitive, and affective components of neighboring. *American Journal of Community Psychology* 13: 139–169.

Upchurch, C. 1996. *Convicted in the Womb: One Man's Journey from Prisoner to Peacemaker*. New York: Bantam Books.

Urban Institute. 1993. At-risk-youth: Identifying adolescents at risk. *Policy and Research Reports* 23: 11–19.

U.S. Dept. of Education. 1998. *Safe and Smart: Making the After-School Hours Work for Kids*. Washington, D.C.: GPO.

U.S. Dept. of Health and Human Services. 1995. National Center on Child Abuse and Neglect. *Child Maltreatment 1993: Reports from the States to the National Center on Child Abuse and Neglect*. Washington, D.C.: GPO.

U.S. General Accounting Office. 1998. *Teen Mothers: Selected Socio-Demographic Characteristics and Risk Factors*. GAO/HEHS-98-141. Washington, D.C.: GPO.

Valentine, G., T. Skelton, and D. Chambers. 1998. Cool places: An introduction to youth and youth cultures. In T. Skelton and G. Valentine, eds., *Cool Places: Geographies of Youth Cultures*, pp. 1–32. London: Routledge.

Van Voorhis, R. 1998. Culturally relevant practices: Addressing the psychosocial dynamics of oppression. In R. R. Greene and M. Watkins, eds., *Serving Diverse Constituencies: Applying the Ecological Perspective*, pp. 97–112. New York: Aldine de Gruyter.

Verhovek, S. H. 1995. Young, carefree, and in love with cigarettes. *New York Times*, July 30, pp. 1, 24.

Video/Action Fund Production Discussion Guide. 1991. *Who's Gonna Sing Our Song?* Washington, D.C.: Video/Action Fund.

Vigil, J. D. 1993. Gangs, social control, and ethnicity: Ways to redirect. In S. B. Heath and M. W. Laughlin, eds., *Identity and Inner-City Youth: Beyond Ethnicity and Gender*, pp. 94–119. New York: Teachers College Press.

Villarruel, F. A. and R. M. Lerner, eds. 1994. Promoting community-based programs for socialization and learning. In *New Directions for Child Development*, vol. 63. San Francisco: Jossey-Bass.

Wade, B. 1998. Hardening the nutcracker: In an inner-city school, the Christmas classic gets a streetwise makeover. *Time*, December 21, p. 8.

Wahl, E. 1995. Youth development: A journey of strength, power and love. In S. Halpern et al., eds., *Contract with America's Youth: Toward a Youth Development Agenda*, pp. 18–20. Washington, D.C.: American Youth Policy Forum.

Walberg, H. J., O. Reyes, R. P. Weissberg, and C. B. Kuster. 1997. Afterword: Strengthening the families, educational, and health of urban children and youth. In H. J. Walberg, O. Reyes, and R. P. Weissberg, eds., *Children and Youth: Interdisciplinary Perspectives*, pp. 363–368. Thousand Oaks, Calif.: Sage.

Waldman, A. 1998. A place for hoops and helping hands. *New York Times*, August 30, p. B15.

Waldorf, D. 1993. *Crack Sales Gangs and Violence: An Exploration* National Institute on Drug Abuse, NIDA grant number DA09106. Rockville, Md.: NIDA.

Walker, K. 1991a. Inner-city midnight basketball discussed. *Arkansas Democrat Gazette*, July 30, p. 9A.

Walker, K. 1991b. Press is on for midnight basketball. *Arkansas Democrat Gazette*, July 31, p. 10A.

Walser, R. 1998. Clamor and community in the music of public enemy. In J. Austin and M. N. Willard, eds., *Generations of Youth: Youth Cultures and History in Twentieth-Century America*, pp. 293–310. New York: New York University Press.

Washington State Child Care Coordinating Committee. Subcommittee on Early Childhood Career Development. 1995. *School-Age Early Childhood Career Development Core Competencies Document*. Olympia, Wash.: Child Care Coordinating Committee.

Watkins, M. and E. Iverson. 1998. Youth development principles and field practicum opportunities. In R. R. Greene and M. Watkins, eds., *Serving Diverse Constituencies: Applying the Ecological Perspective*, pp. 167–197. New York: Aldine de Gruyter.

Watt, P. and K. Stenson. 1998. "The street: It's a bit dodgy around there." Safety, danger, ethnicity, and young people's use of public space. In T. Skelton and G. Valentine, eds., *Cool Places: Geographies of Youth Cultures*, pp. 249–265. London: Routledge.

Weber, B. 1997. Cities are fostering the arts as a way to save downtown. *New York Times*, November 18, pp. A1, A24.

Weick, A., C. Rapp, W. P. Sullivan, and W. Kisthardt. 1989. A strengths perspective for social work practice. *Social Work* 34:350–354.

Werner, E. E. and R. S. Smith. 1982. *Vulnerable but Not Invincible: A Longitudinal Study of Children and Youth*. New York: McGraw-Hill.

Wertz, R. 1994a. Committed, caring, professional leadership. In *Building Resiliency: What Works!* pp. 28–29. Washington, D.C.: National Assembly.

Wertz, R. 1994b. Youth-centered activities in youth-accessible facilities. In *Building Resiliency: What Works!* pp. 30–33. Washington, D.C.: National Assembly.

Whisenhunt W. 1996. The summer search and pryde programs. In P. A. Witt and J. L. Crompton, eds., *Recreation Programs that Work for At-Risk Youth*, pp.195–200. College Station, Pa.: Venture.

White, J. 1998. Arteffects: Blending aerosol artistry and assets in Arizona. *Assets* Magazine, Autumn: 6–8.

Whittaker, J. K. and J. Garbarino, eds. 1983. *Social Support Networks: Informal Helping in the Human Services*. New York: Aldine.

Wiggins, D. K. 1994. The notion of double-consciousness and the involvement of black athletes in American sport. In G. Eisen and D. K. Wiggins, eds., *Ethnicity and Sport in North American History and Culture*, pp. 133–155. Westport, Conn.: Greenwood Press.

Wilgoren, J. 1999. Five teen-agers arrested after slaying that followed basketball game. *New York Times*, January 30, p. A13.

Wilkins, N. O. 1996. Mayor's Night Hoops. In P. A. Witt and J. L. Crompton, eds., *Recreation Programs that Work for At-Risk Youth*, pp. 237–243. College Station, Pa.: Venture.

Will, G. F. 1990. City game. *Chicago Tribune*, October 18, p. 38.

Williams, C. and J. Koney-Li. 1996. The Oakland summer performing arts day camp (OPAC). In P. A. Witt and J. L. Crompton, eds., *Recreation Programs that Work for At-Risk Youth*, pp. 275–286. College Station, Pa.: Venture.

Williams, L. 1999. Progress is a slow train for girls' teams. *New York Times*, January 14, p. C-25.

Williamson, M. 1997. *The Healing of America*. New York: Simon and Schuster.

Willing, R. 1997. Tracking teen crime. *USA Today*, September 18, pp. 1–2.

Willingham, L. 1993. Participants spotlight: Making a difference with area's youth: Pat Jackson uses karate to teach kids the lessons of life, discipline. *Atlanta Journal and Constitution*, December 16, p. K-10.

Willis, S. 1998. Teens at work: Negotiating the jobless future. In Joe Austin and M. N. Willard, eds., *Generations of Youth: Youth Cultures and History in Twentieth-Century America*, pp. 347–357. New York: New York University Press.

Wilson, C. C., II and F. Gutierrez. 1985. *Minorities and Media: Diversity and the End of Mass Communication*. Newbury Park, Calif.: Sage.

Wilson, W. J. 1993. Poverty, health, and adolescent health promotion. In *Promoting Adolescent Health: Symposium on Research Opportunities in Adolescence*, pp. 23–27. Washington, D.C.: CCAD.

Wilson, W. J. 1996. *When Work Disappears: The World of the Urban Poor*. New York: Vintage Books.

Wilson-Brewer, R., ed. 1991. *Violence Prevention for Young Adolescents: A Survey of the State of the Art*. Working papers. Newton, Mass.: Educational Development Center.

Witkin, S. L. 1998. Is social work an adjective? *Social Work* 43: 483–486.

Witt, P. A. and J. L. Crompton. 1996. Major themes emerging from the case studies. In P. A. Witt and J. L. Crompton, eds., *Recreation Programs that Work for At-Risk Youth*, pp. 7–33. College Station, Pa.: Venture.

W. K. Kellogg Foundation, *see* Kellogg Foundation.

Wolfe, W. 1992. Murals help youths picture better world. *Minneapolis Star Tribune*, September 30, pp. 1B, 6B.

Wolfson, J. 1998. Teamwork builds a bridge for kids in L.A. *Youth Today* 7: 23.

Wren, C. S. 1996. Adolescent drug use continues to rise. *New York Times*, December 20, p. B12.

Wright, B. N. 1994. *The Language of Hope: Minneapolis' Neighborhood Safe Art Program*. Minneapolis: Safe Art Spot Project.

Wright, J. H., ed. 1997. *New York Times 1998 Almanac*. New York: New York Times.

Write Now! 1998. Description of Programs. Hollywood, Calif.: Write Now!

Wuthnow, R. 1991. *Acts of Compassion: Caring for Others and Helping Ourselves*. Princeton: Princeton University Press.

Wuthnow, R. 1995. *Learning to Care: Elementary Kindness in an Age of Indifference*. New York: Oxford University Press.

Yin, R. K. 1994. *Case Study Research: Design and Methods*. Thousand Oaks, Calif.: Sage.

Young, T. 1996. Kids get a kick out of camp: Soccer offers lessons in life. *New Orleans Times-Picyune*, July 27, p. B1.

Youniss, J. and M. Yates. 1998. *Community Service and Social Responsibility in Youth.* Chicago: University of Chicago Press.

Zavala, R. 1996. Approach to gang prevention and intervention. In P. A. Witt and J. L. Crompton, eds., *Recreation Programs that Work for At-Risk Youth*, pp. 229–235. College Station, Pa.: Venture.

Zill, N., C. W. Nord, and L. S. Loomis. 1995. *Adolescent Time Use, Risky Behavior, and Outcomes: An Analysis of National Data.* Rockville, Md.: Westa.

Zimring, F. E. 1998. *The Youth Violence Epidemic: Reality or Fantasy?* New York: Oxford University Press.

Zinsmeiter, K. 1990. Growing up scared. *Atlantic Monthly* 265: 49–66.

AUTHOR INDEX

—

SUBJECT INDEX

DATE DUE

OC 12 '03			